Understanding *A Midsummer Night's Dream*

The Greenwood Press "Literature in Context" Series
Student Casebooks to Issues, Sources, and Historical Documents

Understanding
A Midsummer Night's Dream

A STUDENT CASEBOOK TO ISSUES, SOURCES, AND HISTORICAL DOCUMENTS

Faith Nostbakken

The Greenwood Press
"Literature in Context" Series
Claudia Durst Johnson, Series Editor

GREENWOOD PRESS
Westport, Connecticut • London

Library of Congress Cataloging-in-Publication Data

Nostbakken, Faith, 1964–

Understanding A midsummer night's dream : a student casebook to issues, sources, and historical documents / Faith Nostbakken.

p.   cm.—(The Greenwood Press "Literature in context" series, ISSN 1074–598X)

Includes bibliographical references and index.

ISBN 0–313–32213–9 (alk. paper)

1. Shakespeare, William, 1564–1616. Midsummer night's dream—Handbooks, manuals, etc. 2. Shakespeare, William, 1564–1616. Midsummer night's dream—Sources. I. Title. II. Series.

PR2827 .N68   2003

822.3′3—dc21   2002041595

British Library Cataloging in Publication Data is available.

Library of Congress Catalog Card Number: 2002041595

ISBN: 0–313–32213–9

ISSN: 1074–598X

First published in 2003

Greenwood Press, 88 Post Road West, Westport, CT 06881

An imprint of Greenwood Publishing Group, Inc.

www.greenwood.com

Printed in the United States of America

The paper used in this book complies with the Permanent Paper Standard issued by the National Information Standards Organization (Z39.48–1984).

10   9   8   7   6   5   4   3   2   1

Copyright Acknowledgments

The author and publisher gratefully acknowledge permission for use of the following material:

"Guys Just Want to Bulk Up: Teens Go to Extremes to Meet the Poster Boy Ideal," by Steve Bereznai, *Edmonton Journal* (August 14, 2001). He is a contributor to Young People's Press, a news service for youth. Visit www.ypp.net to get involved. Reprinted with permission.

"Fairy Mistakes Put Lovers In a Spin; Shakespeare's Sublime Comedy Sprinkles Magical Confusion through a Forest of Dreams," by Marc Horton, *Edmonton Journal* (May 19, 1999). Reprinted with permission of the *Edmonton Journal*.

Selected paragraphs originally published in chapter 2 of *Understanding Othello: A Student Casebook to Issues, Sources, and Historical Documents* (Greenwood Press, Westport, CT, 2000). Copyright © Faith Nostbakken. Reprinted with permission.

For Linda Woodbridge,
teacher, mentor, friend

Contents

Acknowledgments

I wish to recognize and thank the editors of Greenwood Press for their faith in me as I launched into *Understanding A Midsummer Night's Dream,* my third book in their "Literature in Context" series but my first foray into romantic comedy with all the challenges it has presented. I also gratefully acknowledge Rick Bowers, who has been a faithful and valuable respondent to my work-in-progress through all three Shakespeare projects and who did his best to keep me grounded in comedy during this last endeavor. I thank Linda Woodbridge, whose passion lit the spark that compelled me to pursue this project in the first place, who lent me some of her expertise along the way, and who began teaching me more than she realizes long before the seed of Greenwood's "Literature in Context" series was ever planted.

Introduction: For Students and Teachers

A Midsummer Night's Dream is one of Shakespeare's most purely romantic comedies, dramatizing the wonderment and confusion of characters falling in and out of love under the magical influence of fairies in an enchanted forest on a midsummer night. The term "comedy" identifies the lighthearted nature of the plot but also draws attention to the structure of the play with a story that focuses on community rather than individual characters and an ending that celebrates life by blessing the harmony of multiple marriages. This is a delightful play to watch and includes some of Shakespeare's most lyrical lines of poetry, especially in the speeches of the fairies, whose otherworldliness comes to life in melodious verse.

Perhaps one of the greatest challenges in teaching and studying this play or in addressing its issues involves a delicate balancing point—not always easy to find—between the sheer pleasure of the language and performance and the serious implications of its historical and social milieu. As Shakespearean scholar Linda Woodbridge suggests from her perspective on Shakespearean comedy, "[Its] characters may be violating the rules of society, but they are following the rules of comedy. I would argue that it's every bit as important to know the literary history of comedy as to know the social history of England" (Linda Woodbridge, notes on Shakespearean Comedy, Introduction, p. 2). This guide to understanding *A Midsummer Night's Dream* under the rubric of a series entitled "Literature in Context" devotes much time and space to the "Issues, Sources, and Historical Documents" noted in the book's subtitle. It would be wise to begin, however, with two observations. First, literary and dramatic contexts are necessarily woven into the social and historical discussion at various points along the way because the "rules of comedy" often diverge from or inform the "rules of society." And, second, a word of caution and encouragement: what may be sacrificed or downplayed by the nature of this study is the simple delight and celebration of the play itself. To understand *A Midsummer Night's Dream* more fully, do not forget to focus on the very "playfulness" of the play. Do not lose sight of the laughter and the joy, for to do so would be to misunderstand the gift that Shakespeare shares with us.

In this casebook, an initial chapter establishes some of the dramatic and literary concerns of *A Midsummer Night's Dream*. Following that, four historical chapters engage in a variety of topics that shed light on the historical, social, and political contexts of this play when it was first written and performed in the late sixteenth century, near the end of Queen Elizabeth I's reign. Gender relations, social distinctions, popular culture, and imagination are the overriding subjects of these topical chapters. With love being the thematic center of the play, "Gender Relations" guides us through disparate attitudes towards love and marriage during Shakespeare's time, exploring ways in which not only harmony but also antagonism developed between genders that were wooing and warring simultaneously. The chapter on "Social Distinctions" examines Elizabethan class expectations and regulations as a way to identify more clearly the demarcations between the aristocrats and artisans in *A Midsummer Night's Dream*. A discussion of "Popular Culture" looks at the similarities and differences among holiday customs including May Day and Midsummer's Eve, the lavish entertainments designed for Queen Elizabeth and her courtiers, and the public stage where Shakespeare and other dramatists entertained their main audiences. An inquiry into "Imagination and Beliefs"—another key thematic topic in *A Midsummer Night's Dream*—encompasses diverse subjects from Renaissance psychology of dreams, to Elizabethan beliefs in fairies, to the concept of transformation as it informed responses to witchcraft and shaped superstitions in the sixteenth century.

Because *A Midsummer Night's Dream* focuses so self-consciously on performance with the artisans' play-within-the-play and because drama is a living art form that changes with the times, one chapter is devoted to performance of Shakespeare's play from the 1590s to the present. This chapter addresses questions about how *A Midsummer Night's Dream* has been adapted and interpreted over the centuries in response to social and historical attitudes and values. For example, the propriety of Victorian sentimentality and its portrayal of charming innocent fairies contrast dramatically with some late-twentieth-century productions that emphasize the erotic nature of love between the couples and even suggest deeper sinister qualities. Each new production of the play reinvents the drama and invests it with new powers of imagination, teasing out the possibilities that lie within the text and layering those possibilities onto the social and artistic fabric of a particular time and place.

The final chapter of this casebook looks beyond the boundaries of Shakespeare's text to contemporary issues and human interest stories that invite readers to make connections to *A Midsummer Night's Dream.* The interplay of Shakespeare's comedy with today's topics or events can broaden and challenge our understanding of both the drama and the world around us. The entertainment industry, relationships of love and friendship, and the parameters of dreams and fantasy provide the headlines for this discussion, which encourages an interdisciplinary approach to the study of "literature" in the classroom.

Numerous documents throughout the book, excerpted or in full, invite "hands on" involvement in historical and current topics presented. The range of materials includes the following:

classical Greek and Roman history
sonnets
Elizabethan marriage conduct books
a Tudor political treatise
an Elizabethan legal document regulating artisans
a Puritan pamphlet against holidays
a nobleman's letter describing rural celebrations for Queen Elizabeth I
a Renaissance medical treatise addressing the nature of imagination
an English ballad about Robin Goodfellow
a treatise on witchcraft
stage critics' responses to *A Midsummer Night's Dream*
advice from a stand-up comic
The Teenage Guy's Survival Guide
Freud's and Jung's studies about dreams
excerpts from *The Lord of the Rings* and a Harry Potter book

The end of each section or chapter includes a series of "Questions for Written and Oral Discussion." These questions vary from specific inquiries into details within the excerpted documents that encourage comprehension of the main thoughts or ideas being presented to much broader investigations that connect the documents to Shakespeare's play, historical issues, or present-day concerns. The range of possible approaches in the questions allows for intellectual and artistic involvement through formal responses in paragraphs and essays, to classroom debates about a variety of topics, to assignments that require the use of video cameras, drawings, or musical compositions, to dramatic enactments of a series of scripted or hypothetical scenarios between historical and fictional characters. While many of the topics are quite specific, others are open-ended enough to be adapted for various classroom purposes. *A Midsummer Night's Dream* is one of Shakespeare's plays that is introduced to students in relatively early grades as well as in more senior years. Because the options in the "Questions for Written and Oral Discussion" are extensive, it is hoped that they provide ideas and opportunities for young, new students to engage with Shakespeare's comedy, but also to challenge the more capable and experienced students by nurturing their capacity for insight and imagination.

A Midsummer Night's Dream inspires laughter and celebration. It also bears scrutiny for subtleties of interpretation as it dramatizes responses to love and jealousy, power and playfulness, magic and logic, madness and reason, dreams and comprehension, reality and illusion, play-acting and play-watching, day and night, city and woods, the young and the old, the believable and the incredible and all the range of possibilities that lie in between. As a casebook that strives to foster greater understanding of the play, this study folds back the layers to reveal the richness of the text and the variety of contexts that illuminate it.

Note that all quotations from *A Midsummer Night's Dream* throughout this book come from the Signet Classic version: William Shakespeare, *A Midsummer Night's Dream,* ed. Wolfgang Clemen (1963; New York: Penguin Books, 1998). Spelling and punctuation have been regularized and modernized for clarity where necessary in excerpted documents included in the four historical chapters (2 through 6) of this study.

1 —————————————————————

Dramatic Analysis

This first chapter addresses the dramatic elements of *A Midsummer Night's Dream,* considering what the word "comedy" means, where Shakespeare found his ideas for the plot of the play, and how the poetic and literary patterns work together to give the play meaning and structure.

COMEDY AND THE POPULAR TRADITION

A Midsummer Night's Dream is one of Shakespeare's early comedies, but "comedy," as Shakespeare understood the term, meant much more than a humorous or funny performance, as we might define the word in the simplest terms today. While there are humorous or funny elements in all Shakespeare's comedies, other conventions help to determine what characterizes his comedy as a genre. For example, just as there are dramatic expectations and qualities that define a tragedy, there are different expectations that distinguish comedy from tragedy.

Comedy and Tragedy

Comparing the two genres can be one way to better understand the shape and movement of comedy. Greek philosopher Aristotle (384–322 B.C.), whose definitions of tragedy and comedy influenced playwrights in Shakespeare's time, described the two contrasting dramatic structures by indicating that tragedy begins quietly but ends in horror; comedy, on the other hand, begins with conflict or unrest and ends in peace. This distinction forms some of the other expectations of the two dramatic forms. In tragedy, for example, the individual character is the focus, whereas in comedy the community is central. Typically, in Shakespearean tragedy, the serious struggle of the individual ends in death while the more lighthearted struggles of comedy result in the celebration of life and its cyclical regeneration in which the individual characters are less important than the communal resolution. Consequently, comic characters tend to be less rounded or well developed than tragic characters because tragedy explores the interior mental life while comedy focuses on exterior social, situational aspects of life. Another distinction is that Shakespeare's comedies primarily portray fictional, often domestic plots, whereas his tragedies such as *Hamlet* or *Macbeth* typically rely on historical plots about public figures acting out of political responsibility. The comedies, because of their emphasis on community, often have several overlapping plots happening at the same time; tragedies follow more directly the actions of the central hero to maintain the intensity of the emotion fostered by his struggle.

Shakespeare's comedy *A Midsummer Night's Dream* and his tragedy *Romeo and Juliet* were written about the same time and offer a useful contrast as an illustration of some—although not all—of these distinctions between comedy and tragedy. Both plays enact stories of love between couples, but *A Midsummer Night's Dream* includes not only the two young couples, but also Theseus and Hippolyta and Oberon and Titania, while *Romeo and Juliet* focuses solely on the two title characters. In *A Midsummer Night's Dream,* there are multiple plots, with fairies, tradesmen, and nobles interacting, whereas *Romeo and Juliet* follows a single plot line of the family conflict that divides the two young lovers and their attempts to be united in spite of the forces against them. The tragedy ends in death as the audience watches with horror the suicides of the two lovers, when Romeo, thinking Juliet has already died, kills himself, and she, finding him dead, ends her life. The lovers in *A Midsummer Night's Dream* face a much happier ending when, after much confusion between characters in the middle of the play, three marriages draw the plot to a close in celebration.

Interestingly, "Pyramus and Thisby," the play-within-the-play in *A Midsummer Night's Dream,* parallels the tragic plot of *Romeo and Juliet* with similar family strife leading to the double suicide of the young lovers. By including such a plot in *A Midsummer Night's Dream,* Shakespeare invites obvious considerations of tragic and comic patterns within the play itself. The first scene of *A Midsummer Night's Dream,* in fact, has all the makings of a tragedy. Egeus, Hermia's father, calls for a death sentence on his daughter unless she marries his choice of a husband, and Duke Theseus rules in Egeus's favor, giving Hermia the alternatives of unhappy marriage to Demetrius, a single life in a convent, or death. Little is humorous or lighthearted about the play's beginning.

Before the magic of the fairy world is introduced, *A Midsummer Night's Dream* seems to be a potentially dark play about love in conflict. The plot of "Pyramus and Thisby" reflects that dark pattern. But because the craftsmen bungle their attempt at a tragic performance, their production is transformed into the most humorous business in the play. At the close of their on-stage drama, *A Midsummer Night's Dream* ends with the communal resolution typical of the comic genre as the fairies give their blessing on the noble households and draw even the audience into the final harmony.

Romantic Comedy

Within the comic genre, *A Midsummer Night's Dream* is a specific kind of comedy, a romantic comedy. In short, it is a play about love. More fully, romantic comedy portrays love as a sudden, immediate response for which we might use the modern expressions "falling head over heels in love" or "love at first sight." Such "first sight" infatuation is symbolically represented by the love juice squeezed into the lovers' eyes in Shakespeare's play. This depiction of sudden romantic love seems highly artificial and, therefore, in some respects, unbelievable. Likewise, the motivations of the characters in love appear improbable or impossible. But the characters are portrayed as sympathetic and so their story remains compelling as their mishaps are designed for amusement, tolerance, and self-reflected understanding, not ridicule and judgment. Romantic comedy focuses on young aristocratic characters rather than commoners, and their adventures and misadventures often include a journey out of the city into a forest where things are seldom as they seem, identities become confused, and trickery is involved. The world turns topsy-turvy for a time, but the magical confusion that happens in the forest eventually allows for reentrance into society with the initial tension or conflict being resolved. The plot depends on numerous coincidences and unlikely events to bring about a happy ending, which is always marriage or the promise of marriage and often a celebration with music and dance. Love is portrayed as life-giving, and ideals such as loyalty and gentleness are upheld as important and valued. Describing these features of romantic comedy and comparing tragic and comic forms help to define "comedy" as it applies to *A Midsummer Night's Dream*. Rather than simply being funny, comedy is about the structure and expectations of plot and character. Invariably it also includes humorous elements, but its focus on love and its emphasis on the celebration of life are equally (if not more) significant.

Sources and Traditions

Most of Shakespeare's plays have as the source of their plots another previously written story or portion of history that Shakespeare borrows from another author. Typically, Shakespeare reshapes the original sources according to expectations of stage tragedy or comedy and refashions them according to his own imagination. *A Midsummer Night's Dream* is unusual in that its plot does not derive from another single existing source. It is a play of Shakespeare's own invention. However, numerous poems and stories provide for him the suggestion for various characters or portions of his plot. The "Pyramus and Thisby" story, for example, existed in a variety of forms in his time, deriving originally from the classical Roman poet Ovid (43–17 or 18 A.D.), whose collection of tales entitled *Metamorphoses* included the tragic account of the two lovers. The word "metamorphoses" means changes or transformations. This is a topic that becomes important not simply in the "Pyramus and Thisby" portion of *A Midsummer Night's Dream*, but in the whole play as various characters experience changes in the object or understanding of their love and as Bottom is physically changed when Puck gives him the head of an ass and then later removes it. Shakespeare appears to be influenced by Ovid's idea of "metamorphosis" or change as much as he is indebted to Ovid for the story of two tragic lovers who are "translated" or transformed into the comic characters of the craftsmen's wedding interlude or play.

Other characters in *A Midsummer Night's Dream* existed in previous sources as well. Theseus and Hippolyta are figures from Greek legend who also appeared in English medieval poetry. Oberon is a fairy king from a French prose romance. Titania appears in Ovid's *Metamorphoses,* where she represents Diana, the moon goddess. Puck is a well-known fairy from English Elizabethan folklore. Puck's transformation of Bottom by giving him the head of an "ass" may have been suggested to Shakespeare from another classical Roman writer, Lucius Apuleius, who recounts the story of a man turned into an ass who regains human form with the help of a goddess. Beyond that, the term "jackass" was common slang in the sixteenth century as it is today for a silly person or common butt of jokes. The craftsmen are patterned after typical English artisans from contemporary Elizabethan society. The four young Athenian lovers do not appear to have any specific antecedents, although one of Geoffrey Chaucer's *Canterbury Tales,* the "Knight's Tale," suggests some parallels. Moreover, the lovers as generalized character types rather than carefully individualized characters appear to be suggestive of teenage infatuation as it has existed across societies throughout history. Shakespeare manages to bring together ideas for various characters from many diverse sources, from classical myth, medieval romance, English folklore, and general parlance, as he intertwines them into his own multilayered plot.

There are other more general influences on Shakespeare's play. Early Greek and Roman drama, for example, written by dramatists such as Plautus and Terence in the third century B.C., were taught in English schools in Shakespeare's time in the sixteenth century. From this drama came the idea of artificial rather than realistic plots and specific character types such as old men or fathers who stand in the way of the younger generation. Egeus has his roots in this early drama. From medieval English poetry came the topic of romance and the language of courtly love. Medieval Christian drama from the fifteenth century known as miracle plays provided a pattern for comic structure and an element of humor. The miracle plays enacted a series of stories with biblical characters depicting the Christian movement from the fall into sin to salvation and eternal life. This movement through conflict to a happy resolution became the pattern for much more secular Renaissance comedies, such as *A Midsummer Night's Dream,* where the movement from conflict to resolution is human and immediate rather than divine or cosmic. The evil characters in medieval drama, including the devil, were often presented in a comic light as they enacted their deception and ultimately lost the battle of good over evil. The humorous element of comedy on the Elizabethan stage was influenced by this earlier English drama.

Other influences come from popular folklore and customs that developed or still existed in Shakespeare's own time. A masque was a type of court entertainment often performed for noble weddings and was like drama without having a strong story line but involving music, dance, spectacle, magic, and mythological characters. The music, the dance of the fairies and the craftsmen, the wedding celebrations of the nobles, and the supernatural elements in *A Midsummer Night's Dream* all suggest masquelike elements. Seasonal holiday festivities deriving both from pre-Christian fertility rites and the Christian church year are also reflected in the play with its references to May Day traditions, midsummer night madness, St. Valentine's Day, songs, and feasting. Many of these influences will receive further attention in succeeding chapters about the historical context of the play. Here it is simply important to note that while Shakespeare did not borrow from a specific plot source for his play, characters in previous stories and numerous traditions, customs, and conventions are reflected in the plot, characterization, and themes of *A Midsummer Night's Dream.* The play as comedy, as romance, as celebration, has its roots in Shakespeare's Renaissance surroundings and in literary and ritual patterns from his past.

POETIC AND DRAMATIC PATTERNS

As performance, *A Midsummer Night's Dream* involves the combination of language and gesture working together to engage an audience in the illusion of an invented reality. But as a literary work, the play also includes many patterns in the careful organization of plot and the weaving together of words and images that may not be immediately obvious to audience members attending a stage production. This play is a particularly lyric drama, songlike and poetic, with the art of its language sometimes appearing to rise above the significance of the characters' circumstances and the outcome of the tension and conflict between them. It is worthwhile, therefore, to spend time with the words on the page and to consider how *A Midsummer Night's Dream* is both a literary and a dramatic work of art with word and action complementing each other and contributing to the experience of readers and spectators alike.

Structure

The plot of *A Midsummer Night's Dream* moves according to a very finely structured series of settings. The play begins in the palace of Duke Theseus in the city of Athens where the duke announces his forthcoming marriage to Hippolyta and where Egeus's complaint establishes the initial conflict between Hermia and Lysander's desires and the expectations of law and family. The second setting is also in Athens, at the home of Peter Quince, where the craftsmen gather to prepare a play for Theseus and Hippolyta's wedding night. While these two scenes are quite dissimilar—one characterized by the dignity of the duke's court, the other rustic in its setting and characterized by the coarseness and ignorance of the uneducated laborers—they are united by the focus on Theseus and Hippolyta's marriage and move in the same direction towards the woods where the young lovers intend to escape the decrees of the city and where the artisans plan to rehearse their play.

The next setting, the one that dominates the play, involves the moonlit woods, where Shakespeare introduces the third set of characters, the fairies. Here the second major conflict asserts itself in the argument between Titania and Oberon, the fairy queen and king. They have come to the region near Athens for the same reason that the artisans have planned a play: to celebrate and bless Theseus and Hippolyta's wedding night. In the woods, the separate groups of characters become interconnected as Oberon and Puck use their magic on the young lovers, confusing their identities and purposes; transform Bottom and bring him into relationship with Titania; and settle the dispute with Titania by trickery that allows Oberon to take from her the changeling boy from whom she initially refuses to part. Even Theseus, Hippolyta, and Egeus enter the woods on a hunting trip as morning breaks and discover, to their surprise, what the lovers had planned to achieve, how all their plans have been changed and their conflicts settled by some mysterious happenings of midnight madness. The forest is a setting of enchantment and confusion, but also of possibility and expansive resolution, where the initial problems in the city are solved so that not one marriage but three are ready to be celebrated back at court.

In a symmetrical pattern of movement, the play moves from the woods back to the home of Peter Quince in Athens, where Bottom is reunited with his friends as the rustic characters learn of their opportunity to perform "Pyramus and Thisby" at the court wedding feast. *A Midsummer Night's Dream* then concludes where it began, at the duke's palace for the performance of the artisans' play and for a happy communal conclusion as the fairies enter to bless the night, as well as the three couples ready to unite in marriage. The movement of the plot is deliberately circular, from the palace to Quince's home, to the woods, back to Quince's home, and finally back to the palace. The structure itself is formal, almost like a round dance that the fairies perform, like the fairy rings that enchant the play and bring it to a place of harmony. Shakespeare uses the separate settings to introduce distinct groups of characters whose intentions are all focused on the marriage announced in the first scene and whose lives and actions eventually become intertwined to create the play's entertaining chaos and allow for its festive conclusion.

Language

The language of *A Midsummer Night's Dream* is full of variety and not only enriches the imagination as it describes the settings and activates the play's magic but also helps to characterize the different groups within the three settings. Shakespeare combines poetry and prose, distinguishing characters according to their speech.

Blank verse is a form of poetry common to Shakespeare's plays. It is unrhymed iambic pentameter. "Iambic" indicates the rhythm of the verse line with a pattern in which an unstressed syllable is followed by a stressed syllable. "Pentameter" indicates that there are five patterns of unstressed and stressed syllables or, in other words, ten syllables in the line. This form of poetry closely approximates the natural rhythm of speech, thus bringing together the sound and sense of poetry and prose. Typically, Shakespeare uses blank verse for stately, formal speech and to express emotion and dignity. Theseus, Hippolyta, and Egeus, representatives of the nobility in the play, speak in blank verse. An example of such speech is Egeus's complaint about the relationship between Lysander and Hermia:

> Stand forth, Lysander. And my gracious Duke
> This man hath bewitched the bosom of my child.
> Thou, thou, Lysander, thou hast given her rhymes,
> And interchanged love tokens with my child. (1.1.26–29)

The dialogue between the nobles at court is almost always in blank verse, except when they banter and joke in a lighthearted manner around the banqueting table as they watch the entertainment provided by Bottom and his fellow players.

The lovers are also members of the nobility, and they, too, speak in blank verse, but Shakespeare distinguishes them from the other court characters by having them frequently converse in couplets which are sets of two rhyming lines with the iambic pentameter rhythm. Listen to the rhyme in Helena's distress as she mistakenly thinks Lysander and Demetrius are mocking her with proclamations of their love in the woods:

> Wherefore was I to this keen mockery born?
> When at your hands did I deserve this scorn?
> Is't not enough, is't not enough, young man,
> That I did never, no, nor never can,
> Deserve a sweet look from Demetrius' eye,
> But you must flout my insufficiency? (2.2.123–28)

The rhyme lightens the tone of the language, helping to make Helena's concerns appear less serious, and the lovers' protestations and quarrels, in general, more comic than tragic.

Shakespeare uses prose to identify characters of low stature. The "rude mechanicals," as Puck calls the craftsmen, are uneducated commoners. Their speech, except when they are delivering the lines of "Pyramus and Thisby," is always in prose. The fairies, by contrast, speak in verse, but their language is the most versatile of all the character groups. Oberon and Titania sometimes speak in blank verse befitting the dignity of their status as king and queen of the fairy kingdom. The contrast between Titania's dignified blank verse and Bottom's lowly prose contributes to the humor and absurdity in their scene together. Fairies speak in other styles, too. Oberon's magic spells are in shorter lyrical rhyming lines, conveying the hypnotic sense of enchantment. The other fairies use short lines that create an airy feeling and help to suggest that they are tiny creatures. They also sing songs such as the rhyming lullaby that puts Titania to sleep. And occasionally couplets can be heard not only from the young lovers, but from Oberon and Titania as well. The diversity of the fairies' speech from blank verse to couplets to short rhymes to songs indicates their adaptability as supernatural beings. They are not limited, as the other characters are, by class, mortal distress, and social stature. Shakespeare's deliberate choices in language patterns contribute to characterization and to the distinctions he makes between the various worlds that come together in the unfolding of the plot.

Imagery and Allusion

As one of Shakespeare's most poetic plays, *A Midsummer Night's Dream* relies on imagery and allusions to create setting and atmosphere and to contribute to the exotic qualities in both the natural and the supernatural realms. The play is full of references to the natural world, including names of flowers, descriptions of the sea, and details about the weather. Titania's first long speech in act 2, scene 1 when she meets Oberon explains how their disagreement has disrupted the natural world and brought floods to the land:

> Therefore the winds, piping to us in vain
> As in revenge, have sucked up from the sea
> Contagious fogs; which, falling in the land,
> Hath every pelting river made so proud,
> That they have overborne their continents. (2.1.88–92)

Later, Oberon provides a songlike description of nature's beauty:

> I know a bank where the wild thyme blows,
> Where oxlips and the nodding violet grows,
> Quite overcanopied with luscious woodbine,
> With sweet musk roses, and with eglantine. (2.1.249–52)

The images bring to life the world on stage and the world beyond it, the beauty of the woods and the storms surrounding it, nature and the forces of the supernatural.

Other images reflect the discord, conflict, and chaos among the young lovers and the way their perceptions about love are exaggerated or misrepresented by the fairies' powers. Numerous references to eyes reveal how confused the lovers are about what they see or do not see in each other and suggest that love is both blind and dependent on sight, a paradox that adds to the midsummer night magic and madness. Images of animals, beasts, and monsters contribute to feelings of chaos and danger that the lovers face as they leave the order of the city and enter the dark night of disorder and crisis in the woods and in their own desires and infatuations.

One of the most important images in *A Midsummer Night's Dream* is the moon. Theseus mentions it in the first lines of the play as he chafes against the four nights he has to wait until his wedding day. The moon, waxing and waning, is a reference of time and of mental states. Titania includes the moon in her description of the disorder in nature brought about by her argument with Oberon, saying, "Therefore the moon, the governess of floods, / Pale in her anger, washes all the air, °/ That rheumatic diseases abound" (2.1.103–5). The moon controls the tides and is an important part of the natural world. It also represents a source of madness, with the words "lunacy" and "lunatic" deriving from the word "lunar," meaning "of the moon." This particular representation becomes significant in the middle of the play when magic turns love to madness as the young Athenian couples dash about confusedly in the woods and Titania becomes enamored of an ass-headed Bottom.

Referred to as a character in mythology, the moon also serves as an allusion, which is a reference to a person, place, or event from other literary works. In its mythic form, the moon gives larger-than-life scope to the action of the play. A classical goddess with three forms, the moon is known in heaven as Phoebe or Cynthia; on earth as Diana, the virgin goddess of the forest; and below earth as Hecate, the witch goddess of the underworld. All three names are mentioned in reference to the moon in *A Midsummer Night's Dream,* adding to the complexity of action and understanding throughout the play. The moon represents both chastity and inconstancy; it is a symbol of both virginity and fertility. As an image, a classical allusion, a prop, and even a character in the mechanicals' play, it signifies ambiguities surrounding love and relationship.

Irony

Irony is a literary and dramatic technique that contributes to ambiguity as it focuses on the difference between appearance and reality or knowing and not knowing. The chief form of irony in *A Midsummer Night's Dream* is dramatic irony that exists in the discrepancy or gap between what the audience knows and what the characters know and what some characters know compared to the others. This irony has several layers. At one level, the audience knows that fairies in the woods are using magic to change the perceptions of the young lovers while the lovers are completely oblivious to these supernatural powers. They never do discover the source of their confusion and ultimate reunion through the night's events. The audience also knows that similar magic transforms Bottom and attracts Titania to him. With greater knowledge than the lovers, Bottom at least realizes something about his amorous night with the fairy queen, although he does not know how to describe it. Titania, however, is eventually allowed to see how she has been misled by Oberon's charms. At another level, the audience has its closest ties to Oberon and Puck, who know more than all the other characters and who are aware and deliberate about the actions they take to manipulate and transform the others. But even here, there is an ironic distance between the audience and the two fairies, because the audience knows before Oberon and Puck do that the wrong Athenian man has been enchanted with love juice. Moreover, as humans, the audience vicariously experiences the moral problems to which the fairies seem oblivious. The difference between what the audience knows and what various characters know contributes to the comic effects of the play not only because the audience can laugh at the confusion without being caught in it but because it can experience a delightful sense of involvement in the power of magic that most of the characters simply cannot see. Irony also adds to the dream element in the play because the ambiguity between appearance and reality, what seems and what is, leaves the characters and ultimately the audience, too, with questions about whether events were merely dreamed or really happened.

Stage Conventions

Dramatic irony is related to stage conventions that audiences accept so that they can enjoy the performance on stage, pretending for the sake of entertainment that what they see is "real" although they know the entire play is an act or illusion. A primary stage convention relates to the speeches of the characters who convey information about the plot through dialogue, asides, and soliloquies. Dialogue happens between two or more characters, an aside occurs when one character speaks while others on stage appear not to hear, and a soliloquy is a speech spoken by one character on stage appearing to think out loud so that the audience can hear and know what is evolving. Oberon speaks in soliloquy to describe his plans to enchant Titania with flower juice, and then, upon hearing Demetrius and Helena entering the stage, announces, "I am invisible" (2.1.186). The actor playing Oberon's part does not suddenly disappear, but by convention, the audience accepts that the other two characters on stage cannot see him because he lets us know he is meant to be invisible. Oberon and Puck also engage in many asides, making comments to the audience that the lovers and the "mechanicals" in the wood seemingly cannot hear. In the mad chase in which Puck leads Lysander and Demetrius through bush and briar to exhaust them and prevent them from injuring each other, the audience and performers together engage their imaginations pretending that the two Athenians cannot see each other or Puck and that Puck's voice sounds like either of the two young men. The whole aspect of magic in *A Midsummer Night's Dream* would not be possible without stage conventions, the agreement between audience and performers to accept that what is said and done on stage is believable even though the relationships and contexts are entirely unrealistic.

Burlesque

The importance of imagination for stage conventions that allow the play's action to unfold is given special attention in the "rude mechanicals'" rehearsal and performance of "Pyramus and Thisby," the play-within-the-play. Shakespeare turns this portion of *A Midsummer Night's Dream* into a burlesque, which is a ridiculous imitation meant to mock or ridicule by exaggeration and absurdity. The mechanicals' "Pyramus and Thisby" imitates both the role of imagination in the relationship between audience and actors in the performance of a play and the role of love in the relationships between Shakespeare's other characters. Bottom and his fellow craftsmen do not understand or trust the role of imagination and therefore inadvertently become objects of ridicule as they rely on it. On the one hand, they feel that their audience will not have sufficient imagination to see what does not exist and so they choose to create Wall and Moonshine as characters, not trusting the audience to believe them into existence. On the other hand, the "mechanicals" fear their acting will overstimulate the audience's imagination, creating fears in the female spectators that their lion is a real lion. Consequently, they go to great lengths to explain away the lion's theatrical power. The craftsmen cannot seem to tell the difference between art and life; they do not understand the stage conventions by which an audience and performers agree to believe what is not realistic; and they distort and distrust the powers of imagination completely. The result is a wholly laughing matter whereby Shakespeare's own audience of *A Midsummer Night's Dream* can enjoy the burlesque of the play-within-the-play while appreciating in contrast how Shakespeare as playwright allows imagination to work through his characters in a way that his "mechanicals" interpreting their script do not.

"Pyramus and Thisby" is also a ridiculous imitation of love that enriches the story of Lysander, Demetrius, Hermia, and Helena by ludicrously revealing the potentially darker side of their love relationships. The plot of the mechanicals' play is serious and tragic: two lovers fail to overcome the division between their families symbolized by the Wall and commit double suicide. What turns the performance into a comedy is the great disparity between the subject matter and the manner of acting: the bad verse, misused words, repetitive language, forgotten lines, wild exaggerations, overacting, and ignorance of the subtle nuances of interpretation. Typical of this mangled tragedy is Bottom's big death scene in which he stabs himself repeatedly, calling out, "Now die, die, die, die, die" (5.1.307) but then suddenly recovers to explain to the audience that the wall between the feuding families has been destroyed by the lovers' deaths. Humor is enhanced by the absolute seriousness of the craftsmen as performers and the commentary provided by the on-stage audience of Theseus and his guests. Shakespeare's inclusion of this burlesque interlude draws attention back to the love displayed between various characters in his own play. On the one hand, it affirms the harmony of love achieved by the play's end. But on the other hand, it raises questions about the doting, inconstant, extreme protestations of love expressed by all the play's lovers and serves as a reminder of an outcome that could have been serious and tragic, too, given the rashness of the actions stimulated by the lovers' passions and emotions.

Character

Characters in comedy, especially in a romantic comedy such as *A Midsummer Night's Dream,* are not well rounded, complex, and individualized. In fact,

Shakespeare seems to make the identities of the four young lovers deliberately confusing. Demetrius and Lysander are alike in their status and dress as Athenian nobles, and even Hermia and Helena's names are so similar as to render distinctions difficult. Shakespeare appears to be more interested in generalized character types and the commonness of love infatuation and relationships than in specific character traits. As earlier discussion on "Structure" and "Language" has indicated, *A Midsummer Night's Dream* makes distinctions between four groups of characters—the Athenian rulers, the young lovers, the fairies, and the craftsmen—more clearly than between single characters. Still, attention to the action and interaction of various characters can reveal important patterns of response and connection that contribute to the overall structure, movement, and meaning of the play.

One way to consider significance of character is to look at contrasts and parallels between various types, relationships, and behaviors. There are at least three different examples of love relationships, and even four if Titania and Bottom are included in the list. Compared to the four passionate young lovers, the relationship between Theseus and Hippolyta seems more sedate and dignified, befitting their mature age and roles as heads of state. Oberon and Titania invite comparisons with both these other groups. They seem capable, in spite of their stature as rulers of the fairy kingdom, of letting their emotions dictate extreme actions and reactions, as their quarrel over the changeling boy disrupts their relationship and all of nature besides. They are as passionate and willful in their jealousy as Lysander and Hermia, Demetrius and Helena are in their protestations of love. When Titania "falls in love" with the ass-headed Bottom, the visual absurdity of their relationship as well as the exaggerated difference in their responses to each other illuminate the extremity of behavior between the other couples: Theseus's admission to Hippolyta, "I wooed thee with my sword,°/ And won thy love, doing thee injuries" (1.1.16–17), Lysander and Demetrius's readiness to take up swords in the name of love, and Oberon's willingness to manipulate Titania with magic to settle their dispute. These extreme behaviors reflect Bottom's comment that "reason and love keep little company together nowadays" (3.1.144–45) and give rise to questions about the nature of love, its authenticity, absurdity, and perplexity. Parallels between the various couples lead to insights about what binds two characters together in love and what tears them apart.

The mismatched and transmuting couples, in fact, reveal a series of triangles, not only as conventional relationships reflecting romantic love but also as unconventional relationships counter to it. Initially, Lysander, Demetrius, and Hermia create a conventional triangle that later shifts to replace Hermia with Helena while leading to no distinction in the type of behavior. But Lysander's response to the contest in the first scene suggests a much more unconventional triangle. He says of Hermia, "You have her father's love, Demetrius;°/ Let me have Hermia's: do you marry him" (1.1.93–94), proposing a resolution in which Egeus as father, Demetrius as lover, and Theseus as law-giver create their own triangle based on family tradition and legal power in opposition to romantic love. Oberon and Titania's quarrel also includes unconventional triangles because the source of the couple's conflict is primarily a changeling child rather than another lover, although both the fairy king and queen accuse each other of love ties with Theseus and Hippolyta in double triangles almost as confusing as the overlapping triangles of the young lovers. Then the reunion of the fairy king and queen temporarily involves a mortal, Bottom, as Oberon's replacement in Titania's bower. The triangle, as the typical shape of love in conflict, takes on multiple permutations in *A Midsummer Night's Dream,* characterizing love and lovers in a variety of ways and suggesting that love by its very nature is confusing and multifaceted.

The pairing of characters other than married couples and romantic lovers draws attention to other types of relationship in the play. Helena and Hermia both speak of the long-lasting friendship they have shared since childhood. Demetrius and Lysander also indicate friendly connections prior to their contest for first Hermia, then Helena. As the plot unfolds, it seems that childhood friendship and distressed adult love are in contest with one another as the single-mindedness of the lovers destroys their friendship until it is renewed in the harmony of new coupling at the end of the play. Power is another issue represented by pairings of characters. Clearly power is central to the disagreement between Egeus and his daughter, Hermia. Egeus asserts his fatherly right to command her obedience, while Hermia dares to reply to the duke with a voice of unexpected boldness:

> I do entreat your Grace to pardon me.
> I know not by what power I am made bold,
> Nor how it may concern my modesty,
> In such a presence here to plead my thoughts. (1.1.59–61)

Oberon asserts his power over Puck in giving him orders, over Titania by enchanting her with a magic spell, and over both Athenian young men by changing their vision with flower juice. Even Titania articulates her power over Bottom when she reminds him that he cannot leave the woods against her wishes (3.1.153). The interactions of various individual characters indicate that *A Midsummer Night's Dream* is not simply about love but about relationships of friendship and power and how those relationships connect or conflict with various, changing dynamics of love.

Perhaps one of the most interesting parallels to consider is that between Puck and Bottom. It would be difficult to find two characters so dissimilar. Puck is a fairy with a reputation for causing mischief and a clear delight in being a participant and spectator of chaos and disorder. Bottom, or "bully Bottom" as his companions affectionately call him in a word that signifies "good fellow," is amiable, good-hearted, and harmless though somewhat full of himself, eager to play all the parts, enthusiastic in his engagement with life. Both characters provide humor to the play, Bottom unwittingly and Puck mischievously. If Bottom is somewhat of a foolish clown, Puck is a trickster. More than any other characters in the play, they appear as individuals though they belong to specific groups, the "rude mechanicals" and the fairies. They invite comparison as they turn our attention to magic and dreams, to the way they react to the world around them and invoke the audience's response of sympathy or approval. Considering the two characters together allows us to understand each of their roles more clearly.

Relationships between characters illuminate the significance of action and interaction in *A Midsummer Night's Dream.* Examining the many couples, the multiple triangles, and the various pairings between characters reveals patterns that are important to the play's structure and meaning. Because the characters are deliberately comic and therefore not well rounded, the way they represent topics or themes is much more relevant than specific individualizing character traits.

Theme

A theme is an expressed interpretation of the play's meaning. Because there are many meanings in *A Midsummer Night's Dream,* it is necessary to recognize that there are many potential themes. Character relationships indicate the central significance of love but also the importance of power and friendship and how all three dynamics are interconnected. Love itself is a broad term; beyond stating the obvious, that *A Midsummer Night's Dream* is about love, the greater challenge is to attempt an expression of what the play reveals about love. There are, for example, questions about the relationship of love and reason. When the play concludes, harmony exists only because Demetrius is still under the influence of Oberon's magic spell. When the play begins, however, there is already an indication that love is far from reasonable because Demetrius had loved Helena first before he vowed to marry Hermia, and that inconstancy occurred prior to the presence of the fairies engaging their supernatural power. In many ways, what the night's activities under the influence of the fairies do is intensify what has already been established under the reasoned and ordered civilized arena of Athens. Love can be blind and passionate and powerful. Love can also be an obsession that leads to discord, violent jealousy, inconstancy, and infidelity. Sometimes love is a foolish infatuation as ridiculous as Titania becoming enamored of an ass or as an interlude that is both "merry and tragical," "tedious and brief" at the same time (5.1.58). But ultimately love is also mysterious, a quality of experience that Shakespeare seems to suggest rises above any attempts to explain it reasonably or restrain it lawfully. It transcends language and has the power to transform souls.

While *A Midsummer Night's Dream* is centrally focused on the complexities and ambiguities of love, it also explores other related topics. Contrasts stimulate reflection: the difference between the city and the woods, night and day, sight and blindness, sleeping and waking, performing and being, illusion and reality. These opposites open the way to discussion about the significance of dreams, art, and imagination. Dreams and art both require imagination. The inclusion of "dream" in the title of the play and Puck's closing invitation to the audience to consider the entire performance a dream provide a framework for considering what it is like to experience life at an unconscious level. Dream is a place of confusion and distortion, as the chaos of the night suggests, but it can also be a place of revelation, deep desire, utmost wishes, and fresh insight or understanding, which the lovers and even Bottom attempt to recognize and explain to themselves when the daylight comes. Like love, dreams defy logic and yet have power. Although the events of the midsummer night appear inexplicable to the mortals who experience them, Theseus's dismissal of it all, "I never may believe°/ These antique fables, nor these fairy toys" (5.1.2–3), reveals the limitations° of his own understanding rather than the unreality of what the lovers and even we as audience have experienced. Imagination is crucial, and the burlesque of the play-within-the-play draws attention to its value and importance by indicating just how ridiculous art or play can be when imagination is abused or completely misunderstood. Without imagination that stretches beyond the concrete realm of what can be touched and seen, there can be no love, there can be no dreaming, and, finally, there can be no play. Shakespeare compels a thoughtful conclusion with its own inherent logic. Because an audience watching *A Midsummer Night's Dream* cannot deny the existence of the play, it must accept the reality of imagination and its importance in the way we experience the world. There is more to life than reason; there is more to life than simple common sense; and the sometimes chaotic overflow of emotions cannot necessarily be dismissed or made more orderly by logic.

To address theme is to ask the question "What does the play mean?" or "How does it make me feel?" *A Midsummer Night's Dream* is playful and challenging in the ways it asks us to view the meaning of love, the purpose of dreams, the value of art, and the role of imagination. It invites us to open up our own imaginations in seeking the answers.

TOPICS FOR WRITTEN AND ORAL DISCUSSION

1. Imagine seeing only the first scene of *A Midsummer Night's Dream* and describe how it is like a tragedy. List specific examples. Why do you suppose Shakespeare begins the play so darkly? How does he change the tone, and how soon do you begin to feel that the plot might not be tragic? Provide specific examples.

2. Make a list that summarizes the elements of comedy, recognizing that humor is only one aspect. Then write a description of *A Midsummer Night's Dream* that explains how it fits the rules and patterns of the comic genre. Avoid generalizations as you provide specific examples about character and plot in your response.

3. Discuss how *A Midsummer Night's Dream* fits the patterns of a "romantic comedy." Use specific examples from the play.

• 4. Compare the plot of "Pyramus and Thisby" with the plot of *A Midsummer Night's Dream*. Indicate their similarities and differences. Why do you suppose Shakespeare included the play-within-the-play and how does it add to the overall effect?

5. Humor is an aspect of comedy. Identify some of the sources of humor in *A Midsummer Night's Dream*. Consider the contributions of language, character, and plot.

6. As a small group, choose a comic portion of the play and act it out for the class. Then discuss whether acting the play makes it more humorous than simply reading it and why.

7. How is the woods a significant setting in the play? In answering the question, consider how circumstances for the characters in the court scenes at the beginning and the end of the play are different and how the movement into and out of the woods has affected the change.

8. Setting is achieved through descriptive speeches by various characters. Find two or three examples of such speeches and explain what kind of setting they portray. How is that setting important for the action of the plot?

9. Language is used to distinguish the four groups of characters in the play. Choose examples of various kinds of speech, both poetry and prose, and indicate how these patterns differentiate the character groups.

10. Look for images of nature in *A Midsummer Night's Dream* and discuss how they contribute to the play's tone or atmosphere. Are they pleasant and positive or unpleasant and negative or both?

11. Find references to "eyes" in the play. Why do you suppose Shakespeare includes so many? How are sight and blindness, as opposites, significant in the dramatization of love or perception?

12. Make a list of animal images in the play. How do they add to the atmosphere or tone? Do some characters refer to animals more than other characters? If such a pattern exists, why might that be?

13.   Write an essay about the role of the moon in *A Midsummer Night's Dream*. Research its representation in classical mythology and discuss how that mythology appears in the play. These are some questions you might consider: What does the moon stand for? How do the characters mention it and feel about it? How does it contribute to the play's atmosphere?

14.   Look for examples of dramatic irony in the play—where the audience knows more than one or more characters. What effect does this have on the comedy of the play? Is it possible to see Oberon as a kind of stage manager directing the action and interaction of the other characters? If so, how does this role affect the audience's response to Oberon and their involvement with the other characters?

15.   Choose a scene that includes asides and/or soliloquies as well as dialogue. Draw stage diagrams, indicating where the characters might stand or move as they speak to one another and address the audience. Which characters are meant to hear each other? Which are meant to be unaware of each other? How does that affect where you would place them? Alternatively, act out a scene or portion of a scene, determining where the characters should stand and move as they speak to each other and to the audience.

16.   Consider the effect of comparisons and contrasts between characters and choose one of the following:

  a. Compare Theseus and Hippolyta with Oberon and Titania as ruling couples. Discuss the role of love and power in their relationships.
  b. Compare the triangular relationship between Oberon, Titania, and Bottom with various triangular relationships present among the four lovers. Consider the role of power or jealousy in love.
  c. Compare Puck and Bottom as comic characters in the play. How are they different or similar? How are they like or unlike the character groups they represent?
  d. Compare Oberon's relationship to Titania with his relationship to Puck.
  e. Compare the role of friendship in the relationship between Hermia and Helena and Titania and the Indian votaress of whom she speaks in 2.1.121–37. Alternatively, discuss how relationships of friendship between female characters compare with similar relationships between male characters. Are they different? Do they change in similar or different directions as the play progresses?

17.   Discuss why the performance of "Pyramus and Thisby" is comic. How does the "rude mechanicals'" understanding of imagination contribute to the comedy? Consider language and plot as well as the discussion and explanations the "mechanicals" offer.

18.   Notice the responses of the court characters to the performance of "Pyramus and Thisby." Who makes comments and who does not? Do you find their comments mean and critical or lighthearted and appropriate? Why or why not?

19.   Write a description of how love is portrayed in the play. Focus on only one aspect or argue for the variety of ways love is depicted. Use examples of character interaction to support your position.

20.   Does Shakespeare celebrate love, mock love, or is it possible that he does both at the same time in *A Midsummer Night's Dream*? Address this question as a class debate with one side providing evidence for the celebration of love, the other side providing support for the mockery of love, and a third group listening to both sides and offering its final judgment.

21.   Choose one of the following quotations and explain its significance in the play:

* a) "The course of true love never did run smooth" (1.1.134)
  b) "And yet, to say the truth, reason and love keep little company together nowadays" (3.1.144–45)
  c) "Love looks not with the eyes, but with the mind, And therefore is winged Cupid painted blind" (1.1.234–35)

22.   Describe how imagination has important thematic significance in the play. Consider Theseus's response, "I never may believeº/ These antique fables, nor these fairy toys" (5.1.2–4), but also identify other attitudes towards imagination. What does Hippolyta say in response to Theseus? Does Shakespeare portray imagination as positive or dangerous or both or neither? Explain.

23.   Describe the significance of dreams in the play. Which characters mention dreams and what do they appear to believe? What do you think Shakespeare asks us to believe about dreams? Explain.

24.   Pretend to be a reporter who arrives to interview the lovers the day after their adventures in the woods. Act out the interview in front of the class or write it up. Consider not just what happened but how the lovers might attempt to understand and explain what happened. Remember that none of them ever saw or heard any of the fairies.

25.   Bottom never does offer a ballad of "Bottom's Dream," although he suggests he might. Compose your own version of his "dream" for him. Try to make it suit Bottom's character and speech patterns. Notice, for example, how he often uses a wrong word that sounds similar to the right one. See if you can recreate that pattern.

SUGGESTED READING

Bullough, Geoffrey, ed. *Narrative and Dramatic Sources of Shakespeare.* Vol. 1. London: Routledge, 1973.

Dutton, Richard, et al. *New Casebooks:* A Midsummer Night's Dream. New York: St. Martin's Press, 1996.

Kehler, Dorothea, ed. A Midsummer Night's Dream: *Critical Essays.* New York: Garner Press, 1998.

Pettet, E. C. *Shakespeare and the Romance Tradition.* London: Methuen, 1949.

Salinger, Leo. *Shakespeare and the Traditions of Comedy.* Cambridge: Cambridge UP, 1974.

Swinden, Patrick. *An Introduction to Shakespeare's Comedies.* London: Macmillan, 1973.

Young, David P. *Something of Great Constancy: The Art of "A Midsummer Night's Dream."* New Haven: Yale UP, 1966.

2

Gender Relations: Love, Marriage, and the Battle of the Sexes

A Midsummer Night's Dream is a love story with many unexpected twists and turns. Its characters spend their time and energy falling in and out of love, praising and denouncing love, and being inconstant or remaining true, revealing love's folly and its virtues. Lysander bemoans the dangers and trials that come to lovers, saying, "The course of true love never did run smooth" (1.1.134). Bottom expresses the mystery of love, musing that "reason and love keep little company together nowadays" (3.1.144–45). Amongst all the talk about love, the surrounding action seems to move in two directions: towards love's culmination in marriage or towards love's antagonism in a battle between the sexes—or in the two seemingly opposite directions at the same time. Theseus tells Hippolyta, "I wooed thee with my sword, And won thy love, doing thee injuries" (1.1.16–17). Throughout the play, the relationship between the genders exists in tension, with love and injuries setting up the conflict of the plot. Even within marriage the pattern exists, as Oberon does Titania injuries by making her look foolish with Bottom in order to gain her changeling boy. Even in families the behavior exists, as Egeus and Hermia do each other injuries of trust in their disagreement over law and marriage.

In the play, the paradox of love and injury in the dynamics between men and women can be illuminated by a study of popular attitudes, beliefs, laws, and traditions concerning love, marriage, and gender relationships in sixteenth-century England. Attitudes and expectations were not consistent. Public and private standards sometimes contradicted each other, as did the rules governing church and state. Exploring *A Midsummer Night's Dream* within its historical context can reveal valuable insights into the ideals and customs of the English Renaissance, as well as inconsistencies and complications that challenged the harmony between men and women not simply in the play, but in the culture of its time.

LITERARY CONVENTIONS

Literary conventions provide common assumptions between writers and readers in a way similar to dramatic conventions that allow dramatists and audiences mutually to accept unstated rules or expectations in order to engage imaginations in the unfolding plot. Certain styles, techniques, or forms of expression frame literary and dramatic structure. In Elizabethan times, two literary conventions relevant to the plot of *A Midsummer Night's Dream* were the courtly love tradition and the classical myth of the Amazonian society of warrior women.

The Courtly Love Tradition

Courtly love has its origins in medieval literature from eleventh-century France where poets wrote about romantic adventures. This tradition also spread its influence to England where it later emerged through the voices of Renaissance poets and dramatists. Courtly love in its medieval form reflects an idealized view of love, depicting its supreme value and regarding it as the greatest of human experiences. In this tradition, the female object of love is an exalted Lady who often seems more divine than human. Her beauty is unparalleled and her virtue beyond measure. The man who plays the role of lover often worships the Lady from afar. Indeed, according to the courtly convention, the Lady is often already married and her lover's courtship takes place outside the marriage. His love is an adulterous longing that is not guaranteed or even intended to be fulfilled. The distance between the lover and his beloved is a measure of the purity of their love. Several qualities define the male lover. He demonstrates chivalry, the active service of complete dedication to his beloved. He exemplifies courtesy, which entailed not merely polite behavior but a willingness to prove his worth through dangerous quests, especially in the aid of distressed maidens. Third, he upholds the virtue of humility in his devotion to the woman he worships.

The "Knight's Tale," by Geoffrey Chaucer (c. 1343–1400), one of a collection of his English stories known as the *Canterbury Tales,* is undoubtedly one of the romantic medieval influences on Shakespeare's *Midsummer Night's Dream.* In the tale, two royal cousins of Thebes, Palamon and Arcite, are imprisoned in a tower after Theseus, the ruler of Athens, conquers Thebes. These young men both fall suddenly in love with Queen Hippolyta's sister, Emily, when they see her walking in the garden below the tower. They begin to argue with one another about who has more right to love her. After Arcite is released from prison and Palamon escapes, they meet to fight for Emily's love, but Duke Theseus discovers their plan and instead organizes a tournament between the two with many knights battling on either side. This is a true demonstration of chivalry. The winner will be allowed to marry Emily. Theseus establishes the rules and proclaims that there be no loss of life. In the tournament, which demonstrates the courtly courage and devotion of the two cousins, Palamon is taken prisoner by Arcite's knights and Arcite ruled the winner of Emily's hand. However, Arcite falls from his horse and suffers a mortal injury. At Arcite's death, Palamon is united with Emily. While the tale has a somber tone, it details the high emotions and rash commitments of courtly love that characterize similar interactions between the competing lovers in *A Midsummer Night's Dream.*

As the courtly convention found its way through the centuries to the Renaissance, English writers were especially influenced by Italian love poetry. The poet Petrarch (1304–1374) popularized courtly conventions in his sonnets that depicted women as heavenly creatures, admired for their beauty and perfection. His verse emphasizes the spiritual nature of love, but the character of his male lover differs somewhat from his medieval predecessor. Petrarch's lover demonstrates more dejection than courtesy or chivalry. Miserable in the unfulfilled aspect of his worshipful love, he is more apt to display jealousy than humility in response to his lover (Pettet 19–20). He is willing to die for love, for dying seems the only way to achieve love's true perfection. His language is exaggerated and often fatalistic. Shakespeare became one of the most renowned writers of love sonnets in England, relying on the courtly tradition imported from Petrarch and adapting the conventions to his own imaginative expression. Many of his sonnets were, in fact, written about the relationship of friendship between men, but he also penned sonnets about love between men and women, exploring the relationship rather than simply idealizing it.

Various conventions of the courtly love tradition are incorporated into the language and behavior of characters in *A Midsummer Night's Dream,* especially when the magic of the love-in-idleness flower exaggerates and distorts emotional responses of the four young lovers. From the beginning, Lysander and Hermia display expressions of loyalty and gentleness characteristic of courtly love. But when Lysander and Demetrius both turn their attentions to Helena because of the magic cast upon them, qualities of courtly love become so extreme as to be ridiculous. Lysander manifests extreme dejection when Helena doubts his new advances in the woods, saying, "Why should you think that I should woo in scorn? Scorn and derision never come in tears:°/ Look, when I vow, I weep" (3.2.122–24). Similarly, Demetrius echoes the exalted language of the lover when he awakes and sees Helena with new eyes, calling out,

O Helen, goddess, nymph, perfect, divine!
To what, my love, shall I compare thine eyne?
Crystal is muddy. O, how ripe in show
Thy lips, those kissing cherries, tempting grow!

. . . .

O, let me kiss
This princess of pure white, this seal of bliss! (3.2.137–44)

Helena reacts negatively, believing that these overstated declarations mock her. Shakespeare himself partly mocks the tradition of courtly love as he adopts its language and gesture in an exaggerated form that adds humor to the jealousy and confusion between the four lovers in the woods. Knowing the tradition and its conventions contributes to an understanding of the romance that unfolds in wild directions before it is ultimately restored to harmony.

The Legend of the Amazons

Another literary convention that Shakespeare draws upon in *A Midsummer Night's Dream,* that of the Amazonian warrior women, comes from classical Greek mythology from the fourth and fifth centuries B.C. By tradition, the Amazons were a female society from the region of Scythia who rose to power, conquered the Greeks in many battles, and defended Troy when the city was in danger. According to legend, after Theseus fought and became ruler of Athens, he abducted Hippolyta, Queen of the Amazons, married her, and the two had a son named Hippolytus. When the Amazons tried to take Hippolyta back, they were defeated. The Amazons were said to use men only for procreation, sending sons back to their fathers and keeping only their daughters to train them in their warrior culture.

The Amazons were regarded with a mixture of fascination and suspicion or repulsion in the Renaissance period. On the one hand, they represented all that was the antithesis of the courtly love tradition. Instead of beautiful, divine creatures that men worshipped, protected, and to whom they committed themselves in utter devotion, the Amazons were aggressive warriors, manly in their own way and threatening to men by their skilled martial power. They were also seen as hostile to marriage and therefore a dangerous symbol of barbarism and chaos opposing the values of civilized society. On the other hand, they signified womanly freedom, courage, virtue, and strength. While most Renaissance writers—who were predominantly male—depicted Amazons in a negative light, some saw them as glorious figures of the past and admired their power and skill.

Some who admired the Amazons made direct connections between their own monarch, Queen Elizabeth I, and the Amazonian warriors. A masque or court performance in 1579 during marriage negotiations for the queen included as characters Amazons and male knights who participated in a military tournament at the end of which the men surrendered to the Amazons in a pattern that was certainly contrary to cultural values and expectations. It was a battle of the sexes in which the women won. Comparisons between Elizabeth and warrior Amazons became especially prominent after battle preparations and then the defeat of the Spanish Armada in 1588. The queen visited her troops during that military campaign, before the Spanish ships were destroyed at sea, and is alleged to have said, "I know I have the body of a weak and feeble woman; but I have the heart and stomach of a King, and of a King of England too" (Shepherd 29). As a woman monarch, one with the courage to go to the front lines and visit her troops, she was perceived as the exception to all rules about gender and power in sixteenth-century England. But while some of her subjects were willing to see her as an Amazon warrior, few would have allowed such categories of martial virtue and strength to be identified with other English women. And so the Amazon remained an ambiguous figure, engendering conflicting responses. Shakespeare allows some of this ambiguity to enter into his play where Hippolyta, the Amazon queen, is wooed not by kind words and gentle deeds but by Theseus's military might and is referred to as a "buskin'd warrior," outfitted in the male attire of battle rather than traditional feminine dress.

MARRIAGE LAWS AND CUSTOMS

Examining marriage laws and customs practiced in Shakespeare's England can also help to broaden our understanding of the dynamics between men and women in *A Midsummer Night's Dream.* Almost every age, viewed through the lens of history, reveals elements of transition and change as widely accepted, dominant values and beliefs are subject to resistance, criticism, and challenges from dissenting voices within society. Certainly, this observation appears to be true of gender roles and expectations in sixteenth-century England. Monarchy and patriarchy formed the main political and social power structures, and marriage provided the cornerstone of continuity for each. But within the boundaries of that social system, there were conflicting perspectives about the secular and sacred definitions of marriage, about the balance of individual rights and family expectations in arranging marriages, and about the duties and privileges of husbands and wives.

Patriarchy and Queen Elizabeth

In England's patriarchal system, men were granted supreme authority in politics, community, and family. This male-dominated hierarchy was part of a larger belief system known as the "chain of being," which saw God at the top, moving downward in succession to angels, people, animals, and plants. This official view of "natural" supremacy encouraged a set of parallel relationships that strengthened arguments for a patriarchal society. Just as God was Lord of all and Christ was head of the church, so were kings considered heads of state, and fathers heads of households. Inheritances passed from father to son, and the crown passed from king to prince. The family was seen as a miniature commonwealth mirroring the larger commonwealth or state of England, which, in turn, reflected a God-created universe. It is easy to see that in such a system, women played a necessary but secondary role, subject to their fathers, their husbands, their king, and their God.

Political history in the sixteenth century reveals the prominence of these patriarchal beliefs, but, at the same time, exposes the compromises and contradictions that both established and unsettled peace and order. During Henry VIII's reign (1509–1547), political unrest revolved around his desire for a divorce, his succession of six wives, and his break from the Roman Catholic Church to establish his own authority over the Protestant Church of England. As part of the Reformation, these revolutionary decisions stemmed from Henry's difficulty in producing a male heir to the throne who would satisfy the needs of patriarchy and monarchy. Edward, the only male heir, born to Henry's third wife, died as a young king. Edward VI's short kingship was followed by the stormy reign of his elder half-sister Mary Tudor, known for her reputation as Bloody Mary, and then by the long, relatively peaceful government of his other half-sister, Queen Elizabeth I, who reigned from 1558 to 1603.

Elizabeth's successful political leadership raised many questions about the patriarchal system and its function in marriage and the state. Although she identified herself in masculine terms as "prince" of England, her position as a queen rather than a king commanding obedience from her subjects contradicted the male-dominated assumptions of hierarchy and order. Yet because she was made head of state and governed with political wisdom, she received the authority granted to her royal position. Early in her reign, however, her advisors and subjects were determined to see her married to an appropriate husband, partly because of the perceived need for an heir to continue the monarchy's political stability after her death and partly because of the traditional view that women ought to be wives.

The issue of marriage was complicated and Elizabeth's response was changeable and unpredictable. Politically, she faced not only pressure from her own subjects and advisors to marry and produce an heir but also international pressures to forge an alliance through marriage that would strengthen England in relation to opposing religious positions of various nation-states. Alone, Protestant England was weak and vulnerable to attacks from Catholic strongholds such as Spain. But if Elizabeth were to marry a prince or duke from a European state, she could ensure political strength either by compromising with a Catholic power or joining with a Protestant country. Her advisors thought that such an alliance might stabilize Elizabeth's reign and protect England from international strife. The danger of marrying a foreign prince, however, was that Elizabeth would no longer wield sole power over her own kingdom. Especially as a female ruler in a traditionally male hierarchy, she might be compelled to relinquish some of her authority to her husband. If that husband were a foreign "prince" or king, Elizabeth might ultimately weaken rather than strengthen England's international status.

The other option, marrying an English noble rather than a foreign prince, posed similar problems around the incompatibility of Elizabeth's role as wife and monarch and raised other concerns for her leadership. To wed a subject would diminish her own stature as head of state by breaking down the hierarchy that separated royalty even from nobility and especially from the common people. Elizabeth recognized this dilemma of balancing the need to produce an heir while at the same time maintaining her role as ruler over her people. For several decades—the first half of her reign after her accession in 1558—she played a dangerous but unavoidable political game by courting various foreign princes, as well as an English nobleman or two, without ever committing herself to a marriage contract. This approach provided endless frustration for her political advisors and gained her a reputation as a woman who could never make up her mind. But she was also a ruler who knew how to play for advantage. Her schemes kept her active in several ongoing informal political alliances without having to give up her freedom in submission to a husband, either foreign or English-born.

From early in her reign, Elizabeth tried to avoid the problems associated with the marriage issue by declaring herself married to her kingdom. By the second half of her reign when she was beyond the age of childbearing, she worked hard at fostering an image of herself as the Virgin Queen, turning her status as a single woman into positive political ends. As Protestantism in England grew to ascendancy under her reign, strong advocates of her monarchy encouraged a transfer of some of the Catholic worship of the Virgin Mary to reverence toward the Virgin Queen. This image appeared in public ceremonies surrounding Elizabeth, as well as in literature of the time. In *A Midsummer Night's Dream,* for example, when Oberon describes to Puck a "fair vestal [or virgin] throned by the west" whom Cupid's arrow missed so that "the imperial vot'ress passed on,°/ In maiden meditation, fancy-free" (2.1.158–64),

Shakespeare is most likely referring to Queen Elizabeth. The Virgin Queen imagery, with its roots not only in Catholicism but also in classical mythology of the golden age, helped to maintain support for Elizabeth by characterizing her as an imperial leader who brought to England an age of pure religion, national peace, and economic prosperity.

All the imagery surrounding Elizabeth was complicated and inconsistent. Just as she could be considered both "prince" and queen, she could be viewed as having the masculine qualities of the mythic Amazon warrior and the feminine qualities of a chaste virgin goddess. Just as she could be considered married to her kingdom, she could also portray herself as a mother figure to her subjects. This contradictory language of maternity and virginity, of mortality and immortality, of male and female identity defined Elizabeth's public role until her death in 1603. It characterized a period when the most prominent and powerful figure in the country challenged patriarchy's assumptions about gender, marriage, and authority while providing dramatists and other writers with an unconventional model of female assertiveness.

Chronology of the Tudor Monarchy in Sixteenth-Century England

1509–1547	King Henry VIII rules England.
1547–1553	Henry VIII dies. Edward VI, son of Henry VIII and his wife Jane Seymour, becomes England's king.
1553	King Edward VI dies; Lady Jane Grey is made Queen of England for nine days before being deposed. Mary I, daughter of Henry VIII and Catherine of Aragon, becomes Queen of England. The queen gains a reputation as Bloody Mary.
1554	Princess Elizabeth sent to the Tower because of fears of her rebellion against her sister, Queen Mary I.
1558	Mary I dies; Princess Elizabeth becomes Queen Elizabeth of England.
1571	Elizabeth I negotiates with Henry, Duke of Anjou, for marriage. Plans abandoned a year later.
1588	Spanish Armada defeated in its attempt to conquer England.
1603	Queen Elizabeth I dies and is succeeded by her cousin James VI of Scotland who becomes James I of England.

Courtship and Union

Within this context of tension between the ideals of patriarchy and the reality of a female head of state, other discrepancies and conflicts existed between customs and laws about courtship and marriage. The two issues of individual choice and parental consent that create the conflict in the first scene between Egeus and Hermia reflect friction between legal and traditional expectations which Renaissance England inherited from its past and which was not easily resolved in the unrest of Reformation politics.

On the one hand, the earlier medieval secular view of marriage as an economic, social contract emphasized the parents' role in arranging a match for their children and establishing positive financial conditions. On the other hand, the church, with its increasing influence prior to the Reformation, stressed the binding sacred power of two individuals consenting to a holy union before God without the need for parental influence. After Henry VIII broke away from the Roman Catholic Church and established the Protestant Church of England, conflicting secular and sacred views of marriage continued to co-exist. Church or "canon" law remained the final arbiter, and all that it required legally to make a marriage was the verbal pledge of a man and a woman to each other before witnesses, including the traditional words, "I do." Families, however, maintained a social, if not a legal, influence in directing their children's choices, and even the church firmly advised children to honor and obey their fathers and mothers.

Parental guidance was strongest in upper classes because the economic, social, and political outcome of a marriage was much more significant for people with rank and status. The tradition of parental consent was also stronger for daughters than for sons, because in a patriarchal system, daughters were traditionally recognized as property, making their care and welfare dependent on their husbands' position. Into this mixture of laws and customs, of individual choice and family consent, there was a growing perception that marriage not only could have—but should have—love rather than economic or social gain as its most powerful binding force. Consequently, even when family guidance and approval were recognized and practiced, the feelings of the couple began to be a more important and respected pre-marital consideration. Lysander plays upon this perspective when he argues that not only is he ranked equally in status to Demetrius but more than that, he is "beloved of beauteous Hermia" while Demetrius is not (1.1.104).

Husbands and Wives

In Shakespeare's England, roles of husbands and wives were often addressed in sermons and domestic conduct books that expressed idealistic expectations and practical guidelines for marriage. These popular views invite attention in considering the marriage between Oberon and Titania, who although they are fairies imitate in their interaction the marital relationships of human beings. Within the male-dominated hierarchy of English patriarchy, not only were husbands traditionally granted supreme authority over their wives, but women were also regarded as the weaker sex, physically and morally. Both members of the marriage were expected to fulfill certain duties and responsibilities. The husbands' duties were primarily active and public, involving work outside the home and provision for the family's material needs. In contrast, the wives' responsibilities were more passive and private, including complete obedience to their husbands, as well as bearing and raising children and tending to domestic tasks. Once a woman became married, she surrendered all legal rights and property to her husband, who assumed the control previously exercised by her father.

No doubt, because men were the chief authors of sermons and conduct books articulating these standards and because patriarchy depended on male supremacy, marriage texts often gave more attention to women's roles than to men's. A woman's virginity was considered her greatest virtue before marriage. After marriage, her greatest virtue was her fidelity. She was repeatedly reminded to be silent and submissive. Conduct books and formal debates warned against women being too outspoken and becoming nagging "shrews," while the public harshly condemned adulterous wives, loose women, and unwed mothers. In contrast, a man's adultery was not judged with the same severity, and a husband's honor depended more on his wife's faithfulness than his own. These opposing sexual expectations of husbands and wives presented a double standard that some male writers even in Shakespeare's time began to acknowledge as discriminatory. And yet many others continued to uphold traditional sexual categories as part of the ideal and necessary model of gender relationships.

In fact, against traditional sixteenth-century views of spousal duties, virtues, and indiscretions, opposing perspectives began to emerge with the religious and political changes following the Reformation and during the Renaissance or humanist revival with which it coincided. Historically, the pre-Reformation church viewed marriage as less admirable than a single celibate life, but necessary for procreation and advisable to avoid the temptation of unlawful sexual relations. After the Reformation, leaders within the newly established Protestant church began to stress the social dignity of marriage. A view of marriage that acknowledged the companionship or partnership of the relationship became more popular. The Puritans, a group within the Protestant church, even encouraged private morality and spiritual equality between husbands and wives. Simultaneously, the secular humanism of the Renaissance promoted individualism, recognizing, to a limited degree, the values of freedom and education for women as well as for men. Consequently, although the male hierarchy remained largely intact, women had a greater possibility for self-expression and self-assertion. Nevertheless, traditional assumptions of domestic hierarchy were not simply replaced by growing expressions of individualism and spiritual equality.

These inconsistent historical views of husbands and wives gave Shakespeare scope to explore the nature of male and female relationships in *A Midsummer Night's Dream*. Two of the most fruitful questions to consider are to what extent Shakespeare's play reflects traditional patriarchal attitudes toward love and marriage and to what extent it challenges them. These questions require examination of the marital relationship between Oberon and Titania and the premarital relationship between Theseus and Hippolyta, in the authority and power exercised by the men and the submission or independence demonstrated by the women. The similar issues of male authority and female independence arise in Hermia's relationship to her father and in the four young Athenians' attachments to one another in love and in jealousy. If there is a battle of the sexes as well as an attraction between them, how does that affect the portrayal of gender relations? To love "by doing injury" and to make peace by acknowledging authority are all part of the dynamics that define the tension and resolution of the play.

The excerpted documents and poems that make up the remainder of this chapter help to draw connections between the literary conventions and social history of the English Renaissance and the dramatization of love, marriage, fidelity, and jealousy in *A Midsummer Night's Dream*.

DUKE THESEUS

Plutarch, a Greek biographer (c. 50–120 A.D.), wrote about the legendary Greek and Roman figures of classical mythology. His writings were popular in the Renaissance, translated into French, and then into English in 1579 by Sir Thomas North, a member of the nobility who was renowned for his translation work. Shakespeare relied on North's translation of Plutarch as well as references in Chaucer's "Knight's Tale" for accounts of the life of Duke Theseus. Chaucer depicts Theseus primarily as a noble ruler, wise and compassionate. *Plutarch's Lives* includes some of the same qualities and portrays Theseus as the founder of a great city. But Plutarch also adds details that are at odds with such a description, recording the duke's reputation for treating women badly and for being unfaithful to several of them. The following quotation from North's Plutarch includes three excerpts. The first [1] describes Theseus's role as the new duke of Athens and how he brought peace and order to the city. The second [2] recounts Theseus's capture of Hippolyta and how he treated the Amazons. Note that Plutarch admits to confusion over whether Theseus took Antiopa or Hippolyta. Some writers simply suggest they are two names for the same women. The third [3] excerpt further illustrates Theseus's poor treatment of women, comparing him unfavorably with Romulus, another Greek hero.

Shakespeare was clearly aware of Theseus's mixed reputation, making reference to his deserted women in Oberon's accusation of Hippolyta:

> Didst not thou lead him [Theseus] through the glimmering night
> From Perigenia, who he ravished?
> And make him with fair Aegles break his faith,
> With Ariadne and Antiopa? (2.1.77–80)

These references would have reminded Shakespeare's audiences of Theseus's qualified heroism and thus raise questions about an otherwise straightforward contrast between the "mature" love of Theseus and Hippolyta and the "immature" love or rash infatuation between the young lovers. Shakespeare would seem to suggest that such a contrast between reason and rashness is more ironic than it is simple or straightforward. As you read the following passages consider whether the portrayal of Theseus is consistent or contradictory. Reflect on ways in which Plutarch's Theseus compares with Shakespeare's and whether reading Plutarch's account causes you to see Shakespeare's duke in a different light.

FROM *PLUTARCH'S LIVES OF THE NOBLE GRECIANS AND ROMANS,* TRANS. SIR THOMAS NORTH, VOL. 1 (1579)

(London: J. M. Dent & Co., 1898)

[1] [Theseus] brought all the inhabitants of the whole province of Attica, to be within the city of Athens, and made them all one corporation, which were before dispersed into diverse villages, and by reason thereof were very hard to be assembled together, when occasion was offered to establish any order concerning the common state. Many times also they were at variance together, and by the ears, making wars upon another. But Theseus took the pains to go from village to village, and from family to family, to let them understand the reasons why they should consent unto it. So he found the poor people and the private men, ready to obey and follow his will: but the rich and such as had authority in every village, all against it. Nevertheless he won them, promising that it should be a commonwealth, and not subject to the power of any sole prince, but rather a popular state. In which he would only reserve to himself the charge of the wars, and the preservation of the laws: for the rest, he was content that every citizen in all and for all should bear a like sway and authority.... Now that Theseus was the first who of all others yielded to have a commonwealth or popular state (as Aristotle sayeth) and did give over his regal power.... (63–66)

[2] Touching the voyage he made by the sea Major, Philochorus, and some others hold opinion, that he went thither with Hercules against the Amazons: and that to honour his valiantness, Hercules gave him Antiopa the Amazon. But the more part of the other Historiographers...do write, that Theseus went thither alone, after Hercules' voyage, and that he took this Amazon prisoner, which is likeliest to be true. For we do not find that any other who went this journey with him, had taken any Amazon prisoner besides himself. Bion also the Historiographer, this notwithstanding sayeth, that he brought her away by deceit and stealth. For the Amazons (sayeth he) naturally loving men, did not fly at all when they saw them land in their country, but sent them presents, and that Theseus enticed her to come into his ship, who brought him a present: and so soon as she was aboard, he hoist his sail, and so carried her away.... Afterwards, at the end of four months, peace was taken between them by means of one of the women called Hippolita. For this Historiographer called the Amazon which Theseus married Hippolita, and not Antiopa. Nevertheless, some say that she was slain (fighting on Theseus' side) with a dart, by another called Molpadia. In memory whereof, the pillar which is joining to the temple of the Olympian ground, was set up in her honour. We are not to marvell, if the history of things so ancient, be found so diversely written.... And this is that which is worthy memory (in mine opinion) touching the wars of these Amazons. How the Poet telleth that the Amazons made wars with Theseus to revenge the injury he did to their Queen Antiopa, refusing her, to marry with Phaedra: and as for the murder which he telleth that Hercules did, that me thinks is altogether but device of Poets. It is very true, that after the death of Antiopa, Theseus married Phaedra, having had before of Antiopa a son called Hippolytus, or as the Poet Pindarus writes, Demophon. And for that Historiographers do not

in any thing speak against the tragical Poets: in that which concerneth the ill hap that chanced to him, in the persons of his wife and of his son: we must needs take it to be so, as we find it written in the tragedies. And yet we find many other reports touching the marriages of Theseus, whose beginnings had no great good honest ground, neither fell out their ends very fortunate. . . . (68–73)

[3] . . . Theseus' faults touching women and ravishments, of the twain, had the less shadow and colour of honesty. Because Theseus did attempt it very often: for he stole away Ariadne, Antiope, and Anaxo the Troezenian. Again being steeped in years, and at later age, and past marriage: he stole away Helen in her minority, being nothing near to consent to marry. Then his taking of the daughters of the Troezenians, of the Lacedaemonians, and the Amazons (neither contracted to him, nor comparable to the birth and linage of his own country which were at Athens, and descended of the noble race and progeny of Erichtheus, and of Cecrops) did give men occasion to suspect that his womanishness was rather to satisfy lust, than of any great love. Romulus now in contrary manner, when his people had taken eight hundred or thereabouts, of the Sabine women to ravish them: kept but only one for himself . . . and delivered the rest to his best and most honest citizens. . . . The Athenians contrariwise, by Theseus' marriages, did get neither love nor kindred of any one person, but rather they procured wars, enmities, and slaughter of their citizens, with the loss in the end of the city of Aphidnae. (154–57)

QUEEN ELIZABETH AS AN AMAZON

Some of Queen Elizabeth's subjects compared her to an Amazon warrior, especially after the English faced down the threat of the Spanish Armada. The Spanish fleet of ships headed towards England for war, but were all destroyed in a storm. In the following account, poet James Aske reflects the surge of national support for Elizabeth following the English victory as he gives high praise to his monarch, portraying her as a martial queen, full of courage and a source of encouragement to the English troops as they gathered in August 1588 preparing for the Spanish to attack. Pay attention to words that Aske uses to describe the "triumphant" Elizabeth and what relationship she has with her troops.

FROM JAMES ASKE, *ELIZABETHA TRIUMPHANS* (1588)

(London: Thomas Orwin for Thomas Newman, 1588; STC 847) 22–24

The Drummes, The Fifes, the Trumpets passing shrill,
Do sounded yield such marching forward notes,
As Mars himself with all his train'd-up men,
In Arms are pressed, as if the Goddess Peace
Were coming now to banish him the field.
Which war-like show with that *Mars* thundering noise,
So ravished our princely Sovereign,
(Addicted only then to Martial prowess)
As that she doth (her train forbid therefore)
Most bravely mounted on a stately steed
With Trunchion in her hand (not us'd thereto)
And with her none, except her Lieutenant,
Accompanied with the Lord *Chamberlain,*
Come marching towards this her marching fight,
In nought unlike the *Amazonian Queen,*
Who beating down amain the bloody *Greeks,*
Thereby to grapple with *Achilles* stout,
Even at the time when *Troy* was sore besieg'd.
  . . . .
Thus comes our Queen (our thrice renowned Queen)
A General beseeming such a Camp:
Thus comes our guide, a princely careful guide,
In war-like force to see her warring men,

Who couched had their strong defensive Pikes,
As if they were to fight at push thereof.
She nigh them come, they pitch their fore-couch'd Pikes,
And she stands still to see the Battle set,
With joy to see her men to keep their ranks,

    . . . .

Their Prowess show, then did our sacred Queen
Here signs display of courage wonderful.
For when our Queen (an Amazonian Queen)
Most carefully the Vaward had beheld,
She thence doth go the Rearward for to see,
And takes a view of it two strong set Flanks:
At whose by passing, Lance with Pike are bow'd,
And all yield reverence to her sacred self.
Her officers with all her Soldiers there,
Do tokens show of their made joyful hearts.
She gives them thanks as had she done before
Who nought have done but what their duties hid.
Her stateliness was so with love show'd join'd,
As all there then did jointly joy and fear.
They joy'd in that they see their ruler's love
But fear'd least that in ought they should offend
Against herself, the Goddess of this land.
Thus causing joy and fear, she passed thence
With cheerful heart for this her late viewed sight
Unto the Tent of her Lieutenant there:
Where ready were in readiness each thing,
Which could be fit to entertain a Queen.

SHAKESPEAREAN LOVE POETRY

Shakespeare was a master at writing Renaissance love poetry in the form of sonnets. A sonnet is a fourteen-line poem with an iambic pentameter rhythm and a fixed rhyme pattern. In Shakespeare's sonnets, the last two lines, as rhyming couplets, summarize or reverse the argument or position that has been presented in the previous twelve lines. Of the two sonnets presented here, the first, 18, begins with a question and then proceeds to answer it with images of comparison that attempt to describe the beauty of the speaker's beloved. The last two lines suggest that the words of the poem itself can give lasting memory to the beauty being portrayed. The second sonnet, 130, stands in stark contrast to the first by denying all the traditional images of beauty belonging to the courtly love tradition. Shakespeare is deliberately playing with the courtly tradition, as, indeed, he appears to be in places throughout *A Midsummer Night's Dream.* And yet the conclusion of sonnet 130 is an affirmation of love rather than an argument against it, an affirmation that depends on a realistic rather than idealistic view of love and beauty. Consider how the language of these very different sonnets compares to the expressions of love between Hermia, Lysander, Helena, and Demetrius and which sonnet, if either, is a more convincing approach to love's depth and sincerity.

FROM WILLIAM SHAKESPEARE, SONNETS 18 AND 130
(c. 1590s)

(*The Riverside Shakespeare,* Ed. G. Blakemore Evans et al., Boston: Houghton, 1974) 1752, 1773

Sonnet 18

Shall I compare thee to a summer's day?
Thou art more lovely and more temperate:
Rough winds do shake the darling buds of May,
And summer's lease hath all too short a date;
Sometime too hot the eye of heaven shines,
And often is his gold complexion dimm'd,
And every fair from fair sometime declines,
By chance or nature's changing course untrimm'd:
But thy eternal summer shall not fade,
Nor lose possession of that fair thou ow'st,

Nor shall Death brag thou wand'rest in his shade,
When in eternal lines to time thou grow'st.
> So long as men can breathe or eyes can see,
> So long lives this, and this gives life to thee.

Sonnet 130

My mistress' eyes are nothing like the sun;
Coral is far more red than her lips' red;
If snow be white, why then her breasts are dun;
If hairs be wires, black wires grow on her head.
I have seen roses damask'd, red and white,
But no such roses see I in her cheeks,
And in some perfumes is there more delight
Than in the breath that from my mistress reeks.
I love to hear her speak, yet well I know
That music hath a far more pleasing sound;
I grant I never saw a goddess go,
My mistress when she walks treads on the ground.
> And yet, by heaven, I think my love as rare
> As any she belied with false compare.

THE CONSENT AND CONTRACT OF MARRIAGE

John Dod and Robert Cleaver's *A Godly Form of Household Government* (1598) is one of many handbooks on marriage written in England in the sixteenth and seventeenth centuries. The excerpts included below specifically address the terms of the marriage contract, outlining what constitutes a legitimate marriage and what potential miseries and dangers might result from a hasty or secret marital contract. Note the importance of mutual, voluntary consent between the engaged couple, as well as the rights and limitations of parents in approving or dissolving their children's marriages.

FROM JOHN DOD AND ROBERT CLEAVER, *A GODLY FORM OF HOUSEHOLD GOVERNMENT: FOR THE ORDERING OF PRIVATE FAMILIES, ACCORDING TO THE DIRECTION OF GOD'S WORD* (1598)

(London: 1598. STC 5383)

A Contract, is a voluntary promise of marriage, mutually made between one man and one woman, both being meet and free to marry one another, and therefore allowed so to do by their Parents.

.... [W]e call this promise of marriage, voluntary, because it must not come from the lips alone, but from the well-liking and consent of the heart: for if it be only a verbal promise, without any will at all, (and so mere hypocritical and dissembled) though it bindeth the party that promiseth, to the performance of his promise, made before God and man: yet if the Parents afterwards shall certainly know this, and that there was no will, nor unfeigned meaning at all in the party, neither yet is, but rather a loathing and abhorring of his spouse betrothed, though he be not able to render just and sufficient cause thereof, they may upon this occasion, either defer the day of marriage the longer, to see if God will happily change the mind of the party, or utterly break and frustrate the promise.... Wherefore this promise must be in this respect, at least, willing, and voluntary. For...if it be voluntary and unfeigned, it is enough, and fully sufficient, to make a true contract in the Lord.... Secondly, we call it voluntary, in respect of constraint and compulsion, contrary to a free consent: for if either party be urged, constrained, or compelled, by great fear of their Parents, or others, by threatening of loss or preferment, of health, of limb, of life, or of any such other like, or by any other violent manner of dealing whatsoever, to yield their promise clean contrary to the motion of good liking of their hearts. This kind of promise, as it doth not bind the party to keep it: so it ought to be frustrated and broken by the Parents themselves, or by such masters as may and ought, to command and rule them in such cases. (116–21)

But if [a marriage contract] be mutual, then it doth mutually and inviolably bind both: so that in this regard, neither Parent, Magistrate, nor any other, can or ought to break it. For this being fully performed and accomplished, is one principal cause of making two one flesh.... (123)

...it is a calamity infernal...to be in company with those that a man would not be withall, and yet cannot be separated nor depart from them. Hereof cometh, as we do see in some marriages, so great ruins, so wicked and vile deed, as maims, & murders committed by such desperate persons, as are loath to keep, and yet cannot lawfully refuse, nor leave them: Therefore young folks ought not to be too rash and hasty in their choice, but to have the good advice and direction of their parents and trusty friends in this behalf, who have better judgment, and are more free from the motions of all affections, than they are. And they must take heed, lest following the light and corrupt judgment of their own affections and minds, they change not a short delectation and pleasure, into a continual sorrow and repentance. For we do learn, by great and continual use and experience of things, that the secret contracts made between those that be young do seldom prosper, whereas contrariwise, those marriages that are made and established by the advice of wise and religious parents, do prosper well. (151–52)

THE DUTIES AND RESPONSIBILITIES OF MARRIAGE

Edmund Tilney was the master of the revels who controlled court entertainments and licensed plays for the public. His *brief and pleasant discourse of
duties in Marriage, called the Flower of Friendship* was a popular conduct book
on marriage, published in at least seven editions between 1568 and 1587.
Tilney organizes his book in the form of a dialogue or conversation involving
several male and female characters, some of whom represent prominent historical figures in the sixteenth century, such as Erasmus, the influential humanist thinker. Within the general debate about marriage, the first half of the
narrative addresses a husband's specific virtues and responsibilities, while the
second half considers a wife's parallel virtues and duties. Although the main
argument stresses conventional Elizabethan values, characters occasionally
disagree with one another, raising questions about accepted ideals of marital
harmony. Consequently, the discussion includes seemingly incompatible references, such as the equality or friendship of spouses and the authority of the
husband, or the importance of honesty and the value of pretending or dissembling.

The following selections have been chosen for their potential relevance to
the attitudes and behaviors toward marriage as dramatized in *A Midsummer
Night's Dream*. The excerpts [1] define what constitutes marital equality,
[2] warn against the dangers of jealousy, [3] provide reasons supporting the
husband's domestic authority, and [4] explain the duty of wifely obedience
even when a woman is unjustly treated by her husband. Consider especially
how Oberon and Titania accept and represent these ideals and what consequences follow when they do or do not comply. Also reflect on the relationship between Theseus and Hippolyta as they prepare for marriage and how
they react to one another.

FROM EDMUND TILNEY, *A BRIEF AND PLEASANT DISCOURSE OF DUTIES IN MARRIAGE, CALLED THE FLOWER OF FRIENDSHIP* (1568)

(London: 1568. STC 24076)

[1] [T]he Lady *Julia* desireth to hear of our friendly *Flower,* whereto now I return,
and say, that equality is principally to be considered in this matrimonial amity, as well
of years, as of the gifts of nature, and fortune. For equalness herein, maketh friendli-
ness....

[2] The eighth [virtue] is to be circumspect in matters that concern his honesty, and not to be jealous of his wife. The Stoic philosophers say, that jealousy is a certain care of man's mind, least another should possess the thing, which he alone would enjoy. There is no greater torment, than the vexation of a jealous mind, which, even as the moth fretteth the cloth, doth consume the heart, that is vexed therewith. Two kind of persons are commonly sore sick in this disease, either those that are evil themselves, or they, that in their youth have gone astray, supposing that as other men's wives have done towards them, so will theirs do towards others, which is vanity to think, more folly to suspect, and greatest foolishness to speak of. For as some lewd women be dissolute: so likewise women there be, honest, and very circumspect. If the wife be to be suspected, let the man work as secretly, and closely, as he can to reprehend her, yet all will not peradventure avail. For, trust me, no wisdom, no craft, no science, no strength, no subtlety, yea, no patience suffiseth to enforce a woman, to be true to her husband, if she otherwise determine. Therefore to conclude to be jealous, either needeth not, or booteth not....

[3] Ye say well, Madam, quoth M. *Erasmus.* For indeed both divine, and human laws, in our religion giveth the man absolute authority, over the woman in all places. And, quoth the Lady *Julia,* as I said before, reason doth confirm the same, the man being as he is, most apt for the sovereign being in government, not only skill, and experience to be required, but also capacity to comprehend, wisdom to understand, strength to execute, solicitude to prosecute, patience to suffer, means to sustain, and above all a great courage to accomplish, all which are commonly in a man, but in a woman very rare: Then what blame deserve those men, that do permit their wives to rule all, and suffer themselves to be commanded for company....

[4] For this married woman, whom I have taken upon me to describe, must of duty be unto her husband in all things obedient, and therefore if he, sometimes moved, do chance to chide her, she must forebear. In doing whereof he shall neither eat the more at his dinner, nor she have the less appetite to her supper. This wise woman must consider, that her husband chideth, either without reason, or hath good cause. If reason move him, then of duty she is bound to obey, if otherwise, it is her part to dissemble the matter. For in nothing can a wife show a greater wisdom, than in dissembling with an importunate husband. Her honesty, her good nature, and her praise is showed in nothing more, than in tolerating of an undiscreet man, and to conclude, as the woman ought not to command the man, but to be always obedient: so ought he not to suffer himself to be commanded of his wife.

TOPICS FOR WRITTEN AND ORAL DISCUSSION

1. Familiarize yourself with Chaucer's "Knight's Tale." Explain how Palamon and Arcite fall in love with Emily and how their response to her and to each other fits the courtly love tradition as defined in this chapter.

2. Compare the love of Chaucer's Palamon and Arcite for Emily with Lysander and Demetrius's love in *A Midsummer Night's Dream*. What parallels do you see? How are their circumstances different? Look for specific lines in the "Knight's Tale" that seem to share expressions or behavior with lines in Shakespeare's play.

3. Write a paragraph or two about the relationship between friendship and romantic love in the "Knight's Tale" and *A Midsummer Night's Dream*. (Refer also to the description of "Romantic Love" in chapter 1). Do you think Shakespeare mocks courtly love or takes it seriously? Explain.

4. Referring to excerpts from Chaucer's "Knight's Tale" and *Plutarch's Lives,* describe the qualities that make the Greek hero Theseus a good ruler. Summarize Theseus's faults as they are portrayed in *Plutarch's Lives.* Do these faults appear inconsistent with his qualities as a good leader? Explain why or why not.

5. Considering Chaucer's and Plutarch's descriptions of Theseus, discuss whether Shakespeare characterizes his Theseus in a similar fashion or whether his Theseus is more positively or negatively portrayed than the other two. Use evidence from the play to support your position, referring to Theseus's treatment of Hippolyta and of his other Athenian subjects.

6. What words does James Aske use to describe Queen Elizabeth in *Elizabetha Triumphans*? What traits does he portray in Elizabeth that reflect those of an Amazon warrior?

7. Discuss Elizabeth's relationship to her soldiers in Aske's account. Why do the soldiers respond with both fear and joy? What does that response suggest about Elizabeth's leadership?

8. Aske's description in *Elizabetha Triumphans* is very visual. Draw a poster that captures some of the details included in his account. You may need to look up references to the weapons "lance" and "pike." (See *All Things Shakespeare*)

9. Queen Hippolyta speaks very few lines in *A Midsummer Night's Dream*. Discuss whether you think Shakespeare portrays her as an Amazon in a positive or a negative light, according to her words and the other characters' responses to her, especially Theseus's.

10. Write a few diary entries for Hippolyta in which she reflects on her past glories as an Amazon and expresses her feelings about the marriage to Theseus. Is she happy about her new circumstances or does she yearn for the past? Refer to the play and to the section on "The Legend of the Amazons" in this chapter.

11. Summarize the main comparisons Shakespeare makes in Sonnet 18 between the lover being described and the aspects of nature to which she is being compared. How does the speaker expect to ensure his lover's lasting memory or immortality?

12.   What are the images and metaphors Shakespeare uses in Sonnet 130 as the speaker describes his lover? Do the descriptions seem humorous? If so, why? Why does the speaker use such negative comparisons? How does the conclusion in the last two lines reverse the tone of the earlier description and what does that suggest about the speaker's true feelings for his lover?

13.   Consider Sonnet 130 in terms of the courtly love tradition. What attitude does Shakespeare take towards the tradition in this poem?

14.   Compare Sonnet 18 and Sonnet 130 as poems about love. How are they different? What is the attitude towards love and the lover in each poem? Which one do you like better and why?

15.   Consider either Sonnet 18 or Sonnet 130 in connection with *A Midsummer Night's Dream*. Is the language of either poem like some of the language used by any of the lovers in the play? Find specific examples. Remember also to look at the language used by the "rude mechanicals" as they enact the story of "Pyramus and Thisby."

16.   In *A Godly Form of Household Government,* what do its writers, Dod and Cleaver, consider the main conditions that make a marriage legal and binding? When might a marriage not be binding, and what might parents be allowed to do in such circumstances? How are the conditions Dod and Cleaver describe enacted or challenged in the marriage plans of Hermia and Lysander and Egeus and Demetrius in *A Midsummer Night's Dream?*

17.   What do Dod and Cleaver suggest are the dangers of a hasty marriage? Do you find that their entire discussion is an argument in favor of Lysander and Hermia or of Demetrius and Egeus? Explain your position. Do you think Dod and Cleaver are wise and compassionate in their views of marriage or moralistic and high-handed?

18.   Based on your understanding of Renaissance marriage laws and attitudes, do you find Egeus at all sympathetic in his position? Why or why not? Write several diary entries for Egeus that indicate his feelings after the meeting with Theseus in act 1 and again after Theseus's decision to allow Hermia and Lysander to marry in act 4. Do you think he relents and accepts Hermia's marriage since Demetrius no longer wants to wed her, or do you think he remains stubbornly insistent on his parental authority?

19.   According to Edmund Tilney in *A brief and pleasant discourse of duties in Marriage, called the Flower of Friendship,* what kind of relationship should exist between husbands and wives in Renaissance England? Does his view of male and female roles suggest equality and companionship, a hierarchy based on male dominance and female submission, or both? Explain your position.

20.   Tilney argues against a man's jealousy in marriage but also suggests that the wife must be obedient. Discuss how his views reflect on the relationship between Oberon and Titania. How should the fairy king and queen act toward each other according to Tilney? What happens when they do not?

21.   Hold a debate in which you discuss whether Oberon or Titania seems more blameworthy in their disagreement and whether the resolution is appropriate and satisfactory. One side will argue in favor of Titania and the other side in favor of Oberon.

Use evidence from the play and draw on ideas shared in Tilney's discourse. Let the class decide which side provided the most convincing case.

SUGGESTED READING

Colie, Rosalie L. *Shakespeare's Living Art*. Princeton, NJ: Princeton UP, 1974.

Donaldson, E. Talbot, *The Swan at the Well: Shakespeare Reading Chaucer*. New Haven: Yale UP, 1985.

Dreher, Diane Elizabeth. *Domination and Defiance: Fathers and Daughters in Shakespeare*. Lexington: University of Kentucky Press, 1986. See especially chapter 2, "The Renaissance Background."

DuBois, Page. *Centaurs and Amazons: Women and the Pre-History of the Great Chain of Being*. Ann Arbor: University of Michigan Press, 1982.

Lewis, C. S. *The Allegory of Love: A Study in Medieval Tradition*. Oxford: Oxford UP, 1936. See chapter 1 on courtly love.

Macfarlane, Alan. *Marriage and Love in England: Modes of Reproduction, 1300–1840*. Oxford: Basil Blackwell, 1986. See especially Part III.

Olsen, Kristen. *All Things Shakespeare: An Encyclopedia of Shakespeare's World*. 2 vols. Westport, CT: Greenwood Publishing Group, 2002.

Pettet, E. C. *Shakespeare and the Romance Tradition*. London: Methuen, 1949.

Plowden, Alison. *Marriage with My Kingdom: The Courtship of Elizabeth I*. London: Macmillan, 1977.

Rose, Mary Beth. *The Expense of Spirit: Love and Sexuality in English Renaissance Drama*. Ithaca: Cornell UP, 1988.

Shepherd, Simon. *Amazons and Warrior Women: Varieties of Feminism in Seventeenth-Century Drama*. Sussex: The Harvester Press Ltd., 1981.

Stone, Lawrence. *The Family, Sex, and Marriage in England, 1500–1800*. New York: Harper and Row, 1977.

Valency, Maurice. *In Praise of Love: An Introduction to the Love-Poetry of the Renaissance*. New York: Octagon Books, 1975.

Wayne, Valerie, ed. Introduction. *The Flower of Friendship: A Renaissance Dialogue Contesting Marriage*. By Edmund Tilney. Ithaca, NY: Cornell UP, 1992. 1–94.

Woodbridge, Linda. *Women and the English Renaissance: Literature and the Nature of Womankind, 1540–1620*. Urbana: University of Illinois Press, 1984.

Wrightson, Keith. *English Society, 1580–1680*. London: Hutchinson, 1982. See especially chapters 3 and 4.

Yates, Frances A. *Astrea: The Imperial Theme in the Sixteenth Century*. London: Routledge and Kegan Paul, 1975.

3

Social Distinctions: Royalty, Gentry, and the Common People

In *A Midsummer Night's Dream,* groups of characters in Athens are distinguished by their speech, their dress, their habits and occupations, and their social position. Clear differences divide the nobles at court from the craftsmen who seek to entertain the guests at the Athenian wedding. Even in the fairy world where societal norms do not impose the same rigid standards, the king and queen of this enchanted kingdom exercise a measure of power and authority that sets them above and apart from Puck and the other serving fairies. The degrees of separation in the play deliberately remind audiences that there are those who rule and those who are ruled, those who command and those who serve, those with significant privilege and those with much less who aspire, at times, to more than what they have. The "rude mechanicals" indicate, for example, that they hope to make their fortune by enacting their play before the duke's household. And yet although "Pyramus and Thisby" is received in good humor, the vast social and educational gap between the on-stage audience and the artisan performers indicates just how optimistic and even unrealistic are the craftsmen's hopes and aspirations. Shakespeare's nobles and his common people inhabit separate worlds even as the play draws to a close.

The social distinctions in the play raise questions about the structure of the society in which Shakespeare lived and wrote. What was the relationship between the ruler and the ruled? What set the nobility and gentry apart from the common people? How did the different classes or groups interact with one another? What were their hopes and expectations, their fears and frustrations? Answering these questions can illuminate the social interaction in *A Midsummer*

Night's Dream and even provide a clearer historical context for some of the remarks Titania and Oberon make about the chaos and disorder they cause in the natural and supernatural worlds.

SOCIAL ORDER

Elizabethan England was organized according to a hierarchical system. The section on "Patriarchy and Queen Elizabeth" in chapter 2 has already made reference to the effect of that hierarchy on marital expectations and Elizabeth's obstacles as a female head of state. But the dominant belief system during her reign had religious, political, and social implications far beyond the questions surrounding her need to marry.

Referred to today as the Elizabethan World Picture, the popular view of order in England in the sixteenth century was based on a metaphor of a "chain of being" in which everything in the universe was perceived to be linked vertically and hierarchically from the greatest to the least. As a universal, religious model, this chain moved from God at the top to the lowest inanimate objects at the bottom. As a political model, this chain also provided an explanation for the monarchical system in which the king—or queen, in Elizabeth's case—represented God as the figure at the top of the human hierarchy governing with sole authority over all subjects who ranked from the highest or noblest members to the meanest or lowest sort. In other words, the political model also prescribed a social model in which definite distinctions were made among subjects to explain and to confirm by practice and decree that some subjects were greater and others lesser in relation to each other. Today we easily identify this as a class system. In Elizabeth's time, the language of "class" was not so commonly used but its hierarchical beliefs were both accepted and practiced as a way to ensure order and stability. According to the "chain of being" metaphor, social and cosmic harmony and unity prevailed only when the God-ordained degree and order of hierarchy ensured that all parts—and all people—performed their proper function in their proper place. When any part did not fulfill its function in the hierarchy, chaos and disorder spread through the entire system. The higher in the system the damage occurred, the greater was the measure of chaos.

Royalty

This view of order was encouraged by Elizabeth and her advisors as a means of strengthening her authority as England's royal monarch. In the Middle Ages prior to her father and grandfather's kingship, a feudal system of order existed in which lords had significant power over their own estates and could raise their own armies against one another. After years of civil war, the Tudors, under kings Henry VII and VIII, began to centralize power in the monarchy, and the blood of royalty became far more important as a single ruler began to solicit loyalty from his lords and nobles, creating and responding to an era of growing national consciousness. By the time Elizabeth became queen, the feudal system had passed and the monarchical system was in place.

Yet Elizabeth had to work hard to solidify her position and create an image of power that would foster obedience. All her subjects came to be recognized not only as her responsibility but also as her servants. She had the right to distribute lands, choose advisors, grant peerages or titles to nobles, provide them sources of revenue, or remove them from positions of favor. She could honor and she could punish. She also moved among the common people, travelling in state progresses throughout the country to let her subjects pay her homage and to honor them with her presence. In short, as the royal ruler of England, understood to be God's human representative at the top of the great "chain of being," she was in a class of her own, though she constantly interacted with her subjects, including those of higher and lower degree.

Shakespeare's romantic comedy has no clear monarchical counterpart to Queen Elizabeth, as do many of his histories and tragedies such as *Richard II* and *King Lear*. Shakespeare does recognize and honor his queen, however, in Oberon's reference to a "fair vestal" or Virgin Queen (2.1.158), who was likely Elizabeth, as contemporary audiences would have recognized. He also indicates the authority Duke Theseus as ruler over Athens demonstrates in interpreting the law to which Egeus appeals in demanding his daughter's obedience. Theseus first accepts Egeus's demands, but adds to Hermia's legal alternatives between death and paternal obedience, a lesser, though unappealing punishment of forever living a single life. Ultimately, however, Theseus overturns the law, exercising his prerogative as ruler and demonstrating that his governing power is greater than either the law or Egeus's paternal rights. Finally, the portrayals of Titania and Oberon draw attention not simply to supernatural power but to the concept of hierarchy by indicating just how much damage can occur when those at the top of the order do not behave as they should. Titania provides a litany of disasters in the natural world that have been generated by the discord between the fairy king and queen (2.1.81–117). The world is out of tune. Indeed, harmony and discord recur as thematic words throughout the play, suggesting the tension caused by disobedience, ill judgment, and an unwillingness to adhere to the hierarchical pattern of order.

Gentry

If crowned royalty existed in a class of its own, wealth, power, and lifestyle separated the other two main social groups, those who were gentlemen and those who were not. Apart from the queen, women had status primarily only according to the social positions of their husbands and therefore receive little attention in this discussion. The nobles or aristocrats who were the highest order of gentry were the most powerful social elites in Elizabethan England next to the queen. Their wealth and prestige came from their position as large landowners, from marriage with landowning families, as well as through the queen's special appointments to offices at her court and investment in private ventures and adventures. They had considerable influence not only at court but also at the county level of government where they could fill positions such as clergy, constables, and justices of the peace with relatives or loyal clients. The monarchical government depended on such hierarchical ties of loyalty— the common people to the nobles and the nobles to their queen—because there was no standing army or separate justice system to insure order. Stability came through patronage and a sense that the aristocracy commanded respect and obedience because of their power and influence.

The group recognized as gentry in sixteenth-century English society included not only the small number of wealthiest landowners with titles such as lord or duke, but also other individuals with less personal wealth but enough property or influence to distinguish them from the majority of Elizabethan subjects who labored with their hands. In fact, the third mark of gentlemanly status—along with wealth and power—was lifestyle, defined by leisure and an education in refinement (Sharpe 167). Even the lower order of gentlemen considered "minor gentlemen" could claim this status. Although wealth was the primary factor in measuring social standing, good breeding and good reputation were valued and essential indicators of an elite position in the general population. Ironically, the life of the gentry was an expensive proposition because a life of leisure cost money but, just as importantly, so did the *appearance* of leisure and wealth, which could only be achieved through a public display of riches to foster respect and admiration, allowing the gentry their sense of social superiority.

The Common People

The common people included all those who were socially beneath the gentry or aristocracy, from yeoman and merchants to artisans, laborers, and the unemployed. In other words, there were higher and lower positions within the category of common people just as there were higher and lower sorts of gentlemen. A yeoman was a rural farmer with enough land to be reasonably affluent, while his counterpart, an urban master, was independent enough to run his own business in a town or city, hiring apprentices and often running for public office. Sometimes a yeoman, an urban master, or a merchant could be successful enough or lucky enough to amass greater wealth than the least wealthy of gentlemen, but because they worked with their hands and did not enjoy a life of leisure, they were typically considered distinct from the aristocracy.

Artisans, known as artificers, were craftsmen or tradesmen who had apprenticed for at least seven years in a specific trade, such as those identified with the "rude mechanicals" in *A Midsummer Night's Dream*. For example, a "bottom" is a skein or bobbin used by a weaver and indicates Bottom's trade; a "flute" refers to the fluted bellows of an organ and represents Flute's trade as a "bellows mender." Although the Elizabethans lacked clear, consistent language to distinguish different groups within the larger category of common people, the artisans or craftsmen most likely fall into a group referred to as "the middling sort" as opposed to "the better sort" above them or "the meaner" or "lesser sort" below them. They were neither wealthy nor desperately poor. They had skilled trades that could keep them employed, though some trades generated more income than others. Tailors were proverbially thin, and Shakespeare's character name, "Starveling the Tailor," suggests that such cloth workers were not among the wealthiest of craftsmen.

Artisans were not expected to be refined, as gentlemen were, nor did they have the leisure for extensive education, but many did have at least some grammar school training. Shakespeare's "rude mechanicals" can read well enough to rehearse a script, although Snug the Joiner claims to be "slow of study" and is given the lion's part for it is "nothing but roaring" (1.2.68–70). In short, most artisans were better off than the vast majority of day laborers who toiled long hours in sometimes dangerous conditions. Moreover, the working poor were subject to unemployment because of a seasonal farm economy complicated by a growing unskilled workforce, the result of increasing population. Nevertheless, artisans were still among the lowest level of the hierarchy, those who were to be ruled rather than rule, and they had little direct say in government affairs. Shakespeare makes much fun of the artisans in *A Midsummer Night's Dream* and draws clear distinctions between them and the court characters. From a historical perspective, however, that difference appears to come primarily because the gentry or nobility were granted such high status compared to the non-elites or common people, not because all commoners shared equal conditions or because the "rude mechanicals" represented the very poorest members of society.

SOCIAL MOBILITY

Queen Elizabeth and her supporters in government and religion vocally upheld a view of order based on hierarchy and reminded English subjects to respect their place in the system. Laws and even sermons endorsed obedience as important for stability. Still, the hierarchy was not rigidly fixed; there was some mobility up and down the ranks. Elizabeth herself exercised the right not only to make men lords but also to remove their titles. This, among other favors granted and revoked, caused individuals within the aristocracy to gain and lose social status and significant amounts of money, moving them from higher to lower positions in the gentry or vice versa. More significantly, the large gap between gentry and the common people was sometimes removed as individuals lost or gained status. Because landed nobles left their estates to their eldest sons, younger sons were often sent off to apprentice and learn a respectable trade, becoming craftsmen from an aristocratic family. But if they were successful in their craft, they might earn enough money to purchase country property and settle down to a life of leisure again, returning to the class of landed aristocrats.

Interestingly, by the Elizabethan period, as the "middling sort" began to appear in society, a man who had not been born into the aristocracy could work his way up the ladder and "buy" himself status as a gentleman. Those who obtained a university degree or a military commission allowing them to live without manual labor had the opportunity to become gentlemen. Others could do so through acquiring wealth or land. Shakespeare's family exemplifies this type of social mobility. John Shakespeare, William's father, was a glover and a successful man of property in Stratford. He married the daughter of a wealthy farmer or yeoman in the area and held numerous public offices, including bailiff, the equivalent of mayor of Stratford. John Shakespeare applied to the Herald's College for a coat of arms, which would have elevated him from the wealthy middle-class to the gentry. His application was never completed, however, for he appears to have then fallen on financial hard times before being able to complete the costly process.

William Shakespeare was even more materially successful than his father had been. After he began writing and acting in plays, he became a shareholder in two theater buildings in London, the Globe and the Blackfriars, eventually bought a large home in Stratford, and invested in agricultural lands. His last years appear to have been spent primarily looking after his property interests. If he never displayed a gentleman's coat of arms, he certainly came gradually to live the life of a gentleman rather than a common man. The fortunes of the Shakespeare family indicate the fluidity and ambiguity of social status in sixteenth- and early-seventeenth-century England.

While the governing authorities emphasized that people should be content with their own place in society, some fell through misfortune or mismanagement from higher ranks to more lowly positions, and others who could do so tried to redraw the lines of social hierarchy to their own advantage. The "rude mechanicals" in *A Midsummer Night's Dream* attach personal aspirations to their rehearsal of "Pyramus and Thisby." They hope not simply that the play will be chosen for performance, but that the duke will be so impressed with them that he will award them all a pension of "sixpence a day" so that they shall be "made men" of fortune instead of toiling at their crafts (4.2.15–24). In theory, Elizabethan social status was fixed but in practice there was imprecision and mobility among the ranks.

SOCIAL CONFLICT

Social mobility appears to have been a relatively peaceful dynamic challenging the static ideal of a hierarchical structure. Social conflict, however, was a much more serious upheaval, the threat of which made the government fearful and nervous, while dissenters stirred up trouble hoping to effect some action for one cause or another. The most extreme forms of unrest were plots or rebellions to overthrow the monarchy, even assassinate Queen Elizabeth. Such attempts usually involved nobles and their followers, often motivated by a desire for a return to Catholicism; and each plot failed, though the potential danger was a source of constant vigilance and surveillance. Somewhat less threatening but much more common were riots instigated by the common people who rose up not against the Crown itself but against the gentry and those in local public office. Generally these riots were prompted by specific concerns of the most basic kind—hunger, oppression, or unemployment.

The 1590s, when Shakespeare was actively writing plays, were times of unprecedented economic hardship that saw numerous violent uprisings both in London and in rural areas. Apprentices in the city protested market regulations. There were twelve riots in June of 1595 alone, the year in which it is presumed that Shakespeare wrote *A Midsummer Night's Dream*. A growing population meant that there were too many people for the labor market, and wages were inadequate for those who had work. Taxes were high. These circumstances were aggravated in rural areas by a series of bad harvests from 1594 to 1597 leading to serious food shortages and high grain prices. Food riots were frequent as people gathered to protest their dire conditions and attempt to assert change. For the most part, these riots were local occurrences and therefore were not considered treasonous; violence was directed primarily against property rather than individuals. Often the rioters first tried to persuade authorities to provide affordable food before joining forces to block the passage of grain from landowners to cities and export markets. The government at central and local levels appeared to respond at least in some measure to the hardship, recognizing that a stable hierarchy depended not only on obedience from the ruled but also on care and protection from the rulers. Laws were passed and enforced to allow grain to be sold cheaply to meet some of the desperate needs of the regions.

Still, these were times of civil unrest and the government was not hesitant in punishing dangerous offenders. Many rioters faced fines or imprisonment. The instigators of a failed revolt in 1596 known as the Oxfordshire Rebellion were imprisoned and then executed for their attempt to overthrow gentlemen landowners. The rebels had hoped to gather several hundred supporters but fewer than twenty showed up and were easily identified and captured. The main organizer, Bartholomew Steere, was a carpenter. His brother, a weaver, was also involved. Interestingly, evidence indicates that while rural riots engaged many peasants and townspeople, both men and women, riot leaders were often artisans or craftsmen such as carpenters, weavers, and tanners. Unlike some poor husbandmen or lowly farmers, many craftsmen had no food source of their own, but unlike the unemployed and partially employed day laborers, they had a fixed place of business in the local community rather than a transient existence dependent on seasonal work. Perhaps for these reasons and perhaps because of their dissatisfaction with a "middling" status not quite sufficient to elevate them to gentlemen, they were the prominent members of riots and revolts.

Shakespeare's artisans do not appear to be the restive sort. In fact, they seem especially conscious of the desire not to offend or alarm their courtly audience. Yet that very consciousness may suggest something of the potential social tensions informing the contemporary context of the play. Contrary to the ideal, the hierarchical order of English society was not entirely stable and peaceful. The lower ranks found ways to express their resentment, criticism, and dissent, especially in hard times. The higher ranks felt vulnerable from those climbing the social ladder and those acting out their frustration with force. In the midst of this, Shakespeare writes a comedy about love rather than a political play about power and authority. He shows the kinder face of society, the good intentions of the craftsmen and the tolerant if mocking response of gentry. But he does acknowledge the disorder in the natural world, the floods and unsettled seasons that historically led to bad harvests and food riots. And he does suggest that relations between the ruler and the ruled are not unquestionably harmonious as the "rude mechanicals" reach a unanimous response about the outcome if their roaring lion proves to be too frightening for noble women in their audience. Their distressed perception, "That would hang us, every mother's son" (1.2.78), may seem exaggerated but indicates serious consequences for common people engaging in inappropriate public behavior. If the play ends with ultimate harmony, it intimates that the discord and disorder leading up to the resolution arise not simply the from obvious personal romantic causes but from social implications as well.

The remainder of this chapter includes documents that identify the various parts of the social hierarchy in sixteenth-century England and how they related and reacted to one another.

SOCIAL DISTINCTIONS IN ELIZABETHAN ENGLAND

William Harrison (1534–1593) was a historian writing about his own society in Shakespeare's time. The excerpt below from his *Description of England,* written in the 1560s and first printed in 1587, provides a contemporary perspective on the social distinctions that characterize Elizabethan society. According to Harrison, there are four categories of English subjects: (1) gentlemen; (2) citizens or burgesses, who were townspeople employed in a trade; (3) yeomen, who were farmers with small landholdings; and (4) artificers, who were craftsmen or artisans, along with laborers. Harrison tends to simplify the social order, ignoring, for example, the variations in wealth and skill between craftsmen and laborers. As you read, pay attention to the qualities that Harrison says distinguishes each group or "sort" and look for any inconsistencies in the categories he presents.

FROM WILLIAM HARRISON, *THE DESCRIPTION OF ENGLAND,* IN RAPHAEL HOLINSHED, *CHRONICLES OF ENGLAND, SCOTLAND, AND IRELAND,* VOL. 1 (1587)

(London: 1807; Rpt. New York: AMS Press, 1965) 263–64; 273–75

"Of Degrees of People in the Commonwealth of England"

We in England divide our people commonly into four sorts, as gentlemen, citizens or burgesses, yeomen, which are artificers, or laborers. Of gentlemen the first and chief (next the king) be the prince, dukes, marquesses, earls, viscounts, and barons: and these are called gentlemen of the greater sort, or (as our common usage of speech is) lords and noblemen: and next unto them be knights, esquires, and last of all they that are simply called gentlemen; so that in effect our gentlemen are divided into their conditions, whereof in this chapter I will make particular rehearsal. . . .

Gentleman be those whom their race and blood, or at the least their virtues do make noble and known. The Latins call them Nobiles & generosos, as the French do Nobles or gentlehommes. The etymology of the name expoundeth the efficacy of the word: for as gens in Latin betokeneth the race and surname: so the Romans had Cornelios, Sergios, Appios, Curios, Papyrios, Scipiones, Fabios, Aemilios, Julios, Brutos, etc.: of which, who were Agnati, and therefore kept the name, were also called Gentiles, gentlemen of that or that house and race.

Moreover, as the king doth dub knights, and createth the barons and higher degrees, so gentlemen whose ancestors are not known to come in with William, duke of Normandy (for of the Saxon races yet remaining we now make none account, much less of the British issue), do take their beginning in England, after this manner in our times. Whosoever studieth the laws of the realm, who so abideth in the university giving his mind to his book, or professeth physic and the liberal sciences, or beside his service in the room of a captain in the wars, or good counsel given at home, whereby his commonwealth is benefited, can live without manual labor, and thereto is able and will bear the port, charge, and countenance of a gentleman, he shall for money have a coat and arms bestowed upon him by heralds (who in the charter of the same do of custom pretend antiquity and service, and many gay things) and thereunto being made so good cheap be called master, which is the title that men give to esquires and gentlemen, and reputed for a gentleman ever after. . . .

Citizens and burgesses have next place to gentlemen, who be those that are free within the cities, and are of some likely substance to bear office in the same. But these citizens or burgesses are to serve the commonwealth in their cities and boroughs, or in corporate towns where they dwell. And in the common assembly of the realm wherein our laws are made, for in the counties they bear but little sway (which assembly is called the high court of parliament) the ancient cities appoint four, and the boroughs two burgesses to have voices in it, and give their consent or dissent unto such things as pass or stay there in the name of the city or borough, for which they are appointed.

In this place also are our merchants to be installed, as amongst the citizens (although they often change estate with gentlemen, as gentlemen do with them, by a mutual conversion of the one into the other) whose number is so increased in these our days, that their only maintenance is the cause of the exceeding prices of foreign wares, which otherwise when every nation was permitted to bring in her own commodities, were far better cheap and more plentifully to be had. . . .

Yeomen are those, which by our law are called Legales homines, freemen born English, and may dispend of their own free land in yearly revenue, to the sum of forty shillings sterling, or six pounds as money goeth in our times. . . . [Yeomen] signifieth (as I have read) a settled or staid man, such, I mean, as being married and of some years, betaketh himself to stay in the place of his abode for the better maintenance of himself and his family, whereof the single sort have no regard, but are likely to be still fleeting now hither now thither, which argueth want of stability in determination and resolution in judgment, for the execution of things of any importance. This sort of people have a certain preeminence, and more estimation than laborers and the common sort of artificers, and these commonly live wealthily, keep good houses, and travail to get riches. They are also for the most part farmers to gentlemen . . . or at the leastwise artificers, and with grazing, frequenting of markets, and keeping of servants (not idle servants as the gentlemen do, but such as get both their own and part of their master's living) do come to great wealth, insomuch that many of them are able and do buy the lands of unthrifty gentlemen, and often setting their sons to the schools, to the universities, and to the Inns of the Court; or otherwise leaving them sufficient lands whereupon they may live without labour, do make them by those means to become gentlemen: these were they that in times past made all France afraid. And albeit they be not called master as gentlemen are, or sir as to knights appertaineth, but only John and Thomas, etc.: yet have they been found to have done very good service. . . .

The fourth and last sort of people in England are day laborers, poor husbandmen, and some retailers (which have no free land), copyholders, and all artificers, as tailors, shoemakers, carpenters, brickmakers, masons, etc. As for slaves and bondmen, we have none. . . . This fourth and last sort of people therefore have neither voice nor authority in the commonwealth, but are to be ruled, and not to rule other: yet they are not altogether neglected, for in cities and corporate towns, for default of yeomen they are fain to make up their inquests of such manner of people. And in villages they are commonly made churchwardens, sidemen, aleconners, now and then constables, and many times enjoy the name of headboroughs.

MONARCHY AND THE EDUCATION OF GENTLEMEN

Sir Thomas Elyot was an ambassador and political advisor during the reign of Henry VIII, Queen Elizabeth's father. Elyot's popular treatise, *The Book Named the Governour* (1531), was a guidebook for monarchs and gentlemen. Three excerpted chapters are included below. The first, from chapter II, argues the case for one ruler or monarch as opposed to other political models by providing examples and images to make Elyot's point clear. Note what problems he finds in *Aristocratia* or aristocracy and *Democratia* or democracy compared to government by one sovereign.

The second and third excerpts, from chapters V and VI, describe how young boys should be trained and educated to become gentlemen. Note what subjects and moral values Elyot deems important to a boy's upbringing and why he feels boys should be removed from the presence of women by age seven. Consider how this argument might reflect on the debate between Titania and Oberon about where the changeling boy belongs in their relationship.

FROM SIR THOMAS ELYOT, *THE BOOK NAMED THE GOVERNOUR,* ED. HENRY HERBERT STEPHEN CROFT, VOL. 1 (1531)

(2 vols., London: C. Kegan Paul & Co., 1880)

Chapter II

That one sovereign governour ought to be in a public weal. And what damage hath happened where a multitude hath had equal authority without any sovereign.

Like as to a castle or fortress suffiseth one owner or sovereign, and where any more be of like power and authority seldom cometh the work to perfection; or being all ready made, where the one diligently overseeth and the other neglecteth, in that contention all is subverted and cometh to ruin. In semblable wise doth a public weal that hath more chief governours than one. Example we may take of the Greeks, among whom in divers cities were divers forms of public weals governed by multitudes: wherein one was most tolerable where the governance and rule was alway permitted to them which excelled in virtue, and was in the Greek tongue called *Aristocratia* . . . , in English the rule of men of best disposition, which the Thebans of long time observed.

Another public weal was among the Athenians, where equality was of estate among the people, and only by their whole consent their city and their dominions were governed: which might well be called a monster with many heads: nor never it was certain nor stable: and often times they banished or slew the best citizens, which by their virtue and wisdom had most profited to the public weal. This manner of governance was called in Greek *Democratia...*, in English the rule of the commonality. Of these two governances none may be sufficient. For in the first, which consisteth of good men, virtue is not so constant in a multitude, but that some, being ones in authority, be incensed with glory: some with ambition: other with covetous and desire of treasure or possessions: whereby they fall into contention.... The popular estate, if it anything do vary from equality of substance or estimation, or that the multitude of people have over much liberty, of necessity one of these inconveniences must happen: either tyranny, where he that is too much in favour would be elevate and suffer none equality, or else into the rage of a commonality, which of all rules is most to be feared. For like as the communes, if they feel some severity, they do humbly serve and obey, so where they embracing a license refuse to be bridled, they fling and plunge: and if they once throw down their governour, they order every thing without justice, only with vengeance and cruelty; and with incomparable difficulty and [not] by any wisdom be pacified and brought again into order. Wherefore undoubtedly the best and most sure governance is by one king or prince, which ruleth only for the weal of his people to him subject: and that manner of governance is best approved, and hath longest continued, and is most ancient. For who can deny but that all thing in heaven and earth is governed by one god, by one perpetual order, by one providence? One Sun ruleth over the day, and one Moon over the night; and to descend down to the earth, in a little beast, which of all other is most to be marvelled at, I mean the Bee, is left to man by nature, as it seemeth, a perpetual figure of a just governance or rule: who hath among them one principal Bee for their governour, who excelleth all other in greatness, yet hath he no prick or sting, but in him is more knowledge than in the residue. For if the day following shall be fair and dry, and that the bees may issue out of their stalls without peril of rain or vehement wind, in the morning early he calleth them, making a noise as it were the sound of a horn or a trumpet; and with that all the residue prepare them to labour, and fleeth abroad, gathering nothing but that shall be sweet and profitable, although they sit often times on herbes and other things that be venomous and stinking. (8–12)

Chapter V

The order of learning that a noble man should be trained in before he come to the age of seven years.

Some old authors hold opinion that, before the age of seven years, a child should not be instructed in letters; but those writers were either Greeks or Latins, among whom all doctrine and sciences were in the maternal tongues; by which reason whereof they saved all that long time which at this days is spent in understanding perfectly the Greek or Latin. Wherefore it requireth now a longer time to the understanding of both. Therefore that infelicity of our time and country compelleth us to encroach somewhat upon the years of children, and specially of noblemen, that they may sooner attain to wisdom and gravity than private persons, considering, as I have said, their charge and example, which, above all things, is most to be esteemed. Not withstanding, I would not have them enforced by violence to learn, but according to the counsel of Quintilian, to be sweetly allured thereto with praises and such pretty gifts as children delight in. And their first letters to be painted or limned in a pleasant manner: wherein children of gentle courage have much delectation. And also there is no better allective [enticement] to noble wits than to induce them into a contention with their inferior companions: they sometime purposely suffering the more noble children to vanquish, and, as it were, giving to them place and sovereignty, though indeed the inferior children have more learning.... And it shall be no reproach to a nobleman to instruct his own children, or at leastways to examine them, by way of dalliance or solace, considering that the emperor Octavious Augustus disdained not to read the workers of Cicero and Virgil to his children and nephews. And why should not noblemen rather so do, than teach their children how at dice and cards, they may cunningly lose and consume their own treasure and substance? Moreover, teaching representeth the authority of the prince.... (31–34)

Chapter VI

At what age a tutor should be provided and what shall appertain to his office to do.

After that a child is come to seven years of age, I hold it expedient that he be taken from the company of women: saving that he may have, one year, or two at most, an ancient and sad matron, attending on him in his chamber, which shall not have any young woman in her company: for though there be no peril of offence in that tender innocent age, yet, in some children, nature is more prone to vice than to virtue, and in the tender wits be sparks of voluptuosity: which, nourished by any occasion or object, increase oftentimes into so terrible a fire, that therewith all virtue and reason is consumed. Wherefore, to eschew that danger, the most sure counsel is, to withdraw him from all company of women, and to assign unto him a tutor, which should be an ancient and worshipful man, in whom is approved to be much gentleness mixed with gravity, and, as nigh as can be, such one as the child by imitation following may grow to be excellent. And if he be also learned, he is the more commendable.... How much profited it to King Philip, father to the great Alexander, that he was delivered in hostage to the Thebans? where he was kept and brought up under the governance of Epaminondas, a noble and valiant captain: of whom he received such learning, as well in acts martial as in other liberal sciences, that he excelled all other kings that were before his time in Greece, and finally, as well by wisdom as prowess, subdued all that country....

The office of the tutor is first to know the nature of his pupil, that is to say, whereto he is most inclined or disposed, and in what thing he setteth his most delectation or appetite. If he be of nature courteous, piteous, and of a free and liberal heart, it is a principal token of grace.... Then shall a wise tutor purposely commend those virtues, extolling also his pupil for having of them; and therewith he shall declare them to be of all men most fortunate, which shall happen to have such a master. And moreover shall declare to him what honour, what love, what commodity shall happen to him by these virtues. And, if any have been of disposition contrary, then to express the enormities of their vice, with as much detestation as may be. And if any danger have thereby ensued, misfortune, or punishment, or aggrieve it in such wise, with so vehement words, as the child may abhor it, and fear the semblable adventure. (35–38)

A LAW FOR THE WORKING CLASS

The Statute of the Artificers was a law passed in the Elizabethan House of Commons in 1563 and became an important piece of legislation for the laboring classes for several centuries to follow. The statute, as the introduction below indicates, was meant to bring together and replace many other existing laws. It had a twofold purpose: (1) to ensure fair wages for employees at a time when wages were not adequately keeping pace with the cost of living; and (2) to legislate social order and stability by ruling that people had an obligation to work while setting limits on mobility from one place to another.

Of the forty sections of the law, the first five are included below. The wording is in the cumbersome language of legal documents but essentially specifies some simple terms for employment: (II) that those employed in crafts and trades must work for a full year term; (III) that those unmarried and under the age of thirty who did not own land or have an inheritance should not refuse work where work was available and needed; (IV) that masters and servant were bound to one another and each deserved fair warning for the termination of a contract; and (V) that all persons between the ages of twelve and sixty, with some qualifications, should be required to work where they were needed. Watch for these basic terms in the provisions below. These are the regulations under which Elizabethans such as Shakespeare's "rude mechanicals" would have worked.

FROM THE STATUTE OF ARTIFICERS (1563), IN *TUDOR ECONOMIC DOCUMENTS: BEING SELECT DOCUMENTS ILLUSTRATING THE ECONOMIC AND SOCIAL HISTORY OF TUDOR ENGLAND,* EDS. R. H. TAWNEY AND EILEEN POWER, VOL. 1.

(London: Longmans, Green, 1924) 338–41

An Act Touching Diverse Orders for Artificers, Laborers, Servants of Husbandry, and Apprentices

Although there remain and stand in force presently a great number of Acts and Statutes concerning the retaining, departing, wages, and orders of Apprentices, Servants, and Laborers, as well in husbandry, as in diverse other Arts, Mysteries and occupations: yet partly for the imperfection and contrariety that is found and do appear in sundry of the said Laws, and for the variety and number for them, and chiefly for that the wages and allowances limited and rated in many of the said statutes are in diverse places too small and not answerable to this time, respecting the advancement of prices of all things belonging to the said servants and laborers, the said laws cannot conveniently without the great grief and burden of the poor laborer and hired man, be put in good and due execution: and as the said several Acts and Statutes were at the time of the making of them thought to be very good and beneficial for the commonwealth of this Realm as *diverse of them yet are,* So if the substance of the many of the said laws as are meet to be continued shall be digested and reduced into one sole law and statute, And in the same an uniform order prescribed and limited concerning the wages and other orders for apprentices, servants, and laborers, there is good hope that it will come to pass that the same law, being duly executed, should banish idleness, advance husbandry, and yield unto the hired person both in the time of scarcity and in the time of plenty a convenient proportion of Wages.

I. *Be it therefore enacted*…That as much of all the estatutes heretofore made, and every branch of them as touch or concern the hiring, keeping, departing, working wages, or order of servants, Workmen, Artificers, apprentices, and laborers, or any of them, and the penalties and forfeitures concerning the same shall be from and after the last day of September next ensuing repealed.

II. And be it further enacted…that no manner of person or persons after the foresaid last day of September…shall retain, hire, or take into service, or cause to be retained, hired or taken into service, nor any person shall be retained, hired, or taken into service, by any means or color to work for any less time, or term, than for one whole year in any of the sciences, crafts, mysteries, or arts of clothiers, woolen cloth weavers, tuckers, fullers, Cloth workers, Shearmen, dyers, hosiers, Tailors, shoemakers, Tanners, Pewterers, Bakers, Brewers, Glovers, Cutlers, Smiths, Farriers, Curriers, Saddlers, spurriers, Turners, Cappers, Hatmakers or feltmakers, Bowyers, fletchers, arrowhead makers, Butchers, Cooks, *or* Millers.

III. …That every person being unmarried, and every *other* person being under the age of thirty years, that after the Feast of Easter next shall marry, and having been brought up in any of the said Arts, crafts or sciences, or that hath used or exercised any of them by the space of three years or more, and not having lands, Tenements, Rents, or Hereditaments, Copyhold, or Freehold of one estate of inheritance, or for term of any Life or Lives of clear yearly value of forty shillings, nor being worth of his own Goods the clear value of ten pounds, and so allowed by two Justices of the peace of the County [etc.]…nor being retained with any person in husbandry, or in any of the aforesaid Arts…nor lawfully retained in any other Art or Science, nor…in household, or in any office with any nobleman, gentleman, or others, according to the laws of this Realm, nor having a convenient farm, or other holding in tillage, whereupon he may employ his Labor, shall, during the time that he or they shall so be unmarried, or under the said Age of 30 years, upon request made by any person using the Art or mystery, wherein the said person so required hath been exercised, as is aforesaid, be retained and shall not refuse to serve according to the tenor of this statute, upon pain and penalty hereafter mentioned.

IV. …That no person which shall retain any servant shall put away his or her said servant and that no person retained according to this statute shall depart from his Master, Mistress, or Dame before the end of his or her term, upon pain hereafter mentioned, unless it be fore some reasonable and sufficient cause or matter to be allowed before two Justices of Peace, or one at the least, within the said County or before the mayor or other chief officer of the city Burrough or town corporate where in the said Master [etc.] inhabiteth, to whom any of the parties grieved shall complain, which said Justices [etc.] shall have and take upon them or him the hearing and ordering of the matter, betwixt the said Master [etc.] and servant according to the equity of the cause. And that no such Master [etc.] shall put away any *such* servant, at the end of his term, or that any such Servant shall depart from his Master [etc.] at the end of his term, without one quarter warning given before the end of his said term, either by the said Master [etc.], or servant, the one to the other, upon the pain hereafter ensuing.

V. ... Every person between the age of Twelve years and the age of Threescore years, not being lawfully retained, nor apprentice[d] with any fisherman or mariner haunting the Seas, *nor being in Service with any Kiddier or Carrier of any corn, grain, or meal for provision of the city of London,* nor with any husbandman in husbandry, nor in any City, Town Corporate, or Market Town, in any of the arts or Sciences... appointed by this Estatute to have or take apprentices, nor being retained by the year or half the year at the least, for the digging, seeking, finding, getting, melting fining, working, trying, making of any Silver, Tin, Lead, Iron, Copper, Stone, sea-coal, stone-coal, moor-Coal, or Charcoal, nor being occupied in *or about* the making of any glass, nor being a gentleman born, nor being a student or scholar *in any* of the universities or in any school, nor having lands [etc. as above in Section III]... *nor having a father or mother then living or other Ancestor whose heir apparent he is,* then having lands [etc.] of the yearly value of ten pounds, or above or Goods or cattle of the value of forty pounds, being a necessary or convenient officer or servant lawfully retained as is aforesaid, nor having a convenient farm, or holding whereupon he may or shall employ his labor, *nor being otherwise lawfully retained according to the true meaning of this Statute,* shall... by virtue of this estatute, be compelled to be retained to serve in husbandry by the year, with any person the keepeth husbandry, and will require any such person to serve within the same shire where he shall be so required.

TOPICS FOR WRITTEN AND ORAL DISCUSSION

1. Identify the different types of gentlemen in William Harrison's divisions of social groups in *The Description of England*. What are the qualifications that grant an Englishman status as a gentleman?

2. According to Harrison, what distinguishes citizens and burgesses from yeomen? It may also be useful to look up the terms in a dictionary. How is the fourth and final sort of people different from the others?

3. Look for any inconsistencies in Harrison's categories of English people. Can you identify ways in which the hierarchical system was not static but dynamic with movement from one group to another? What allows for or causes the changes to take place?

4. In *The Book Named the Governour*, Thomas Elyot argues in favor of a monarchy in which one sovereign rules. Identify the two examples of alternative governments he describes and summarize why Elyot thinks they are inferior. What points does he make in support of one governor or monarch?

5. Describe the type of government in Athens in Shakespeare's *Midsummer Night's Dream*. How does Duke Theseus exercise authority? Does he seem like a just and good leader? Explain your response.

6. Compare Theseus and Oberon as rulers of their worlds. Do they treat their subjects fairly? Do they use power appropriately or abuse it? Provide examples and draw conclusions. What roles do Hippolyta and Titania play in the government of Athens and the fairy world and how does that affect your response to the two male leaders?

7. Elyot's book provides guidelines for educating boys belonging to the class of gentry or nobility. According to the excerpt from Chapter V of his book, what does he feel boys should be taught before they reach the age of seven years and what are his reasons? According to Chapter VI, what is the role of a tutor?

8. Why does Elyot suggest boys be removed from the company of women at seven years? What is your response to his argument?

9. In the context of Elyot's Chapter VI, consider the disagreement between Titania and Oberon about the changeling boy. Does Elyot's position help you understand and support Oberon in his actions or do you favor Titania's perspective? Pretend you are an attorney and write a defense for either Oberon or Titania about who should have the changeling boy.

10. From Elyot's Chapters V and VI, find information to help you define the qualities of a sixteenth-century gentleman.

11. Describe the characteristics of the gentlemen in *A Midsummer Night's Dream*. Who are they? Consider indications of their social status, power, good breeding, and their display of courtesy or nobility. Do the gentlemen act in a "gentlemanly" fashion or not? Provide examples. Discuss how Shakespeare defines the group as a social class and note distinctions between the duke as ruler and his noble subjects.

12. William Shakespeare rose from middle-class status to attain the wealth and property of a gentleman after years of working in the theater business. Write a diary entry for him in which he muses about the change in his status and how it affects his relationship to his less financially successful theater comrades or his view towards his father, who had earlier tried to enter the gentry but failed through financial hardship.

13. What does the introduction to the Statute of the Artificers indicate as the main purpose for the legislation?

14. Summarize the main points of the Statute of the Artificers and discuss whether it seems to be of greater benefit to the employer, the laborer, or the state, or whether it seems to have the best interests of everyone in mind. Explain reasons for your conclusion.

15. Imagine yourself as a newspaper reporter covering national government news in 1563 when the Statute of the Artificers was passed as sweeping legislation. Write a newspaper article about the legislation. Try to come up with a flashy title and an angle that will grab headlines and foster public reaction.

Alternatively, write an editorial and one or two "letters to the editor" expressing opinion about the introduction of the legislation. Perhaps one of your letters could be from the perspective of a master or mistress employing servants and the other could be from a craftsman, for example, Bottom the Weaver or Snug the Joiner.

16. The government in Shakespeare's time upheld a hierarchical system in which order was maintained if all subjects stayed in their places and had no ambitions to change their circumstances. Do you think action in *A Midsummer Night's Dream* supports this view or challenges it? You may want to consider causes for disorder in the play, the references to "discord" and other imagery of chaos, the relationship between Oberon and Titania or between the court people and craftsmen or "mechanicals" at Athens, and the way the play ends.

17. Review the interaction between the nobles and the "mechanicals" in act 5. Do you find the responses of the nobles to the players pleasantly lighthearted or mean and condescending? Provide examples to support your view. Discuss how your understanding of the class system in Elizabethan England affects your response.

18. Titania's speech in Act 2.1.81–117 depicts a world in disorder with floods ruining harvests and seasons out of tune, not unlike the mid-1590s in Shakespeare's England. Choose one of the following writing exercises:

    a) Explain how this speech reflects the view of hierarchical order in Elizabethan England according to the ideal of the "chain of being" described in this chapter.

    b) Write a diary entry for a poor English farmer or his wife suffering the outcome Titania describes, indicating the mood, hopes, and fears of these people in the face of hardship.

19. Food riots were common in England in the 1590s, expressing the frustration and desperation of the common people against landowners and gentlemen who not only were better off but also controlled the movement and sale of scarce grain commodi-

ties. In the failed Oxfordshire Rebellion of 1596 mentioned in this chapter, Bartholomew Steere, the organizer, sought recruits among weavers, including his own brother. Imagine that Steere solicits Bottom's involvement in the plot. Bottom seems to be a law-abiding citizen but he also appears ambitious enough to seek financial advancement through a play performed before the duke. Write a dialogue between the two men that describes their encounter. What are Bottom's reasons for refusal? Fear? Loyalty to the duke? Honor? Is he tempted at all to support the other tradesmen in their revolt? How does Steere try to convince him?

SUGGESTED READING

Amussen, Susan Dwyer. *An Ordered Society: Gender and Class in Early Modern England.* Oxford: Basil Blackwell, 1988.

Bindoff, S. T., J. Hurstfield, and C. H. Williams. *Elizabethan Government and Society.* London: The Athlone Press, 1961.

Clark, Peter, and Paul Slack. *English Towns in Transition: 1550–1700.* Oxford: Oxford UP, 1976.

Haigh, Christopher. *Elizabeth I.* New York: Longman, 1988.

Paster, Gail Kern, and Skiles Howard, eds. A Midsummer Night's Dream: *Texts and Contexts.* Bedford, England: St. Martin's, 1999.

Sharp, Buchanan. *In Contempt of All Authority: Rural Artisans and Riot in the West of England, 1586–1660.* Berkeley: University of California, 1980.

Sharpe, J. A. *Early Modern England: A Social History, 1550–1760.* London: Edward Arnold, 1987.

Stone, Lawrence. *The Crisis of the Aristocracy, 1558–1641.* Oxford: Oxford UP, 1965.

Tillyard, E. M. W. *The Elizabethan World Picture.* New York: Random House, 1944.

Wright, Louis B. *Middle-Class Culture in Elizabethan England.* Chapel Hill: University of North Carolina Press, 1935.

Wrightson, Keith. *English Society, 1580–1680.* London: Hutchinson, 1982.

4

Popular Culture: Holidays, Court Entertainments, and Play-Acting

The popular culture of a nation and its communities reflects the way its people spend their time apart from labor and economic pursuits. In what pastimes or recreations do the people participate? What form of entertainment and celebration defines their culture? In Elizabethan England, a society made up of different classes or sorts of people—as the last chapter has indicated—defined the popular culture of its subjects as partly determined by economic distinctions. How the queen and her courtiers engaged in festivities and rituals, for example, did not necessarily imitate or replicate the pastimes of commoners in their rural or urban communities. Yet the customs and cultural practices of the elite and nonelite segments of English society sometimes intersected or merged in recreations that temporarily broke down the barriers imposed by economic status and bloodlines, creating common grounds for a national and communal identity, allowing people freedom to mingle together temporarily in a world where they were otherwise defined and separated by their social status. Going to plays, for example, was an activity that spanned the different groups in society; Shakespeare and other dramatists wrote for a broad audience including members from the common laboring class to the queen herself.

A Midsummer Night's Dream enacts and alludes to various elements of popular culture in Elizabethan England. Though the setting is intended to be Athens, many English traditions are incorporated into the play. Even as Shakespeare designed the comedy as entertainment for his English audiences, the plot focuses on the rituals and festivities that entertain its characters so that what goes on in the play mirrors to a certain extent what went on in the community of spectators outside the play. While the wedding at court is the primary celebration, other holiday recreations figure in the play's events. The title is the first clue, drawing attention to Midsummer's Eve, an occasion annually recognized and celebrated as part of English culture. The significance of the title can be better understood by exploring Elizabethan customs connected to that day and to other holidays mentioned in the play. Along with holidays and court entertainments, considerable attention to the play-acting of Shakespeare's craftsmen raises questions about how drama and theater fit into the popular culture of the 1590s, providing the immediate context for *A Midsummer Night's Dream*. The following discussion addresses some of the practices and beliefs surrounding holidays, court entertainments, and play-acting, offering historical references for the events and allusions in the play and examining how these different aspects of cultural practice related to one another.

HOLIDAYS

Shakespeare's comedies, in general, have a holiday spirit about them. They enact celebrations; they are full of merriment and good humor. They often enter a time apart from the everyday work routine, a time of topsy-turvy and possibility, of reversals or the questioning of usual authority.

Midsummer's Eve

A Midsummer Night's Dream draws attention in its title to a specific holiday time with all the connotations of celebration, freedom, and good spirits it generates. Midsummer's Eve is on June 23, the summer solstice, marking the longest day of the year. It is also one of the oldest celebrations on record, with a history reaching back to primitive times and pagan practices acknowledging the power of the sun. In Elizabeth's reign in sixteenth-century England, many of the ancient impulses still existed. Midsummer was recognized as a time to celebrate fertility, both in the natural world of planting and harvesting and in the human world of courtship, marriage, and sexuality. Communities celebrated by building bonfires that were considered to bring good luck, by lighting torches, and by gathering plants that were thought to have medicinal or magical powers (Young 20–22). Released from usual restrictions, they enjoyed drinking, music, and outdoor festivities. Midsummer's Eve was also believed to be a time when young maidens might discover through dreams who would be their true love, thus suggesting associations with marriage. It was seen as a time of superstition and magic, when spirits from the supernatural world might roam about and when "midsummer madness" might affect the community, especially young lovers. All these associations with Midsummer's Eve would have been commonplace to Shakespeare's audiences, who undoubtedly participated regularly in the holiday spirit of the occasion. Thus the title of the play sets the tone for what is to follow: love and magic, the gathering of powerful flowers and herbs, and the wandering of supernatural beings, the fairies of another world.

Valentine's Day and May Day

Interestingly, however, Midsummer's Eve is never specifically mentioned in the play itself, while two other days receive attention, Valentine's Day and May Day. Lysander tells Hermia to meet him "in the wood, a league without the town,°/ Where I did meet thee once with Helena,°/ To do observance to a morn of May,°/ There will I stay for thee" (1.1. 165–68). Later, when the hunting party of Theseus and Hippolyta finds the lovers asleep in the woods after daybreak, Theseus also refers to May Day, saying, "No doubt they rose up early to observe°/ The rite of May; and, hearing our intent,°/ Came here in grace of our solemnity" (4.1.135–37). He adds, "Good morrow, friends. Saint Valentine is past:°/ Begin these wood birds but to couple now?" (4.1.142–43). Valentine's Day, then as now, was associated with lovemaking, romance, and coupling. By tradition, women were free to approach men on St. Valentine's Day rather than the other way around. But there was also a randomness in love choices, with lots being drawn to join young lovers together, and a belief that the first person one saw upon waking up on February 14 would be one's Valentine. The magic of the woods in *A Midsummer Night's Dream* leads to a randomness in lovers' choices and a coupling that confuses Theseus as he wonders that the young people should seem to be enacting Valentine celebrations at a later date, which he appears to identify as May Day, when the rites of May took place.

What were the rites or rituals of May Day? Like Midsummer's Eve, May Day or May 1 focused on celebrations of coupling and of a view of love that often tended towards infatuation. May Day was also an ancient fertility festival. It was a seasonal holiday that marked spring and the new life that comes with that season. It was a festivity especially meant for young people. They would rise shortly after midnight and go into a neighboring wood, accompanied by music and the blowing of horns. There they would collect branches from hawthorn trees, adorn themselves with flowers, and then return home around sunrise, decorating their houses by covering their doors and windows with the branches and flowers. This activity was called the "bringing home of May." Garlands were hung in the streets. There were bonfires, pipers, bell-ringers, game-players, and dancers. One dance was called the morris dance, which receives mention in *A Midsummer Night's Dream* when Titania documents the damage her argument with Oberon inflicts on the natural world, which includes among other disasters that "The nine men's morris is filled up with mud" (2.1.98). The rains, in other words, had spoiled the place on the village green where morris dancers gathered as a group of characters impersonating, among others, Maid Marian, a Fool, a piper, and St. George, who danced in lively kicks and jumps. The other important dance included all the villagers, who would gather and perform a ritual dance around a tall pole known as a Maypole. There was also a village feast at which a Lord and Lady of May were chosen to host the community.

It might be easy to think that Shakespeare had his days and dates mixed up when he called his play *A Midsummer Night's Dream* but makes reference to May Day in the drama itself. In fact, however, "maying"—as the celebrations of May Day were called—was not limited to May Day alone. Records indicate that maying occurred at various times throughout the late spring season, including Midsummer's Eve (Barber 119–20). The dancing, the trips into the woods, the garlands and music, the emphasis on love and matchmaking were all part of the general celebration of springtime and new life. Shakespeare was not necessarily linking his play to a specific festival but rather conjuring up the spirit of love and license and green world adventures associated with two popular holidays in his time, with Midsummer's Eve having more direct references to the supernatural world and May Day having more emphasis on fertility and youth.

Popularity and Debate

The widespread popularity of these holidays in the 1590s is open to debate. There were supporters, but there were also detractors. The supporters saw the events as signs of communal harmony and unity, as a source of a healthy break or freedom from the constraints of the work routine. The detractors were representatives both of local civic authorities and of the Puritan strain of Protestant religion with its emphasis on holy living and upright behavior. Local authorities were nervous about the fact that spirited holiday celebrations sometimes led to outbreaks of violence and destructiveness as the crowd mentality carried the activities beyond mere harmless entertainment to riots incited by commoners. Devout Puritans were critical of the holidays for their pagan origins and for sexual license that the emphasis on love, coupling, and young people's nighttime trips into a neighboring wood or forest tended to encourage.

Beyond this debate, there was also a sense that the purpose and meaning of holidays seemed to send mixed messages. Holiday rhythms and celebrations in Elizabethan England derived from two sources: the seasons of the year, associated with pagan origins and the agricultural patterns of planting and harvesting; and the calendar of the church year, associated with its festivities including Christmas and Easter but also many other feast days. The two holidays described, Midsummer's Eve and May Day, appear to have primarily pagan origins, but the Church attempted to adopt and regulate those days by tying Midsummer's Eve to the religious feast of St. John and May Day to the feast of St. Philip and St. James. Even while trying clerically to legitimize the holiday events, the Elizabethan government remained suspicious of traditional practices as they attempted to reinvent the church year according to a post-Reformation Protestant perspective rather than the pre-Reformation Catholic rituals. In general, however, the community celebrators of the holidays mentioned in *A Midsummer Night's Dream* tended to practice the traditions associated with the secular customs rather than those with religious significance. They gathered to have fun, not to be devout. Thus, there remained a growing ambivalence or mixture of attitudes about holidays, their purpose, and their meaning. Typically, the commoners or nonelites initiated the events of these special days, and the authorities—national, local, and ecclesiastical—could say what they would with little impact on the events that occurred. As in Shakespeare's comedy, couples did what they would do, in spite of the counsel and orders of fathers and government leaders.

COURT ENTERTAINMENTS

If the dominant impulse for many holiday celebrations came from the lower classes guided by tradition, court entertainments were the domain of the elites—lords, gentlemen, and especially Queen Elizabeth, who was the focus and often the instigator of numerous rituals and festivities.

Masques

One such court event was the masque, a semidramatic performance that became popular in Henry VIII's reign and then grew to a much more sophisticated presentation in King James I's time following the Elizabethan era. This form, however, enjoyed popularity during the government of England's long-reigning female monarch. A masque was a formal entertainment with elaborate dress and decoration. It combined song, dance, and pageantry and included allegorical characters such as Peace and Malice; mythological characters such as Mars and Venus, Neptune, or Diana the moon goddess; and folklore characters such as fairies and nymphs. The primary purpose of the masque was to honor and entertain the monarch, whose presence as spectator was crucial to the meaning of the performance. She became incorporated into the plot, as did other courtiers who not only were spectators but often danced with the masquers. Unlike plays, masques were guided more by music and visual spectacles than by story line. Masque characters were closely connected to the nobles performing the parts, reflecting the actual life and relationships of elite political society rather than offering illusion removed from reality.

One element of the masque became known as the antimasque, which involved a grotesque dance preceding the courtly masque performance. The antimasque provided contrast to and variety from the staid, sophisticated action of the masque. In *A Midsummer Night's Dream,* the craftsmen's court entertainment is reminiscent of the antimasque form, although not by intention. The "rude mechanicals" see their performance of "Pyramus and Thisby" and the following dance as a dignified courtly offering, but the onstage spectators recognize it for what it is, a bumbling, awkward attempt at serious classical drama that turns the tragic into the comic. The contrast between the mechanicals' entertainment and fairy dances in the woods and around the court provides similar variety as the antimasque does for the masque in English court entertainment, except that within Shakespeare's play the fairies with their folklore and mythological associations are as "real" as the court characters whom they come to honor, celebrate, and bless.

Pageantry

Another form of court entertainment was the rite and ritual of pageantry offered to Queen Elizabeth. This pageantry, in the form of solemn jousting tournaments, recreated or renewed the medieval feudal allegiances of chivalry but linked the expression of knightly loyalty closely to the Crown rather than to feudal lords. The tournaments conjured up images of King Arthur and his knights with their heroic deeds, but shifted imagery to express it in feminine terms. Elizabeth was validated as the fair lady or mistress and primary audience whom her lords and knights honored as the heroine of life's romance. The lords rode into the tiltyard on decorated pageant carts or horses, sometimes disguised in symbolic costumes. They or their squires or servants recited songs and verses as a tribute to Elizabeth and then two knights jousted with lances in a sport designed to prove their martial prowess and their loyalty to their monarch.

From early in Elizabeth's reign, this pageantry began to take on national proportions as the court, and especially the queen herself, instigated a new holiday known as Accession Day on November 17, the anniversary of Elizabeth's ascent to the throne after her sister Mary's reign. A tournament at court on November 17 became a huge public spectacle open to everyone. Even for those who could not attend the court festival, celebrations spread throughout the country to every community where some of the typical holiday activities such as bell-ringing, feasting, rural sports, and bonfires were enjoyed but where people also went to church to hear sermons thanking God for Elizabeth's reign. She was portrayed not only as a Virgin Queen and Amazon warrior (as described in chapter 2) but also as Deborah and Judith, who were biblical female heroines; as Astrea, the ancient goddess of justice; and as the Fairy Queen, a magical figure of English folklore and the name of Edmund Spenser's national epic published late in Elizabeth's reign. Although the imagery was mixed and contradictory, it served to generate popularity, support, and loyalty throughout the kingdom. Ballads, tracts, and prayer books were published praising Elizabeth's virtues. This short example sets the tone for such works:

> Adore November's sacred Seventeenth Day,
> Wherein our second sun began her shine:
> Ring out sounding Bells; on Organs play;
> To Music's Mirth, let all Estates incline:
> Sound Drums and Trumpets, rending Air and Ground,
> Stringed Instruments, strike with melodious sound. (Strong 123)

Elizabeth became the object of devotion, and by the middle of her reign, celebrations also spread to her birthday on September 7, and to November 19, a religious feast day for St. Elizabeth, which became instead a remembrance of the defeat of the Spanish Armada in 1588 with credit going to the queen. These holidays, although stage-managed from court with idealized imagery that became a form of political propaganda, helped to break down barriers between the court and the common people for temporary periods of celebration among all Elizabeth' subjects. These political festivities added to the holidays of the seasons and the church year a whole new form of holiday with national significance that contributed to Elizabeth's popularity as monarch even among those who never saw her or had opportunity to honor her in person.

Progresses

Queen Elizabeth not only accepted the affirmation of loyalty from subjects who honored her in London and local communities on Accession Day, but she also traveled throughout the country in elaborate progresses giving villagers an opportunity to pay her tribute as she passed. The progresses were summer journeys to royal palaces and the great houses of the nobility and gentry. The queen left London partly to escape its unhealthy summer heat, partly to visit relatives and courtiers, and partly as a public relations exercise to encourage support among her subjects (Wilson 38–39). At the great houses she visited, lavish entertainments were organized for her pleasure and at great cost to the host, although the queen's arrival also vastly increased the host's prestige among his neighbors and dependents as well as at court.

The events sponsored for Elizabeth's visits were varied and catered to her interests. There were masques, plays, feasts, concerts, fireworks, hunting, and other rural pastimes. The queen was the chief audience and the aristocrats were secondary spectators, but the neighboring public was also welcome to attend, free of charge. Local artisans were even called upon to perform shows before their monarch as part of the festivities. Including the play by Bottom and his companions at a list of wedding entertainments for the aristocrats in *A Midsummer Night's Dream* was like a page out of the history books, for evidence indicates that Elizabeth appeared quite willing to enjoy an awkward performance of local craftsmen amongst the more sophisticated events offered by the hosts of her summer progresses. The festival time of her travels broke the boundaries of everyday social order to allow harmony among princes, aristocrats, and the common people celebrating together even if social boundaries were reinstated when the celebrating was over. Elizabeth even rode out to the woods to "gather May" one year near the end of her life, showing her support for a popular festival and helping to establish the goodwill with her subjects that characterized the image she fostered in pageants and progresses throughout her reign.

PLAY-ACTING

A Midsummer Night's Dream draws attention not only to holidays and court entertainments that were celebrated during the Elizabethan period, but also to play-acting, another element of popular culture in late-sixteenth-century England. With so much stage time given to the rehearsal and performance of "Pyramus and Thisby," *A Midsummer Night's Dream* is one of Shakespeare's most self-conscious plays about drama and the theater.

Play-acting falls somewhere between the popular festivities of holiday time represented by the communal rites of May Day and Midsummer's Eve and the formal court entertainments organized for Queen Elizabeth and her royal attendants. Like holiday time, a play provides license to pretend, improvise, and create an imaginary world apart from the everyday where fairies can be real and lovers can be touched by magic, where common people—the players—can become kings and queens like the summer Lord and Lady of May Day. Like court entertainments, play-acting includes formal elements of prepared speech and costumes and requires an audience, though not necessarily the specific audience of the queen. Like masques, plays could be performed at a specific occasion. While no definitive evidence exists, there is much historical speculation suggesting that *A Midsummer Night's Dream* was first enacted on the occasion of a court wedding where aristocrats and possibly even Queen Elizabeth were present. But *A Midsummer Night's Dream* was also performed in London's public theaters that drew audiences from both the common people and the gentry, reflecting the community orientation of popular holidays, the communal spirit of entertainments on royal progresses, and the general popularity of Shakespeare's drama.

Theater therefore challenged social boundaries and as it grew to become a vastly popular enterprise in the 1580s, 1590s, and beyond Elizabeth's reign, it became a source of controversy, too, with some of the same detractors as those who invoked religious propriety and civic order against the mirth and disorder associated with holiday time. Theater buildings grew up on the south side of the Thames River in London, outside the city's boundaries, to displace complaints of local civic authorities. Plays were disallowed on Sundays, a regulation that did virtually nothing to satisfy the strong disapproval of Puritan religious leaders, who saw theaters as places of corruption and drama as a repository of anti-Christian idleness. Nevertheless, audiences came and plays flourished.

Craft Guilds

Emphasis on play-acting in *A Midsummer Night's Dream* represents both a testament to the success of theater and a humorous critique of drama unsuccessfully delivered. "Pyramus and Thisby" is performed by amateur craftsmen. Their theatrical endeavor harks back to early medieval drama acted by craft guilds for the religious festival of Corpus Christi, which honored and remembered the body of Christ. Each guild that organized and represented a particular trade or craft was responsible for a certain play or interlude as part of a whole series recounting biblical history from the creation of the world to the resurrection of Christ. The dramatic series was enacted on pageant wagons throughout the town in places such as York and Coventry. The guilds covered the expenses of their plays, the wagons, and costumes, and amateurs performed annually for the community. When Edward VI and then Elizabeth I attempted to rid England of the trappings of Catholicism under their Protestant regimes, they banned Corpus Christi plays. Yet, in spite of government regulation, the religious dramatic cycles continued to be performed well into the 1570s in some areas of England and formed part of the history of the secular theater emerging at that time. Quince, Bottom, and their fellow craftsmen are a reminder of the historic association between drama, tradesmen, and the community.

Master of the Revels

Philostrate is the minor character in *A Midsummer Night's Dream* who reads out the list of optional entertainments for Theseus and Hippolyta's wedding day and offers advice and commentary. His role is reminiscent of the Master of the Revels, a regulatory office that was created by the Tudors and grew to prominence as play-acting moved from amateur street performances to professional theatrical stages. Initially, the court-appointed figure who headed the Revels Office was only responsible for selecting and paying entertainers for court, as Philostrate does. But gradually the Master of the Revels' responsibilities grew to include studying the content of all plays, acting as censor in determining which plays could be performed publicly, and licensing acting companies. What that meant for playwrights and actors was the assertion of official guidelines or limitations about what they could write and perform. Political and religious themes were especially risky or prohibited. The fears that the "rude mechanicals" express about the aristocrats' response to various parts of their play reinforce a self-conscious expression of the need for restraint by playwrights and actors engaged in entertainment regulated by a licensing, censoring body.

At the same time, the Revels Office allowed some actors the privilege of official permission to perform, which others did not receive. This distinction helped lead to the rise of professional acting troupes. Whereas actors held no clear social status and were often considered to be in the same maligned class as vagabonds and beggars, they became more socially acceptable when stamped with government approval and invited to bring their plays to court as well as perform them in London's theaters and on rural tours. Shakespeare became part of the Chamberlain's Men, an acting troupe under the patronage of Lord Hunsdon, the queen's Lord Chamberlain. The troupe rose to become one of the most prestigious and successful acting companies at the height of Elizabethan theatrical success.

Amateurs and Professionals

As a play self-consciously about play-acting, *A Midsummer Night's Dream* points to two performances—the first and obvious one being the "rude mechanicals'" "Pyramus and Thisby," and the second, less noticeable reference being to Shakespeare's comedy itself as Puck appeals to the audience in the final lines, inviting applause: "Give me your hands, if we be friends, And Robin shall restore amends" (5.1.439–40). Shakespeare creates in the two references a contrast between amateur or poorly acted drama and successful, professionally effective performance. In the 1570s and 1580s as professional acting was only beginning to develop, plays were performed by amateur groups. There were boy companies organized at St. Paul's Cathedral and the Chapel Royal where boys' choirs also became performers acting out plays written specifically for them for public and court entertainment. Young law students studying at the Inns of Court and university students at Oxford and Cambridge also included amateur theatricals as part of their education to refine their skills at elocution and debate. These actors were amateur both in the strict sense that they did not make their living from the stage and in the more conventional sense that their skill in performance was not as refined as the ability of professional actors coming into their own in the 1590s.

Shakespeare's constructed contrast between "Pyramus and Thisby" and his own comedy that frames it is humorously critical not only of amateur players but of the plays they performed. University and Inns of Court drama tended to be more speech-oriented than story-oriented, with a declamatory style that was formal and exaggerated. The language and the acting were highly artificial. The excesses of speech and embellished action in "Pyramus and Thisby" reflect this outdated style that was being replaced in Shakespeare's time with a much more realistic manner of delivery and a more integrated sense of story. Even the full paradoxical title, "The most lamentable comedy, and most cruel death of Pyramus and Thisby" echoes the title of a formerly popular university play, "A lamentable tragedy mixed full of pleasant mirth, containing the life of Cambises King of Persia, from the beginning of his kingdom unto his death, his one good deed of execution, after that many wicked deeds and tyrannous murders, committed by and through him, and last of all, his odious death by God's Justice appointed, done in such orders as followeth. By Thomas Preston" (1569). In light of Shakespeare's farcical inclusion of his play-within-the-play, it is difficult to imagine anyone taking seriously Thomas Preston's title—or his play. Even Pyramus's death seems to make fun of such overdone scenes as Cambises's death. Compare Pyramus's words with the tyrant Cambises:

Pyramus: Thus did I, thus, thus, thus.
Now am I dead,
Now am I fled;
My soul is in the sky.
Tongue, lose thy light;
Moon, take thy flight...
Now die, die, die, die, die. (5.1.301–7)

Cambises: I feel myself a-dying now, of life bereft am I,
And Death hath caught me with his dart, for want of blood, I spy.
Thus gasping here on ground I lie, for nothing I do care.
A just reward for my misdeeds my death doth plain declare.
(*Here let him quake and stir*).

(*Cambises* ll. 1168–70 in *Tudor Plays: An Anthology of Early English Drama,* ed. Edmund Creeth. New York: Doubleday, 1966, 501)

Like Pyramus, Cambises seems more inclined to speak to the audience than to act before it. The words explain and therefore diminish the experience of the performance. Absurdities in "Pyramus and Thisby" not only are humorous in light of the tightly-knit symmetrical action in the larger play, *A Midsummer Night's Dream,* but also deliberately reveal by farce and mockery ineffective, outdated plays while indicating the growing maturity of drama and the professionalism of the theater for which Shakespeare was in part responsible.

The remainder of this chapter includes excerpted documents that provide historical descriptions, attitudes, and responses to various forms of popular culture in Shakespeare's time.

HOLIDAY FESTIVITIES IN LONDON

John Stow was a sixteenth-century English historian (1525?–1605). In *A Survey of London* (1598), he provides an account of May Day and Midsummer's Eve in Henry VIII's time, describing an atmosphere of festivity in which the holiday activities reflect a spirit of harmony and goodwill. His positive perspective makes one wonder why any contemporaries would have objected to holidays as times of disruption and disorderly conduct, although he does refer to an insurrection of youth that led to the Maypole being less frequently used for a period. Stow recounts a May Day celebration in which Henry VIII and Queen Katherine happen upon a group of subjects in the woods pretending to be the folk hero Robin Hood and his men. Royalty and the commoners unite for a display of archery and a forest feast in which social barriers come down for the sake of communal celebration. His description of Midsummer's Eve focuses on the transformation of city houses for the occasion and the pageantry in which men marched through London streets with weapons, trumpeters, and drums honoring civic order in a display like a military parade. Notice the variety of activities that characterized the holiday festivities and the sense of social harmony Stow conveys.

FROM JOHN STOW, *A SURVEY OF LONDON* (1603), INTRODUCTION AND NOTES BY CHARLES LETHBRIDGE KINGSFORD, VOL. 1 (1908 EDITION)

(Reprinted from the text of 1603. Oxford: Clarendon Press, 1908)

From "Sports and pastimes of old time used in this City."

In the month of May, namely on May day in the morning, every man, except impediment, would walk into the sweet meadows and green woods, there to rejoice their spirits with the beauty and savour of sweet flowers, and with the harmony of birds, praising God in their kind, and for example here of *Edward Hall* hath noted, that K. *Henry* the eight, as in the [third year] of his reign and diverse other years, so namely in the seventh of his reign on May day in the morning with Queen *Katherine* his wife, accompanied with many Lords and Ladies, rode a Maying from Greenwich to the high ground of Shooters hill, where as they passed by the way, they espied a company of tall yeoman clothed all in Green, with green hoods, and with bows and arrows to the number of 200. One being their Chieftain was called *Robin Hood,* who required the king and his company to stay and see his men shoot, whereunto the king granting, *Robin Hood* whistled, and all the 200 Archers shot off, loosing all at once, and when he whistled again, they likewise shot again, their arrows whistled by craft of the head, so that the noise was strange and loud, which greatly delighted the King, Queen, and their Company. Moreover, this *Robin Hood* desired the King & Queen with their retinue to enter the green wood, where, in harbours made of boughs, and decked with flowers, they were set and served plentifully with venison and wine, by *Robin Hood* and his many, to their great contentment, and had other Pageants and pastimes as ye may read in my said Author. I find also that in the month of May, the Citizens of London of all estates, lightly in every Parish, or sometimes two or three parishes joining together, had their several mayings, and did fetch in Maypoles, with diverse warlike shows, with good Archers, Morris dancers, and other devices for pastime all the day long, and towards Evening they had stage plays, and Bonfires in the streets....

These great Mayings and Maygames made by the governors and Masters of this City, with the triumphant setting up of the great shaft (a principal May-pole in Cornhill, before the Parish Church of S. *Andrew*) therefore called Undershaft, by mean of an insurrection of youths against Aliens on may day, 1517, the ninth of *Henry* the 8 have not been so freely used as afore, and therefore I leave them, and will somewhat touch of the watches as also of the shows in the night. (98–99)

From "Of watches in this City, and other (Matters) commanded, and the cause why."

In the Months of June, and July on the Vigils of festival days, and on the same festival days in the Evenings after the Sun setting, there were usually made Bonfires in the streets, every man bestowing wood or labour towards them: the wealthier sort also before their doors near to the said [Bonfires], would set out Tables on the Vigils, furnished with sweet bread, and good drink, and on the Festival days with meats and drinks plentifully, whereunto they would invite their neighbors and passengers also to sit, and be merry with them in great familiarity, praising God for his benefits bestowed on them. These were called Bonfires as well of good amity amongst neighbours that, being before at controversy, were there by the labour of others, reconciled, and made of bitter enemies, loving friends, as also for the virtue that a great fire hath to purge the infection of the air. On the Vigil of Saint *John Baptist,* and on Saint *Peter* and *Paul* the Apostles, every man's door being shadowed with green Birch, long Fennel, Saint John's Wort, Orpin, white Lilies, and such like, garnished upon with Garlands of beautiful flowers, had also Lamps of glass, with oil burning in them all the night, some hung out branches of iron curiously wrought, containing hundreds of Lamps lit at once, which made a goodly show, namely in new Fishstreet, Thames street, &c. Then had ye besides the standing watches, all in bright harness in every ward and street of this City and Suburbs, a marching watch, that passed through the principal streets.... The marching watch contained in number about 2000 men, part of them being old Soldiers, of skill to be Captains, Lieutenants, Sergeants, Corporals, &c. Wilflers, Drummers, and Fifes, Standard and Ensign bearers, Sword players, Trumpeters on horseback, Demilances on great horses, Gunners with hand Guns, or half hakes, Archers in coats of white fustian signed on the breast and back with the arms of the City, their bows bent in their hands, with sheafs of arrows by their sides, Pike men in bright Corslets, Burganets, &c....there were also diverse Pageants, Morris dancers...the Mayor himself well-mounted on horseback, the sword bearer before him in fair Armour well mounted also, the Mayor's footmen, & the like Torch bearers about him, Henchmen twain, upon great stirring horses following him....

This Midsummer Watch was thus accustomed yearly, time out of mind until the year 1539 the 31 of *Henry* the 8th in which year on the eight of May, a great muster was made by the Citizens, at the Miles end all in bright harness with coats of white silk, or cloth and chains of gold, in three great battles, to the number of 15000, which passed through London to Westminster, and so through the Sanctuary, and round about the Park of S. *James,* and returned home through Holborn. King *Henry* then considering the great charges of the Citizens for the furniture of this unusual Muster, forbade the marching watch provided for, at Midsummer for that year, which being once laid down, was not raised again till the year 1548 the second of *Edward* the sixth, Sir *John Gresham* then being Mayor, who caused the marching watch both on the Eve of Saint *John Baptise,* and of S. *Peter* the Apostle, to be revived and set forth, in as comely order as it had been accustomed, which watch was also beautified by the number of more than 300.... Since this Mayor's time, the like marching watch in this City hath not been used, though some attempts have been made thereunto, as in the year 1585 a book was drawn by a grave citizen, & by him dedicated to sir *Thomas Pullison,* then Lord Mayor and his Brethren the Aldermen, containing the manner and order of a marching watch in the City upon the Evenings accustomed, in commendation whereof, namely in times of peace to be used, he hath words to this effect. The Artificers of sundry sorts were thereby well set a work, none but rich men charged, poor men helped, old Soldiers, Trumpeters, Drummers, Fifes, and ensign bearers with such like men, meet for Prince's service kept in ure, wherein the safety and defense of every commonwealth consisteth. Armour and Weapon being yearly occupied in this wise the Citizens had of their own readily prepared for any need, whereas by intermission hereof, Armorers are out of work, Soldiers out of ure, weapons overgrown with foulness, few or none good being provided, &c. (101–4)

AN OPPONENT OF HOLIDAY CELEBRATIONS

Philip Stubbes (1555?–1593) was a Puritan pamphleteer who held strongly negative views of holiday celebrations in stark contrast to John Stow's account. In *Anatomy of Abuses* (1583), Stubbes offers a vivid description of May Day festivities but does so as a scathing criticism of the practices. As a religious extremist, he condemns any activity that appears idolatrous and does not lead to moral behavior. Harsh as his criticisms are, he may be raising a legitimate concern about some of the excesses encouraged by holiday liberties. Pay attention to words and phrases that indicate Stubbes's opinion of May Day activities.

FROM PHILIP STUBBES, *THE ANATOMY OF ABUSES* (1583)

(London: J. Kingston for R. Jones, 1583; STC 23376) M3v

The Fruits of Maygames

Against May[day], Whisunday, or other time, all the young men and maids, old men and wives run gadding over night to the woods, groves, hills, and mountains, where they spend all the night in pleasant pastimes, and in the morning they return, bringing with them birch and branches of trees, to deck their assemblies withal, and no marvel, for there is a great Lord present among them, as superintendent and Lord over their pastimes and sports, namely Satan, prince of hell: But the chiefest jewel they bring from thence is their Maypole, which they bring home with veneration, as thus. They have twenty or forty yoke of oxen, every ox having a sweet nosegay of flowers placed on the tip of his horns, and these oxen draw home this Maypole (this stinking idol, rather) which is covered all over with flowers, and herbs bound round about with strings from the top to the bottom, and sometimes painted with variable colours, with two or three hundred men, women and children following it with great devotion. And thus being reared up with handkerchiefs and flags hovering on the top, they straw the ground round about, bind green boughs about it, set up summer halls, bowers, and arbors hard by it. And then they fall to dance about it like as the heathen people did at the dedication of the idols, whereof this is a perfect pattern, or rather the thing itself. I have heard it credibly reported . . . by men of great gravity and reputation, that of forty, threescore, or a hundred maids going to the wood over night, there have scarcely the third part of them returned home again undefiled. These be the fruits which these cursed pastimes bring forth.

QUEEN ELIZABETH'S KENILWORTH PROGRESS, 1575

Robert Laneham is an Elizabethan subject who witnessed one of the most lavish summer progresses in the queen's reign, at Kenilworth Castle in 1575, where the host, Robert Dudley, Earl of Leicester, entertained his monarch for three weeks. Laneham records in exhaustive detail the variety of activities and spectacles organized to honor Elizabeth. Excerpts included here describe the stately welcome of the queen, Sunday's fireworks, Monday's deer hunting, and the second Sunday's popular show by amateur Coventry players that combined drama with warlike pageantry. Notice Elizabeth's response to the players and consider how this compares to the hopes and aspirations of Shakespeare's amateur troupe of "rude mechanicals." Consider also Elizabeth's participation in the aristocratic hunt as it parallels the intentions of Theseus and Hippolyta the morning they come upon the four lovers in the woods. Pay attention to the way Kenilworth's entertainments combined courtly and popular elements.

FROM *ROBERT LANEHAM'S LETTER: DESCRIBING A PART OF THE ENTERTAINMENT UNTO QUEEN ELIZABETH AT THE CASTLE OF KENILWORTH IN 1575* (1575), EDITED WITH INTRODUCTION BY F. J. FURNIVALL (1907 EDITION)

(London: Chatto and Windus, 1907) 1–33

Unto my good friend, Master Humphrey Martin, Mercer.

After my heart commendations, I commend me heartily to you. Understand ye, that since through God and good friends, I am placed at Court here (as ye wot) in a worshipful room: whereby I am not only acquainted with the most, and well known to the best, and every officer glad of my company: but also have power, [on] days (while the Council sits not,) to go and to see things sight worthy, and to be present at any show or spectacle only where this Progress represented unto her Highness: And of part of which sports, having taken some notes and observations, (for I cannot be idle at any hand in the world,) as well to put from me suspicion of sluggardly, as to pluck from you doubt of any [of] my forgetfulness of friendship: I have thought it meet to impart them unto you, as frankly, as friendly, and as fully as I can....

On Saturday, the ninth of July ... it was eight o'clock in the evening ere her highness came to Killingworth. Where, in the Park, about a flightshoot from the Braize, and first gate of the Castle, one of the ten Sibyls, ... comely clad in a pall of white silk, pronounced a proper poesy in English rhyme and meter: of effect, how great gladness her goodness presence brought into every stead where it pleased her to come, and [especially] now into that place that had so long longed after the same: [the poem] ended with prophecy certain, of much and long prosperity, health, and felicity: this, her Majesty benignly accepting, passed forth unto the near gate of the Braize, which...they call now the Tiltyard, where a Porter, tall of person, big of limb, and stern of countenance, wrapt also all in silk, with a club and keys of quantity according, had a rough speech, full of passions, in meter aptly made to the purpose.... Trumpeters...stood upon the wall of the gate there, to sound up a tune of welcome.... this music maintained from them very delectably while her highness all along this tiltyard rode unto the inner gate next [to] the base court of the Castle: where the Lady of the Lake (famous in King Arthur's book) with two Nymphs waiting upon her, arrayed all in silks, attending her highness' coming: from the midst of the Pool, where, upon a movable Island, bright blazing with torches, she, floating to land, met her Majesty with a well penned meter....

This Pageant was closed up with a delectable harmony of Hautboys, Shalms, Cornets, and such other loud music, that held on while her Majesty pleasantly so passed from thence toward the Castle gate: whereunto, from the base court over a dry valley cast into a good form, was there framed a fair Bridge of a twenty foot wide and a seventy foot long....

Over the Castle gate was there fastened a Table, beautifully garnished above with her highness' arms, and fealty with Ivy wreathes bordered about: of a ten foot square: the ground black, whereupon, in large white Capital Roman, fair written, a Poem mentioning these Gods and their gifts thus presented unto her highness....

So passing into the inner Court, her Majesty (that never rides but alone) there set down from her Palfrey, was conveyed up to chamber: when after, did follow so great a peal of guns, and such lightning by firework a long space together, as Jupiter would show himself to be no further behind with his welcome than the rest of his Gods: and that would he have all the country to know: for indeed the noise and the flame were heard and seen a twenty mile off....

On Sunday: the forenoon occupied (as for the Sabbath day) in quiet and vacation from work, and in divine service and preaching at the parish church: The afternoon in excellent music of sundry sweet instruments, and in dancing of Lords and Ladies, and other worshipful degrees, uttered with such lively agility and commendable grace, as, whether it might be more strange to the eye, or pleasant to the mind, for my part indeed I could not discern: but exceedingly well was it (me thought) in both.

At night late, as though Jupiter the last night, had forgot for business, or forborn for courtesy and quiet, part of his welcome unto her highness appointed...displays me his main power: with blaze of burning darts, flying to and fro,...streams and hail of fiery sparks, lightnings of wildfire,...flight and shoot of thunderbolts: all with such countenance, terror, and vehemency that the heavens thundered, the waters surged, the earth shook.... This ado lasted while the midnight was past....

Monday was hot; and therefore her highness kept in till five o'clock in the evening: what time it pleased her to ride forth into the Chase to hunt the Hart of force: which found anon, and after sore chased, and chafed by the hot pursuit of the hounds, was fain, of fine force, at last to take soil. . . . with the stately carriage of his head in his swimming...like the sail of a ship: the hounds harrowing after, as...to the spoil of caravel: the tone no less eager in purchase of his prey, than was the other earnest in safeguard of his life: so as the earning [baying] of the hounds in continuance of their cry, the swiftness of the Deer, the running of the footmen, the galloping of the horses, the blasting of the horns, the halloing and hueing of the huntsmen, with the excellent Echoes between whiles from the woods and waters in valleys resounding, moved pastime delectable in so high a degree, as for any person to take pleasure by most senses at once. . . . Well, the Hart was killed, a goodly Deer. . . .

A Sunday opportunely, the weather broke up again, and after divine services in the parish church for the Sabbath day, and a fruitful sermon there in the forenoon: at afternoon, in worship of this Kenilworth Castle . . . a solemn bride-ale of a proper couple was appointed: set in order in the tiltyard, to come and make their show before the Castle in the great court, where as was [set up] a comely quintain for feats of arms, which, when they had done, to march out: at the north gate of the Castle, homeward again into the town. . . .

Many such a gay games were there among these riders: who by and by after, upon a greater courage, left their quintaining, and ran one at another. There to see the stern countenance, the grim looks, the courageous attempts, the desperate adventures, the dangerous courses, the fierce encounters, whereby the buff [blow] at the man, and the counterbuff at the horse, that both sometime came toppling to the ground. . . .

And hereto followed as good a sport (me thought) presented in an historical cue, by certain good hearted men of Coventry, my Lord's neighbors there: who, understanding among them the thing that could not be hidden from any, how careful and studious his honour was, that by all pleasant recreations her highness might best find herself welcome, and be made gladsome and merry, (the groundwork indeed, and foundation of his Lordship's mirth and gladness of us all), made petition that they might renew now their old storial show: Of argument, how the Danes whilom [once] here in a troublesome season were for quietness born withall, and suffered in peace, that anon, by outrage and importable insolency, abusing both Ethelred, the king then, and all the estates everywhere besides: at the grievous complaint and counsel of Huna, the king's chieftain in wars on Saint Brice's night, Ann. Dom. 1012 . . . that falleth yearly on the thirteenth of November, were all dispatched and the Realm rid. And for because the matter mentioneth how valiantly our English women for love of their country behaved themselves: expressed in actions and rhymes after their manner, they thought it might move some mirth to her Majesty the rather.

. . . But aware, keep back, make room now, here they come! And first, captain Cox, an odd man I promise you: by profession a Mason, and that right skilfull, very cunning in fence[ing], and hardy as Gawain [a medieval knight] . . . great oversight hath he in matters of story. . . .

Captain Cox came marching on valiantly before, clean trussed, and gatered above the knee, all fresh in a velvet cap . . . flourishing with his tonsword, and another fence-master with him: thus in the forward making room for the rest. After them proudly pricked on foremost, the Danish lanceknights on horseback, and then the English: each with their alder poll martially in their hand. Even at the first entry the meeting waxed somewhat warm: that by and by kindled with courage a both sides, grew from a hot skirmish unto a blazing battle: first by spear and shield, outrageous in their races as rams at their rut, with furious encounters, that together they tumble to the dust, sometimes horse and man: and after fall to it with the sword and target, and good bangs a both sides: the fight so ceasing; but the battle not so ended: followed the foot-men, both the hosts, t'one after t'other: first marching in ranks, then warlike turning, then from ranks into squadrons, then into triangles; from that into rings, and so wind-ing out again: A valiant captain of great prowess, as fierce as a fox assaulting a goose, was so hardy to give the first stroke: then get they grisly together: that great was the activity that day to be seen there a both sides: t'one very eager for purchase of prey, t'other utterly stout for redemption of liberty: thus, quarrel enflamed fury a both sides. Twice the Danes had the better; but at the last conflict, beaten down, overcome and many led captive for triumph by our English women.

This was the effect of this show, that as it was handled, made much matter of good pastime: brought all indeed into the great court, e'en under her highness' window to have been seen: but (as unhappy it was for the bride) that came thither too soon. . . . For her highness beholding in the chamber delectable dancing indeed: and herewith the great throng and unruliness of the people, was cause that this solemnity of the Bride-ale and dancing, had not the full muster was hoped for: and but a little of the Country plea her highness also saw: commanded therefore on the Tuesday following to have it full out: as accordingly it was presented, whereat her Majesty laughed well: they [the players] were the jocunder, and so much the more because her highness had given them two bucks [deer], and five mark in money, to make merry together: they prayed for her Majesty, long, happily to reign, and oft to come thither, that oft they might see her: and what, rejoicing upon their ample reward, and what, triumphing upon the good acceptance, they vaunted their play was never so dignified, nor ever any players afore so beatified [blessed].

Thus though the day took an end, yet slipped not the night all sleeping away: for as neither office nor obsequy ceased at any time to the full, to perform the plot his honour had appointed: So, after supper was there a play presented of a very good theme, but so set forth by the Actors well handling, that pleasure and mirth made it seem very short, though it lasted two good hours and more. . . .

After the play out of hand, followed a most delicious and . . . Ambrosial banquet. . . .

Unto this banquet there was appointed a masque: for riches of array, of an incred-ible cost: but the time so far spent, and very late in the night now, was cause that it came not forth to the show. . . .

QUEEN ELIZABETH HONORED AT ELVETHAM, 1591

Another significant Elizabethan progress took place at Elvetham, hosted by the Earl of Hereford in 1591. Although not nearly as lavish as Kenilworth, it remains one of the most spectacular on record. On the fourth day of entertainments, a masquelike show was performed for Elizabeth in the garden as she watched from her gallery window. Elizabeth is portrayed in the show as Elisa, a favorite of the Fairy Queen. Coming four years before *A Midsummer Night's Dream,* this entertainment may well have been a source for or influence on Shakespeare's play. The outdoor performance is linked to the chivalric behavior of romance and the characterization of myth as Elisa receives a chaplet or wreath of flowers and is almost worshipped in her association with Phoebe, also known in classical mythology as Diana, the moon goddess. Connecting Elizabeth with the fairy world conveys an unearthly, and therefore powerful but delicate, quality about her monarchy. Notice the many ways in which action and imagery parallel the fairy kingdom of Shakespeare's play. Note: Nereus is the god of the sea and Sylvan gods are gods of the forest.

FROM "THE HONORABLE ENTERTAINMENT GIVEN TO THE QUEEN'S MAJESTY IN A PROGRESS, AT ELVETHAM IN HAMPSHIRE, BY THE RIGHT HONORABLE EARL OF HEREFORD, 1591" (1591) IN *ENTERTAINMENTS FOR ELIZABETH I,* ED. JEAN WILSON (1980)

(Woodbridge: Brewer, 1980) 115–16

On Thursday morning, Her Majesty was no sooner ready and at her Gallery window looking into the Garden, but there began three Cornets to play certain fantastic dances, at the measure whereof the Fairy Queen came into the garden, dancing with her maids about her. She brought with her a garland, made in form of an imperial crown; within the sight of her Majesty she fixed upon a silvered staff, and sticking the staff into the ground, spake as followeth:

... I that abide in places underground,
Aureola, the Queen of Fairy land,
That every night in rings of painted flowers
Turn round, and carol out Elisa's name:
Hearing, that Nereus and the Sylvan gods
Have lately welcomed your Imperial Grace,
[I opened] the earth with this enchanting wand,
To do my duty to your Majesty,
And humbly to salute you with this chaplet,

Given to me by Auberon, the Fairy King.
Bright shining Phoebe, that in human shape
Hid'st Heaven's perfection, vouchsafe t'accept it:
And I Aureola, beloved in heaven,
(For amorous stars fall nightly in my lap)
Will cause that Heavens enlarge thy golden days,
And cut them short, that envy at thy praise.

   After this speech, the Fairy Queen and her maids danced about the Garden, singing a Song of Six parts, with the music of an exquisite consort; wherein was the lute, bandora, bass-viol, cittern, treble-viol, and flute. And this was the Fairies' song:

Elisa is the fairest Queen
That ever trod upon this green.
Elisa's eyes are blessed stars,
Inducing peace, subduing wars.
Elisa's hand is crystal bright,
Her words are balm, her looks are light.
Elisa's breast is that fair hill,
Where Virtue dwells, and sacred skill.
O blessed be each day and hour,
Where sweet Elisa builds her bower.

REGULATIONS FOR PLAY-ACTING

The following proclamation appeared in the second year of Elizabeth's reign and established standards for performances of interludes or plays throughout the kingdom. Although it does not specifically mention the Revels Office or the Master of the Revels, it indicates how regulations limited dramatic activity and describes the penalties for disregarding the rules. The government's apparent need to monitor such entertainments suggests that they had a potentially powerful and political effect on spectators, participants, and the public at large.

FROM PROCLAMATION 509 BY THE QUEEN (1559), IN E. K. CHAMBERS, *ELIZABETHAN STAGE,* VOL. 4 (1923)

(Oxford: Clarendon, 1923) 263–64

The Queen's Majesty doth straightly forbid all manner Interludes to be played either openly or privately, except the same be notified beforehand, and licensed within any City or town corporate, by the Mayor or other chief officers of the same, and within any shire, by such as shall be Lieutenants for the Queen's Majesty in the same shire, or by two of the Justices of peace inhabiting within that part of the shire where any shall be played.

And for instruction to every of the said officers, her majesty doth likewise charge every of them, as they will answer: that they permit none to be played wherein either matters of religion or of the governance of the estate of the commonwealth shall be handled or treated, being no meet matters to be written or treated upon, but by men of authority, learning and wisdom, nor to be handled before any audience, but of grave and discrete persons: All which parts of this proclamation, her majesty chargeth to be inviolably kept. And if any shall attempt to the contrary: her majesty giveth all manner of officers that have authority to see common peace kept in commandment, to arrest and imprison the parties so offending, for the space of fourteen days or more, as cause shall need: And further also until good assurance may be found and given, that they shall be of good behavior, and no more to offend in the likes.

And further her majesty giveth special charge to her nobility and gentlemen, as they profess to obey and regard her majesty, to take good order in this behalf with their servants being players, that this her majesty's commandment may be duly kept and obeyed.

ELIZABETHAN ACTING STYLES

Just as Shakespeare uses the craftsmen in *A Midsummer Night's Dream* to comment by example on good and poor acting styles, he later comments again on theatricality and acting styles through the words of Hamlet, in *The Tragedy of Hamlet, Prince of Denmark* (1600–1601). Hamlet wants a troupe of travelling players to perform a play before King Claudius, the content of which will help Hamlet confirm Claudius's guilt by his response to the play-within-the-play. While instructing the actors about which play to perform and how to act it, he offers his own perspective on effective and ineffective stage demeanor. It is likely that Shakespeare had real examples in mind as he wrote the lines. Hamlet argues for balance and subtlety. Pay attention to the extreme behaviors he cautions the players to avoid and think of how the "rude mechanicals" might have benefited from his instruction.

FROM WILLIAM SHAKESPEARE, *HAMLET* (1600–1601)

(*The Riverside Shakespeare,* Ed. G. Blakemore Evans et al. Boston: Houghton, 1974) 1161–62

Hamlet: Speak the speech, I pray you, as I pronounc'd it to you, trippingly on the tongue, but if you mouth it, as many of our players do, I had as live the town-crier spoke my lines. Nor do not saw the air too much with your hand, thus, but use all gently, for in the very torrent, tempest, and, as I may say, whirlwind of your passion, you must acquire and beget a temperance that may give it smoothness. O, it offends me to the soul to hear a robustious periwig-pated fellow tear a passion to totters, to very rags, to spleet the ears of the groundlings, who for the most part are capable of nothing but inexplicable dumb shows and noise. I would have such a fellow whipt for o'erdoing Termagant, it out-Herods Herod, pray you avoid it.

Player: I warrant your honor.

Hamlet: Be not too tame neither, but let your own discretion be your tutor. Suit the action to the word, the word to the action, with this special observance, that you o'erstep not the modesty of nature: for any thing so o'erdone is from the purpose of playing, whose end, both at the first and now, was and is, to hold as 'twere the mirror up to nature: to show virtue her feature, scorn her own image, and the very age and body of the time his form and pressure. Now this overdone, or come tardy off, though it makes the unskillful laugh, cannot but make the judicious grieve; the censure of which one must in your allowance o'erweigh a whole theatre of others. O, there be players that I have seen play—and heard others [praise], and that highly—not to speak it profanely, that, neither having th'accent of Christians nor the gait of Christian, pagan, nor man, have so strutted and bellow'd that I have thought some of Nature's journeymen had made men, and not made them well, they imitated humanity so abominably. (3.2.1–35)

TOPICS FOR WRITTEN AND ORAL DISCUSSION

1. What is the main event John Stow describes in his account of May Day pastimes? How do the participants interact and behave with one another? What indication does Stow give that May Day festivities were not always harmonious?

2. According to Stow, in what ways did London people typically celebrate Midsummer's Eve? What was the Midsummer Watch and what seems particularly festive about it? Stow concludes by suggesting a practical purpose for the Watch. What was it?

3. Philip Stubbes protests the practice of May games and May Day celebrations. What are the main grounds for his criticism and to what specific practices does he object?

4. Does Stubbes's description of May games, as opposed to his reaction to them, seem attractive or unappealing? Do you think his description assists or hinders his arguments against the festivities?

5. Compare Stubbes's account of May Day to the references and actions in *A Midsummer Night's Dream* that appear to imitate May Day celebrations. Do any of Stubbes's objections appear justified in light of the lovers' interactions in the forest? Why or why not?

6. Imagine Philip Stubbes and Shakespeare's Egeus having a dialogue together after the morning that Theseus and Hippolyta discover the four lovers in the woods. Do you think they will be like-minded or dissimilar in their attitudes? Script or act out a conversation between them.

7. From the information in this chapter, make a list of activities associated with holiday celebrations in sixteenth-century England. Can you recognize any parallels with activities we engage in today to mark holidays or special occasions? Does your community have any specific annual celebrations? Describe what happens at them.

8. Describe how Queen Elizabeth was welcomed to Kenilworth Castle on her summer progress in 1575. What kind of atmosphere did the host try to create? What are Sibyls and Nymphs? What kind of image do they help generate for Elizabeth?

9. Compare Robert Laneham's description of the deer hunt with Theseus and Hippolyta's discussion about hunting as they enter the woods in act 4, scene 1. What roles do sound and music play? How is the hunt portrayed as an enjoyable pastime?

10. How is "the hunt" symbolic of the nighttime activities in the woods in *A Midsummer Night's Dream*? Find images and examples in the play that support the symbolism.

11. The Coventry players who come to entertain the queen at Kenilworth perform "a storial show." What is the basic plot of the "story" and in what respect does the entertainment appear to be more of a "show" or "display" than a "story"?

12. The Coventry players are craftsmen, amateur performers. Compare their skill at performance with the that of the "rude mechanicals" in *A Midsummer Night's Dream*.

Which troupe is presented in a more positive light and how? How do the responses of Queen Elizabeth and Shakespeare's onstage aristocrats differ? Are they at all alike?

13. Imagine Laneham's "Captain Cox" and Shakespeare's Bottom swapping stories about their performances before aristocratic audiences. What are their hopes and expectations prior to the performance, how do they approach their task of acting, and how might they feel when it is over? Compose or act out a dialogue based on the details provided in Laneham's letters and Shakespeare's play.

14. What atmosphere is created by the performance for Queen Elizabeth at Elvetham in 1591? What words and images help to set the tone? How is the show like a masque?

15. Flattery was an important part of shows given before the queen. Compare and contrast the Coventry players' show at Kenilworth with the "Fairy Queen" show at Elvetham. What different attributes do they appeal to in the public image Elizabeth tried to fashion for herself? How does each show flatter her?

16. The queen was the subject of flattery and heroic representations in sixteenth-century England. Do we have heroes or heroines in our culture today whom we flatter, honor, or idealize? Do they come from government or from elsewhere?

17. What connections do you see between the Elvetham show and *A Midsummer Night's Dream*? Consider, for example, characters, imagery, poetry, mythology, setting, and dance.

18. Imagine you are Shakespeare and that you have seen the Elvetham "Fairy Queen" performance. Pretend the show sparks an idea for a play about fairies and write a series of notes to yourself about how the Elvetham entertainment sets your creative energies in motion for a drama eventually to be called *A Midsummer Night's Dream.* If you have seen the movie *Shakespeare in Love,* you may appreciate from that fictionalized account how difficult and intense the creative process of playwriting could be in Shakespeare's time. You may even want to act out a humorous mini-play as a group assignment, portraying the steps Shakespeare goes through to reach the final version of *A Midsummer Night's Dream.* What false starts and brilliant ideas enter into the process?

19. The "rude mechanicals" are overly sensitive about potential responses from their audience, but Elizabethan playwrights and players did have reasons to be cautious about reactions to their work. What limitations does the Royal Proclamation of 1559 impose? What topics were playwrights to avoid and what were the penalties for disregarding the rules?

20. Hamlet is critical of a particular style of acting. What is his chief criticism? What does he feel good acting should achieve and how does he believe the purpose can be attained?

21. Imagine Hamlet has seen the "rude mechanicals" rehearsing "Pyramus and Thisby." He does not suffer fools gladly and he takes the craftsmen to be fools. Act out a scene in which he enters and responds to their rehearsal. Alternatively, write a

response for Hamlet in which he details his criticism. Is he mocking or dismissive, angry or disgusted?

22. What role would Hamlet play as a guest at the final performance of the craftsmen's play if he were to join Theseus's company? Do you find yourself sympathizing with the actors or the audience? Explain why. Are the aristocrats themselves at all sympathetic, generous, or kind in their responses? Provide examples.

23. Choose a speech from one of the characters in *A Midsummer Night's Dream*—excluding the craftsmen—and overact it following Hamlet's description of bad acting or the examples provided by the "rude mechanicals" themselves. Then redo the speech in a more effective and natural style. Discuss the results with audience members from your class.

24. As a group assignment, perform the craftsmen's "Pyramus and Thisby." Remember that the more badly you act the play-within-the-play, the closer you will be to Shakespeare's intention for it.

SUGGESTED READING

Barber, C. L. *Shakespeare's Festive Comedy: A Study of Dramatic Form and Its Relation to Social Custom.* New York: Meridian Books, 1959.

Bradbrook, M. C. *The Rise of the Common Player: A Study of Actor and Society in Shakespeare's England.* London: Chatto and Windus, 1962.

Cressy, David. *Bonfires and Bells: National Memory and the Protestant Calendar in Elizabethan and Stuart England.* London: Weidenfeld and Nicolson, 1989.

Dunlop, Ian. *Palaces and Progresses of Elizabeth I.* London: Jonathan Cape, 1962.

Happe, Peter. *English Drama before Shakespeare.* London: Longman, 1999.

James, Mervyn. *Society, Politics and Culture: Studies in Early Modern England.* Cambridge: Cambridge UP, 1986.

Laroque, Francois. *Shakespeare's Festive World: Elizabethan Seasonal Entertainment and the Professional Stage.* Trans. Janet Lloyd. Cambridge: Cambridge UP, 1991.

Montrose, Louis. *The Purpose of Playing: Shakespeare and the Cultural Politics of the Elizabethan Theatre.* Chicago: University of Chicago Press, 1996.

Strong, Roy. *The Cult of Elizabeth: Elizabethan Portraiture and Pageantry.* London: Thames and Hudson, 1977.

Welsford, Enid. *The Court Masque: A Study in the Relationship between Poetry and the Revels.* Cambridge: Cambridge UP, 1927.

Wiles, David. *Shakespeare's Alamanac:* A Midsummer Night's Dream, *Marriage, and the Elizabethan Calendar.* Woodbridge: D. S. Brewer, 1993.

Wilson, Jean. *Entertainments for Elizabeth I.* Woodbridge: D. S. Brewer, 1980.

Yates, Frances A. *Astrea: The Imperial Theme in the Sixteenth Century.* London: Routledge and Kegan Paul, 1975.

Young, David P. *Something of Great Constancy: The Art of "A Midsummer Night's Dream."* New Haven: Yale UP, 1966.

5

Imagination and Beliefs: Dreams, Fairies, and Transformation

A Midsummer Night's Dream is a play about imagination. It describes a nighttime dream experience that its characters cannot absorb and understand by simple reason and common sense. It creates a kingdom of fairies, creatures who cannot be seen or heard by ordinary human senses. It portrays a supernatural experience of transformation where lovers touched by powers beyond their comprehension fall in love with those they hate and hate those with whom they fall in love. Transformation also touches a craftsman who suddenly wears the head of an ass, and when his human form returns he senses beyond the grasp of words that the experience has somehow changed him. The play-within-the-play draws further attention to the relationship between imagination and art, and Shakespeare makes the role of imagination in his comedy all the more self-conscious by having his characters debate and discuss their views about the effects and limitations of the mind's eye. Theseus appears to see only the limitations and dismisses all "antique fables," "fairy toys," as the "tricks" of "strong imagination" (5.1.3,18). Hippolyta leaves room to believe what cannot be comprehended, suggesting that "fancy's images" of that midsummer night "grow to something of great constancy;°/ But, howsoever, strange and admirable" (5.1.25–27). Steeped as the play is in the power and confusion of imaginary worlds, it invites questions about how the imagination was perceived in Shakespeare's time, how those perceptions—reflected in ideas about dreams, fairies, and transformation—shape the boundaries of Shakespeare's play, and how Shakespeare's play in response sometimes challenges the boundaries of belief surrounding it.

Imagination, in late-sixteenth-century England, was primarily understood as one of three faculties, filling the middle role in a hierarchy between the intellect above it and the senses below it. Because of its middle position, it was perceived to be a bridge between the physical body that sensed the world around it and the mind that comprehended the information it received. As long as the hierarchy remained in order, imagination was recognized for its necessary role in acquiring knowledge by transferring accurate sensory images from the physical to the intellectual realm. But the imagination was also seen as potentially dangerous because it could too often gain power over the mind, work against reason, and lead to excesses of passion and appetite. When this happened, imagination no longer transmitted accurate information but imparted false information by misrepresenting what was real. The result could lead to momentary illusion or, at worst, insanity. The "lunacy" or lunar madness of the lovers in the woods in *A Midsummer Night's Dream* depicts a circumstance in which imagination or "fantasy" has achieved the upper hand, and reason, its opposite, has lost control.

If imagination was considered by many as a suspicious though necessary faculty of human comprehension, it had its supporters among poets and storytellers who recognized that imagination could create a world of beauty and pleasure beyond the boundaries of reason or logic. To counter the arguments that imagination was the source of lying and deception, some borrowed from ancient beliefs that imagination was a higher power that set human beings apart from other living creatures. In this view, imagination provides the source of invention rather than deception. Though Theseus stands as a strong supporter of reason over imagination, much within the play works from the power to create and invent worlds beyond reason that compel belief, express beauty, and spark pleasure that are as much a part of being human as the concrete capacity to think and to reason. The following discussion of dreams, fairies, and transformation explores this world of invention, experience, and belief where reason does not always assume the superior role.

THE PSYCHOLOGY OF DREAMS

Dreams originate in the unconscious part of the mind where reason has no power to order and contain experience. They fascinate because they are a universal phenomenon of such mysterious proportions and puzzling significance. There is no doubt that dreams are meant to be somehow central to *A Midsummer Night's Dream*. Not only does the word appear in the title, but there are multiple references and experiences within the play itself. Hermia awakes suddenly in the woods after Lysander has departed and describes a dream—a nightmare, in fact—in which a serpent is at her breast eating her heart away while Lysander smiles cruelly (2.2.145–56). This is the only "real" dream in the play. But the lovers also awake the next morning and at first believe that their nighttime adventures have been a dream, except that they all seem to have had the same experience, which is not how dreams usually work upon the mind. Bottom, too, describes his amorous night with Titania as a dream, deciding to honor its perplexing significance by calling it "'Bottom's Dream,' because it hath no bottom" (4.2.220–21). Finally, Puck closes the play by inviting the audience to see the whole play, not just the nighttime adventures in the woods, as a dream, and therefore to receive it kindly without harsh judgments about its rational or realistic development.

What did Shakespeare's contemporaries and those watching his play know or believe about dreams? The question is simpler than the answer. The dream psychology of the Renaissance period appears to have grown out of much earlier traditions, from classical scholars of ancient Greece and Rome, from the Christian biblical accounts of prophetic dreams and visions, and from the medieval English literary device of the dream frame narrative, used by Chaucer among others, in which a character enters into a dream experience that reveals a deeper awareness, understanding, or wisdom concerning rational experience.

From the classical Greek and Roman cultures came lengthy works of dream analysis, some of which were printed and reprinted centuries later during the Renaissance. Such longevity indicates their lasting popularity and authority. These works classified dreams in a variety of ways, often creating a hierarchy in which serious dreams of significant revelation defined the top level while utterly mundane dreams of no significance whatsoever fell into the bottom category. Ancient dream theory presented a great deal of ambiguity about dreams, their causes, and their meanings. Dreams could be inspired by evil and demonic sources or angelic and divine causes. They could therefore offer deception or truth. They should be approached, then, with caution but potentially with enthusiasm. The views of one ancient writer, Gregory the Great, indicate just how confusing dream analysis could be, for he suggested that dreams could come to the soul because of an empty stomach or a full one, because of illusion—a false source—or revelation—a true source—or a combination of thought with illusion or revelation (Kruger 45). Dreams could, therefore, have their basis in physical conditions or physiology; in psychology, the workings of the mind; in philosophy, the understanding of human beings within their world; and in theology, the relationship between the human and the divine.

The Christian biblical tradition, which some ancient writers as well as the early modern minds of the Renaissance accepted, focused on the theological basis of dreams. These dreams could be prophetic in that they revealed to the dreamer something about the unfolding of the future. They could also be allegorical, meaning that their parts signified or represented meaning beyond themselves. Egypt's Pharaoh in the Old Testament dreams of seven lean cows that eat seven fat cows, and Joseph, the dream artist, interprets for him that the cows represent seven years of plenty followed by seven years of famine in Egypt. The interpretation of the allegory allows Pharaoh to prepare for scarcity in the land. Hermia's dream of the serpent in *A Midsummer Night's Dream* follows a similar tradition. Serpents are a sign of evil, especially from biblical tradition in which the serpent caused the temptation and fall in the Garden of Eden. The vision of Lysander laughing cruelly while the serpent eats Hermia's heart away both symbolizes and prophesies, indicating that Lysander has left her and, by laughing at her distress, is about to treat her harshly and cruelly. Nobody in the play provides this interpretation, but the awareness of dream significance, its layers of allegory or symbolism, and its capacity to predict or prophesy, would have been immediately recognized by an English Elizabethan audience. We even recognize such dream possibilities today because our modern understanding of dreams still includes such ancient traditions.

The literary device of the dream frame narrative of the medieval period preceding the Renaissance forms yet another aspect of interpreting and understanding dreams in Shakespeare's time. The dream narrative is not a real dream of the mind but an artificial dream created by a writer as a way to reveal some fundamental truth, wisdom, or higher knowledge that comes to the fictionalized dreamer and leads to his or her fuller harmony with the world which before the dream held confusion or caused despair. The dream fiction takes the form of a kind of transforming journey. In some ways, "Bottom's Dream" both reflects and parodies this literary tradition. The dream of his night with Titania is no dream at all. But he believes it is. And it is a transforming journey in which he is literally changed physically and then restored again. He also gains some wisdom but is naive enough not to comprehend the depth of the experience, the magic of it all, that he—more than the others—at least recognizes because he has been allowed to experience it, though he cannot find the words for it. His confused parody of a biblical passage brings the theological element of dreams into play, too, as he humorously mixes all the senses, saying, "The eye of man hath not heard, the ear of man hath not seen, man's hand is not able to taste, his tongue to conceive, nor his heart to report, what my dream was" (4.1.214–17; from 1 Corinthians 2:9). Bottom elicits laughter, but he also offers the possibility of wonder because of the power that dreams can have to change perceptions of reality.

Dream analysis in the Renaissance borrowed from these numerous earlier traditions, but skeptics of the time simply approached dreams with suspicion. Because of the connection between dreaming and imagination—from whence the dream images derived—dreams were seen as sources of illusion or the unreal, of false information or misunderstanding. They derived from shadow rather than from substance and thus were sometimes compared with or seen as parallel to plays on the stage, which were also considered to be based on "illusion" or pretense rather than reality. Puck draws this comparison as he suggests that Shakespeare's entire play is a dream. But his comparison is both an apology and a request for applause: "Give me your hands, if we be friends" (5.1.439). Shakespeare embraces the ambiguity that the understanding and interpretation of dreams represent. If one doubts the power of dreams, one must doubt the power of the play; if either the dream or the play is criticized, the other one must be dismissed. Shakespeare leaves his audience with this paradox. But Theseus, the most skeptical character about the fantasies of the night, offers an unusually inconsistent perspective when in response to the ridiculousness of "Pyramus and Thisby," he says of the incompetent actors, "The best in this kind are but shadows; and the worst are no worse, if imagination amend them" (5.1.212–13). He seems to suggest here not skepticism but a view that the audience can use their imaginations to a positive end, embracing the play, accepting the dream, and capturing from illusion some source of truth or pleasure or wonder.

FAIRIES

Fairies, like dreams, demand belief in what cannot be seen, and, as such, they too draw upon the imagination. Though there were some skeptics who discounted magic, many Elizabethans, especially among the common people, believed in fairies as real creatures who inhabited the English countryside, living among caves, mountains, and hills. Precisely what kind of creatures they were, however, is unclear. The word "fairy" comes from the word "fay," which comes from "Fata," meaning "goddess of fate." This association suggests a relationship of fairies to Fates or Norns, supernatural goddesses or mythical creatures. Elizabethans believed fairies to be of ordinary human size, some with extraordinary beauty in an array of colors including blue, green, red, white, and especially black. All were thought to have supernatural powers that they could exert over human beings with positive or negative results. Views about their origins varied, however. They were seen alternately as ghosts, evil spirits, wicked monsters, or the devil himself. They were considered fallen angels, the souls of dead men and women, or beings inhabiting a third kingdom between heaven and hell (Latham 41–46). But one pre-Shakespearean belief was consistent: that fairies were not benign but sinister beings. There were many superstitions about how to behave to protect oneself from their wiles and charms.

Creatures included in the fairy kingdom ranged from the heroic or aristocratic trooping fairies of the Celtic and Romantic tradition who could ride on horseback, to the more domestic types who were concerned with household cleanliness, to mermaids, giants, monsters, and hags (Briggs *Anatomy* 15). Some common characteristics of fairies were their ability to change themselves into different shapes, their power to transport themselves overseas, their love of music and dancing, their fondness for mischief, their intolerance of lust, their tendency to lead travelers astray, and their ability to cause dreams. They were thought to be most powerful and active on May Day and Midsummer's Eve. Clearly, Shakespeare's fairy kingdom incorporates a number of these viewpoints. The single most common belief about fairy interaction with the human world was that fairies stole babies and replaced them with changelings, who were deformed and unintelligent. Fairies were also thought to abduct human beings and turn them into witches. Indeed, there is a close connection between witchcraft and fairies, for convicted witches often claimed familiarity with fairies, and fairies were thought capable of bewitching humans not only by causing disease and blindness but by destroying crops and cattle, an influence Titania acknowledges in her description of the effects of her quarrel with Oberon in Shakespeare's play.

The influence of the fairies was not all bad, however, for though their punishments of human behavior that they found offensive ranged from severe pinchings to abductions to death, they also offered rewards and were thought to be generous to their favorites. It was thought that they sometimes left money or jewels in a person's shoes or basin, that they knew herbal remedies and could cure diseases, and that they could see into the future and might give this second sight to humans. For all their power, though, they depended on mortals for food and water, and while they might bring good favor on those who left them a pail of clean water or a bowl of cream at night before going to bed, they would bring mischief to those who deprived them. Elizabethans with strong beliefs in fairy lore, therefore, practiced a number of cautionary measures. They tried to avoid any land that they thought fairies occupied, especially the fairy rings where fairies danced; they avoided trying to see fairies; and they avoided speaking to fairies on pain of death or speaking of them to other people lest they lose the reward or favor they might have received.

While Shakespeare incorporates some of the qualities of Elizabethan fairy enchantment into *A Midsummer Night's Dream,* he invents his own fairy kingdom that stands in stark contrast to some of the prominent fairy beliefs of his time. Oberon declares to Puck, "But we are spirits of another sort" (3.2.387), and much of what Shakespeare does is indeed of another sort. From a purely physical standpoint, he turns his fairies into tiny creatures, small enough to hide in acorn cups or fan themselves with butterfly wings. Equally significantly, he makes the fairies far more kind and benevolent to human beings than the sinister nature of their counterparts in English folklore. Titania does not steal a child but looks after a changeling boy out of love and loyalty to his dead mother. The fairies still have power to do harm and Puck certainly is mischievous at heart, but Titania and Oberon come to bless, not harm, the wedding couple of Athens, and Oberon attempts to set right the love sickness of the young Athenian people. Though Puck enjoys the confusion he causes in mistaking Lysander for Demetrius, the deed is accidental rather than intentional, and Shakespeare makes it appear more humorous than dangerous.

Puck, in fact, is one of Shakespeare's innovations. Though a traditional and famed figure in English folklore, Puck, alias Robin Goodfellow or Hobgoblin, belonged in a category of demons or devils separate from fairyland. He was a supernatural being with a love for practical jokes. Relishing any mishap or domestic accident deemed his doing, he was called "Goodfellow" to appease his anger and stay in his favor. An individual folk spirit, he was best known for his sense of humor and his laughter, but he also had associations with witches and dark powers. Shakespeare captures the exuberance of Robin Goodfellow in *A Midsummer Night's Dream,* but incorporates the character into the fairy kingdom where he becomes mischievous henchman to King Oberon.

Interestingly, while Shakespeare's portrayal of fairies strayed from standard contemporary folklore beliefs, his influence was significant for views about fairies that succeeded his play. When we think of fairies today as tiny, harmless creatures—the tooth fairy, for example—we owe more than we realize to the vision that Shakespeare created and that folklore and literature adopted from him in the decades and centuries that followed.

TRANSFORMATION

Transformation is a central theme in Shakespeare's play, including not only the lovers' changing views of one another, but especially Bottom's transformation into an ass-headed creature who is later returned to his own human form. The fairies are instrumental in this change, and Puck reports the success of his task to Oberon with great delight, "My mistress with a monster is in love" (3.2.1). For Elizabethans, the topic of transformation had literary and folk origins. "Metamorphosis" means change or transformation, and the collection of tales entitled *Metamorphoses* by the classical Roman writer, Ovid, is considered one of the mythical sources for *A Midsummer Night's Dream.* In it, for example, the goddess Circe, called Titania by Ovid, turns Ulysses and his men into swine by offering them a magical drink (Paster and Howard 277).

This kind of magical power was not only recognized as mythical and literary, however. Transformation could be the result of witchcraft. The Elizabethan period of English history was a time fraught with witch hysteria, anxiety, and superstition. When experiences or outcomes happened beyond human control and natural explanation, there seemed to be two believable causes. The first was that God was acting with divine power to punish or judge individuals for their sins by bringing tragedy or deformity upon them. The second was that a witch using magic imposed the misfortune for wicked and spiteful reasons. Often it was easier to accept the second explanation than the first because no one wanted to be seen as deserving or experiencing God's wrath. Furthermore, witches could be judged and punished, whereas God could not. Consequently, many women were the subjects of anxiety or terror that led to witch trials and burnings resulting in innocent lives being lost.

A third source of negative transformation from healthy humanity to deformity or monstrosity was the imagination itself. We return again to the Renaissance view that the imagination was considered a dangerous human faculty when it rose in power and influence over the superior guidance of reason. If this imbalance occurred, birth deformities could be explained by a woman's overactive imagination during conception and pregnancy. Curiously enough, all three of these sources for negative transformation—mythological story, witchcraft, and an overactive imagination—focus on the power of women to govern or control the physical appearance and experience of men. They suggest an anxiety about gendered roles at a time when men were seen to be superior to women in the hierarchy of order. A woman's ability to control or manipulate a man was considered a threat to the accepted world view and an unnatural demonstration of power.

In Shakespeare's *A Midsummer Night's Dream*, however, the male fairies Oberon and Puck are the main instruments of Bottom's deformity and the unnatural relationship between him and Titania. And yet in this comedy in which all's well that ends well, order and harmony rely on the restoration of male hierarchy: Titania gives up the changeling boy to Oberon; Hippolyta, the warrior queen, weds Theseus, who remains in command of his city-state; and of the lovers, Puck provides a male bias, saying, "Jack shall have Jill;°/ Nought shall go ill;°/ The man shall have his mare again, and all shall be well" (3.2.461–63). Reason seems to gain control in the balance of human relationships; and yet imagination is celebrated in the wonder of love, fairy magic, and dreams "[m]ore strange than true" (5.1.2). Shakespeare engages the belief system of the world around him, following some of its patterns but also raising questions, challenging settled ideas, and leaving his audience and readers to wonder what to know and what to believe, what to understand and what to simply accept and experience.

The remainder of this chapter includes excerpted documents that reflect some of the varied views about the power of the imagination in Shakespeare's time and explores what people believed about dreams, fairies, and transformations.

THE EFFECT OF IMAGINATION

Robert Burton (1577–1640) was an Anglican vicar who is widely known for writing *The Anatomy of Melancholy* (1621), a lengthy medical treatise that addresses the disease of melancholy, also known as the "black distemper" and sometimes understood simply as "irrationality." Burton studied its causes, symptoms, and cures, treating it as an illness caused by immoderate heat, according to a medical understanding of the body as being made up of four humors, distinguished by the four physical elements, earth, air, water, and fire. In the excerpt below, Burton discusses the inner senses, of which he says there are three: common sense, fantasy—which is also imagination—and memory. Pay attention to the balance Burton describes between the three parts and what happens when the balance is lost in melancholy. Notice how he understands the experience of dreams and what role he conceives fantasy or imagination playing. Consider how this "medical" approach to dreams and imagination compares with Shakespeare's dramatic, poetic approach in *A Midsummer Night's Dream*.

FROM ROBERT BURTON, *THE ANATOMY OF MELANCHOLY,* ED. A. R. SHILLETO, VOL. 1 (1621)

(3 vols. 1621; London: George Bell and Sons, 1903) 182–83

Subject 7.—Of the Inward Senses

Inner senses are three in number, so called, because they be within the brain-pan, as *common sense, fantasy, memory.* Their objects are not only things present, but they perceive the sensible species of things to *come, past, absent,* such as were before in the sense. This *common sense* is the judge or moderator of the rest, by whom we discern all differences of objects; for by mine eye I do not know what I see, or by mine ear that I hear, but by my *common sense* who judgeth of sounds and colours: they are but the organs to bring the species to be censured; so that all their objects are his, and all their offices are his. The fore-part of the brain is his organ or seat.

Fantasy, or imagination . . . is an inner sense which doth more fully examine the species perceived by *common sense,* of things present or absent, and keeps them longer, recalling them to mind again, or making new of his own. In time of sleep this faculty is free, and many times conceives strange, stupend, absurd shapes, as in sick men we commonly observe. His *organ* is the middle cell of the brain; his *objects* all the species communicated to him by the *common sense,* by comparison of which he feigns infinite others unto himself. In *melancholy* men this faculty is most powerful and strong, and often hurts, producing many monstrous and prodigious things, especially if it be stirred up by some terrible object, presented to it from *common sense* or *memory.* In Poets and Painters *imagination* forcibly works, as appears by their several fictions, anticks, images.... In men it is subject and governed by *reason,* or at least should be; but in brutes it hath no superior, and is *ratio brutorum,* all the reason they have.

Memory lays up all the species which the sense have brought in, and records them as a good *register,* that they may be forth-coming when they are called for by *fantasy* and *reason.* His object is the same with *fantasy,* his seat and *organ* the back part of the brain.

The affections of these senses are *sleep* and *waking,* common to all sensible creatures. *Sleep is a rest or binding of the outward senses, and of the common sense, for the preservation of body and soul*...for when the common sense resteth, the outward senses rest also. The fantasy alone is free, and his commander, reason: as appears by those imaginary dreams, which are of diverse kinds, *natural, divine, demoniacal, etc.,* of which *Artemidorus, Cardan,* and *Sambucus,* with their several interpretators, have written great volumes. This ligation of senses proceeds from an inhibition of spirits, the way being stopped by which they should come; this stopping is caused of vapours arising out of the stomach, filling the nerves by which the spirits should be conveyed. When these vapours are spent, the passage is open, and the spirits perform their accustomed duties; so that *waking is the action and motion of the senses, which the spirits dispersed over all parts cause.* (Part I, Section I, Member II, Subsection VII, 182–83)

THE DREAMING MIND

Thomas Nashe (1567–1601) was both a poet and a prose writer. His *Terrors of the Night* (1594) is a study of dreams, demonology, and witchcraft. In the passage below he describes what he thinks a dream is and what its causes are. He mentions the role of imagination as well as the influence of daytime thoughts—or "conceits" and "cogitations"—which enter into the night and cause distress and suffering. Along with these thoughts, there are also nighttime sounds and disturbances, which add to the experience of the dream. Nashe's language is vivid with images and metaphors. Try to pay attention to his use of these literary techniques to convey his ideas about the significance of dreams. Note, for example, his description of the arrow, the contrast between the sun and shadows, the wounded man and the surgeon. Look for other images, as well. Determine, as you read, whether Nashe takes dreams seriously or not, and how his language conveys his attitude.

FROM THOMAS NASHE, *THE TERRORS OF THE NIGHT OR, A DISCOURSE OF APPARITIONS* (1594), IN *THE WORKS OF THOMAS NASHE*, ED. RONALD B. MCKERROW, VOL. 1 (1910)

(London: Sidgwick and Jackson, Ltd. 1910) 355–57

A dream is nothing else but a bubbling scum or froth of a fancy, which the day hath left undigested; or an after feast made of the fragments of idle imaginations.

How many sorts there be of them no man can rightly set down, since it scarce hath been heard there were ever two men that dreamed alike. Divers have written diversely of their causes, but the best reason among them all that I could ever pick out, was this, that as an arrow which is shot out of a bow, is sent forth many times with such force, that it flyeth far beyond the mark whereat it was aimed; so our thoughts intensively fixed all the day time upon a mark we are to hit, are now and then over-drawn with such force, that they fly beyond the mark of the day into the confines of the night. There is no man put to any torment, but quaketh and trembleth a great while after the executioner hath withdrawn his hand from him. In the day time we torment our thoughts and imaginations with sundry cares and devices; all the night time they quake and tremble after the terror of their late suffering, and still continue thinking of the perplexities they have endured. To nothing more aptly can I compare the working of our brains after we have unyoked and gone to bed, than to the glimmering and dazzling of a man's eyes when he comes newly out of the bright Sun into the dark shadow.

Even as one's eyes glimmer and dazzle when they are withdrawn out of the light into darkness; so are our thoughts troubled & vexed when they are retired from labor to ease, and from skirmishing to surgery.

You must give a wounded man leave to groan while he is in dressing: Dreaming is no other than groaning while sleep our surgeon hath us in cure.

He that dreams merrily is like a boy new breeched, who leaps and danceth for joy his pain is past: but long that joy stays not with him, for presently after his master the day, seeing him so jocund and pleasant, comes and does as much for him again, whereby his hell is renewed.

No such figure of the first Chaos whereout the world was extraught, as our dreams in the night. In them all states, all sexes, all places are confounded and meet together.

Our cogitations run on heaps like men to part a fray, where every one strikes his next fellow. From one place to another without consultation they leap, like rebels bent on a head. Soldiers just up and down they imitate at the sack of a City, which spare neither age nor beauty: the young, the old, trees, steeples, & mountains, they confound in one gallimaufry.

Of those things which are most known to us, some of us that have moist brains make to ourselves images of memory: on those images of memory whereon we build in the day, comes some superfluous humour of ours, like a Jack-anapes in the night, and erects a puppet stage, or some such ridiculous idle childish invention.

A Dream is nothing else but the Echo of our conceits in the day.

But other-while it falls out, that one Echo borrows of another: so our dreams (the Echoes of the day) borrow of any noise we hear in the night.

As for example; if in the dead of the night there be any rumbling, knocking, or disturbances near us, we straight dream of wars, or of thunder. If a dog howl, we suppose we are transported into hell, where we hear the complaint of damned ghosts. If our heads lie double or uneasy, we imagine we uphold all heaven with our shoulders like *Atlas*. If we be troubled with too many clothes, then we suppose the night mare rides us.

I knew one that was cramped, and he dreamt that he was torn in pieces with wild horses; and another, that having a black sant brought to his bedside at midnight, dreamt he was bidden to dinner at Iron-mongers Hall.

Any meat that in the daytime we eat against our stomachs, begetteth a dismal dream. Discontent also in dreams hath no little predominance: for even as from water that is troubled, the mud dispersingly ascendeth from the bottom to the top; so when our blood is chased, disquieted, and troubled, all the light imperfect humours of our body ascend like mud up aloft into the head.

The clearest spring a little touched, is creased with a thousand circles: as those momentary circles for all the world, such are our dreams. When all is said, melancholy is the mother of dreams, and of all terrors of the night whatsoever.

THE FAIRY KINGDOM

John Aubrey was a seventeenth-century English scientist and historian (1626–1697). In two excerpts that follow, he records memories and stories about the fairy kingdom. His account in *The Remains of Gentilism and Judaism* (1688) offers some of the popular beliefs about fairies and their relationship to mortals when he was young. Note that in the title of his work "gentilism" refers to classical paganism and "Judaism" refers to ancient Hebrews (Paster and Howard 309).

The second account, "The Wiltshire Fairies" (1686), describes an experience that a curate named Mr. Hart had with fairies one night and raises a question about fairy changelings. Pay attention to Aubrey's tone. He seems so scientific in his explanation of the fairy rings and yet his all his observations taken together raise uncertainty about whether he does or does not believe in fairies.

FROM JOHN AUBREY, *THE REMAINS OF GENTILISM AND JUDAISM,* IN *THREE PROSE WORKS,* ED. JAMES BRITTEN (1688)

(1688; London: Satchell, Peyton, and Co., 1881) 29–30

They were wont to please the fairies, that they might do them no shrewd turns, by sweeping clean the Hearth and setting by it a dish of fair water.... whereon was set a mess of milk sopt with white bread. And on the morrow they should find a groat of which.... if they did speak of it they never had any again. That they [fairies] would churn the cream &c. Mrs. H., of Hereford had as many groats, or 3ds. this way made a little silver cup or bowl, of (I think) 3lbs value, which her daughter preserves still.

That the Fairies steal away young children and put others in their places; verily believed by old women of those days; and by some yet living.

Some were led away by the Fairies, as was a Hind riding upon Hackpen with corn, led a dance to the Devises. So was a shepherd of Mr. Crown, of Winterburn-Basset: but never any afterwards enjoy themselves. He said that the ground opened, and he was brought into strange places underground, where they used musical Instruments, viols, and Lutes, such (he said) as Mr. Thomas did play on.

And in Germany old women tell the like stories received from their Ancestors, that a Water-monster, called the Nickard, does enter by night the chamber, where a woman is brought to bed, and stealeth when they are all sleeping, the the [sic] new-born child and supposeth another in its place, which child growing up is like a monster and commonly dumb. The remedy where of that the Mother may get her own child again. The mother taketh the Supposititium, and whips it so long with the rod till the said monster, the Nickard brings the Mother's own child again & takes to himself the Supposititium which they call Wexel balg.

FROM JOHN AUBREY, "THE WILTSHIRE FAIRIES" (1686),
IN *ILLUSTRATIONS OF THE FAIRY MYTHOLOGY OF
"A MIDSUMMER NIGHT'S DREAM,"* ED. JAMES
ORCHARD HALLIWELL (1853)

(1687; London: Bradbury and Evans, 1853) 235–37

In the year 1633–4, soon after I had entered into my grammar at the Latin School at Yatton Keynel, our curate Mr. Hart was annoyed one night by these elves or fairies. Coming over the downs, it being near dark, and approaching one of the fairy dances, as the common people call them in these parts, viz. the green circles made by those sprites on the grass, he all at once saw an innumerable quantity of pigmies or very small people dancing round and round, and singing, and making all manner of small odd noises. He, being very greatly amazed, and yet not being able, as he says, to run away from them, being, as he supposes, kept there in a kind of enchantment, they no sooner perceive him but they surround him on all sides and, what betwixt fear and amazement, he fell down scarcely knowing what he did. And thereupon these little creatures pinched him all over, and made a sort of quick humming noise all the time. But at length they left him and, when the sun rose, he found himself exactly in the midst of one of these fairy dances. This relation I had from him myself, a few days after he was so tormented; but when I and my bedfellow Stump went soon afterwards at nighttime to the dances on the downs, we saw none of the elves or fairies. But indeed it is said they seldom appear to any persons who go to seek for them.

As to these circles, I presume they are generated from the breathing out of a fertile subterraneous vapour, which comes from a kind of conical concave, and endeavours to get out at a narrow passage at the top, which forces it to make another cone inversely situated to the other, the top of which is the green circle. Every tobacco-taker knows that 'tis no strange thing for a circle of smoke to be whiffed out of the bowl of the pipe, but 'tis done by chance. If you dig under the turf of this circle, you will find at the roots of the grass a hoar or moldiness. But as there are fertile streams, so contrary-wise there are noxious ones which proceed from some minerals, iron, etc., which also as the others, *cateris paribus,* appear in a circular form. *Mem[orandum].* that pigeon's dung and nitre, steeped in water, will make the fairy circles; it draws to it the nitre of the air and will never wear out.

Let me not omit a tradition which I had many years since, when I was a boy, from my great uncles and my father's baily, who were then old men; that in the harvest time, in one of the great fields Warminster, at the very time of the fight at Bosworth Field in Leicestershire between King Richard III and Henry VII, there was one of the parish (I have forgot whether he was not a natural fool) who took two wheat-sheaves, one in one hand, and the other in the other hand, and said that the two armies were engaged. He played with the sheaves, crying with some intervals, "Now for Richard!" "Now for Henry!" At last lets fall Richard, and cried, "Now for King Henry, Richard is slain!" And this action of his did agree with the very time, day, and hour. Query, might not this boy have been one changed by the fairies. The vulgar call them changelings.

ROBIN GOODFELLOW, ALIAS PUCK

While Shakespeare's approach to the fairy kingdom ran counter to a variety of common folk beliefs in his culture, his portrayal of fairies in *A Midsummer Night's Dream* strongly influenced traditions and literature that came after his play. His characterization of Puck contributed to heightened interest in this folk figure—otherwise known as Robin Goodfellow—in the early seventeenth century. Whereas Puck had in earlier times been closely associated with the devil, after *A Midsummer Night's Dream* appeared, he became less malignant in reputation, noted for his good humor and helpfulness, as well as his practical jokes. The following ballad is likely an example of the way Shakespeare's creation of his dramatic character shaped public perception of this lively prankster. Ballads were part of oral culture, shared in community celebrations, and remembered, in part, because of the music that accompanied the verse. The tune for this ballad, "Dulcina," was a common melody used for many ballads in the early seventeenth century (Paster and Howard 317). As you read, consider how much the persona of Robin Goodfellow in this ballad sounds like Shakespeare's character. Listen for echoes not only of content but also of language and style.

FROM "THE MAD MERRY PRANKS OF ROBIN GOOD-FELLOW" (C. 1600), IN *THE EUING COLLECTION OF ENGLISH BROADSIDE BALLADS,* ED. JOHN HOLLOWAY. (1971)

(c. 1600; Glasgow: University of Glasgow Publications, 1971) 325–26

To the Tune of, Dulcina.

From *Oberon* in Fairy Land,
    the King of Ghosts and shadows there,
Mad *Robin* I at this command,
    am sent to view the night-sports here.
        What revel-rout
        Is kept about,
In every corner where I go,
        I will o'ersee,
        And merry be,
And make good sport with, ho ho ho.

More swift than lightning can I fly,
    and round about this air welkin soon;

And in a minute's space descry
   each thing that's done beneath the moon.
     There's not a Hag,
     nor Ghost shall wag,
Nor cry goblin where I do go;
     but *Robin* I,
     their feats will spy,
And fear them home with, ho ho ho.

If any wanderers I meet,
   that from their nightsports do trudge home,
With counterfeiting voice I greet
   and cause them on with me to roam;
     through woods, through lakes,
     through bogs, through brakes,
O'er bush and briar with them I go,
     I call upon
     them to come on,
And went me laughing, ho ho ho.

Sometimes I meet them like a man,
   sometimes an Ox, sometimes a hound.
And to a horse I turn me can,
   to trip and trot about them round;
     but if to ride,
     my back they stride,
More swift than wind away I go,
     o'er hedge, and lands,
     through pools and ponds,
I whirry laughing, ho ho ho.

When Lads and Lasses merry be,
   with possets and with junkets fine,
Unseen of all the company,
   I eat their Cakes and sip the Wine;
     and to make sport,
     I fart and snort,
And out the Candles I do blow.
     the Maids I kiss,
     they shriek, who's this?
I answer nought but, ho ho ho.

Yet now and then the Maids to please,
   I card at midnight up their wool;
And while they sleep, snort, fart, and sneeze,
   with wheel to thread their flax I pull.

I grind at Mill
their Malt up still,
I dress their hemp, I spin their tow;
if any awake
and would me take,
I wend me Laughing, ho ho ho.

The second Part, to the same Tune.

When House or hearth doth sluttish lie,
I pinch the Maids there black and blue
And from the bed the bedclothes I,
pull off and lay them naked to view;
'twixt sleep and wake
I do them take,
And on the key-cold floor them throw,
If out they cry,
then forth fly I,
And loudly Laugh, ho ho ho.

When any need to borrow aught,
we lend them what they do require,
And for the use demand we nought,
our own is all we do desire.
if to repay
they do delay,
Abroad amongst them then I go,
and night by night,
I them affright,
With pinching, dreams, and ho ho ho.

When lazy queans have nought to do,
but study how to cog and lie,
To make debate and mischief too,
'twixt one another secretly:
I mark their gloze
and do disclose
To them that I had wronged so.
when I have done,
I get me gone,
And leave them scolding, ho ho ho.

When men do traps and engines set
in loopholes where the vermin creep,

That from their folds and houses set,
>   their ducks and geese, their lambs & sheep,
>   *I* spy the gin,
>   and enter in,
And seems a vermin taken so,
>   but when they there
>   approach me near,
I leap out laughing, ho ho ho.

By Wells and Gills in Meadow green,
>   we nightly dance our hey-day guise,
And to our Fairy King and Queen,
>   we chant our Moonlight harmonies.
>   when Larks 'gin sing,
>   away we fling,
And babes newborn steal as we go.
>   an elf in bed
>   we leave instead,
And wend us laughing, ho ho ho.

From Hay-bred *Merlin's* time have *I,*
>   thus mighty revelled to and fro,
And for my pranks men call me by
>   the name of *Robin Good-fellow.*
>   Fiends, Ghosts, and Sprites,
>   that haunt the nights,
The Hags and Goblins do me know,
>   and Beldams old,
>   my feats have told,
So *Vale, Vale,* ho ho ho.

FROM MAN TO BEAST

Reginald Scot (1538?–1599) is best known for his book, *The Discovery of Witchcraft* (1584), the first English treatise of its kind to examine and explain the phenomenon of witchcraft. Scot countered the popular tide of superstition by explaining away the fears of witches from a rational perspective. According to Scot, witches were either imposters or victims of public paranoia. In the segment included here, Scot records the story of a man turned into an ass by a witch, and then proceeds to explain why the story, told by the French writer Jean Bodin, among others, must be discredited and dismissed. The story is much more engaging than Scot's arguments against it, which are presented in a dry rhetorical style. The primary argument included here is that only God has power above human beings to perform supernatural deeds. This story of the English sailor is considered a possible influence on Shakespeare's tale of Bottom's transformation. Look for clues about the similarities between the two stories.

FROM REGINALD SCOT, *THE DISCOVERY OF WITCHCRAFT* (1584)

(1584; Arundel: Centaur Press, 1964) 95–98

Chapter III

Of a man turned into an ass, and returned again into a man by one of Bodin's witches: St. Augustine's opinion thereof.

It happened in the city of *Salamin,* in the kingdom of Cyprus . . . that a ship loaden with merchandise stayed there for a short space. In the meantime many of the soldiers and mariners went to shore, to provide fresh victuals. Among which number, a certain Englishman, being a sturdy young fellow, went to a woman's house, a little way out of the city, and not far from the seaside, to see whether she had any eggs to sell. Who, perceiving him to be a lusty young fellow, a stranger, and far from his country (so as upon the loss of him there would be the less miss or inquiry) she considered with herself how to destroy him; and willed him to stay there awhile, whilest she went to fetch a few eggs for him. But she tarried long, so as the young man called unto her, desiring her to make haste: for he told her that the tide would be spent, and by that means, his ship would be gone, and leave him behind. Howbeit, after some detracting of time, she brought him a few eggs, willing him to return to her, if his ship were gone when he came. The young fellow returned towards his ship; but before he went aboard, he would needs eat an egg or twain to satisfy his hunger, and within short space he became dumb and out of his wits (as he afterwards said). When he would have entered into the ship, the mariners beat him back with a cudgel saying; What a murrain lacks the ass? Whither the devil with this ass? The ass or young man (I cannot tell by which name I should term him) being many times repelled, and understanding their words that called him ass, considering that he could speak never a word, and yet could understand everybody; he thought that he was bewitched by the woman, at whose house he was. And therefore, when by no means he could get into the boat, but was driven to tarry and see her departure; being also beaten from place to place, as an ass; he remembered the witch's words, and the words of his own fellows that called him ass, and returned to the witch's house, in whose service he remained by the space of three years, doing nothing with his hands all that while, but carried such burthens as she laid on his back; having only this comfort, that although he were reputed an ass among strangers and beasts, yet that both this witch, and all other witches knew him to be a man.

After three years were passed over, in a morning betimes, he went to town before his dame; who upon some occasion . . . stayed a little behind. In the meantime being near to a church, he heard a little sacring-bell ring to the elevation of a morrow-mass, and not daring to go into the church, lest he should have been beaten and driven out with cudgels, in great devotion he fell down in the churchyard, upon the knees of his hinder legs, and did lift his forefeet over his head, as the priest doth hold the sacrament at the elevation. Which prodigious sight when certain merchants of Genoa espied, and with wonder beheld; anon cometh the witch with a cudgel in her hand, beating forth the ass. And, because . . . such kinds of witchcrafts are very usual in those parts; the merchants aforesaid made such means, as both the ass and the witch were attached by the judge. And she being examined and set upon the rack, confessed the whole matter and promised, that if she might have liberty to go home, she would restore him to his old shape; and being dismissed, she did accordingly. So as notwithstanding they apprehended her again, and burned her; and the young man returned into his country with a joyful and merry heart.

Upon the advantage of this story . . . *Bodin,* and the residue of the witchmongers triumph; and specially because St. *Augustine* subscribeth thereunto; or at the least to the very like. . . . I say . . . that, how much *Augustine* saith he hath seen with his eyes, so much I am content to believe. Howbeit St. *Augustine* concludeth against *Bodin.* For he affirmeth these transubstantiations to be but fantastical, and that they are not according to the verity, but according to appearance. And yet I cannot allow of such appearances made by witches, or yet by devils: for I find no such power given by God to any creature. . . . General councils and the pope's canons, which *Bodin* so regardeth, do condemn and pronounce his opinions in this behalf to be absurd; and the residue of the witchmongers, with himself in the number, to be worse than infidels. And these are the very words of the canons, which elsewhere I have more largely repeated; Whosoever believeth, that any creature can be made or changed into better or worse, or transformed into any other shape, or into any other similitude, by any other than by God himself the creator of all things, without all doubt is an infidel, and worse than a pagan. And therewithal this reason is rendered, to wit: because they attribute that to a creature, which only belongeth to God, the creator of all things.

Chapter IV

....

But where was the young man's own shape all these three years, wherein he was made an ass? It is a certain and a general rule, that two substantial forms cannot be in one subject..., both at once....

But to proceed unto the probability of this story. What luck was it, that this young fellow of *England,* landing so lately in those parts, and that old woman of *Cyprus,* being both of so base a condition, should both understand one another's communication: *England* and *Cyprus* being so many hundred miles distant, and their languages so far differing?

MONSTERS AND IMAGINATION

Ambroise Paré was a sixteenth-century French surgeon who wrote a medical text that included *Of Monsters and Marvels* (1573) explaining the causes of human deformity. Some causes were natural and others were supernatural. The excerpt below describes as a "monster" an infant that is born deformed and then provides one of the supernatural causes for this defect: the role of the imagination during conception. His explanation provides the imagination with a kind of "scientific" value or recognition, giving it a degree of power difficult to believe in our own age of scientific study and research.

FROM AMBROISE PARÉ, *OF MONSTERS AND MARVELS,* TRANS. JANIS L. PALLISTER (1634)

(Chicago: University of Chicago Press, 1982)

The Preface

Monsters are things that appear outside the course of Nature (and are usually signs of some forthcoming misfortune), such as a child who is born with one arm, another who will have two heads, and additional members over and above the ordinary. (3)

Chapter IX

An Example of Monsters That are Created through the Imagination

The ancients, who sought out the secrets of Nature . . . have taught of other causes for monstrous children and have referred them to the ardent and obstinate imagination [impression] that the mother might receive at the moment she conceived—through some object, or fantastic dream—of certain nocturnal visions that the man or woman have at the hour of conception. . . .

Whether true or not, Heliodorus . . . writes that Persina, the Queen of Ethiopia, conceived by King Hidustes—both of them being Ethiopians—a daughter who was white and this [occurred] because of the appearance of the beautiful Andromeda that she summoned up in her imagination, for she had a painting of her before her eyes during the embraces from which she became pregnant.

Damascene, a serious author, attests to having seen a girl as furry as a bear, whom the mother had bred thus deformed and hideous, for having looked too intensely at the image of Saint John [the Baptist] dressed in skins, along with his [own] body hair and beard, which picture was attached to the foot of her bed while she was conceiving.

...As a result, it is necessary that women—at the hour of conception and when the child is not yet formed...—not be forced to look at or to imagine monstrous things; but once the formation of the child is complete, even though the woman should look at or imagine monstrous things with intensity, nevertheless the imagination will not then play any role because no transformation occurs at all.... (38–40)

TOPICS FOR WRITTEN AND ORAL DISCUSSION

1. In *Anatomy of Melancholy,* what does Robert Burton identify as the three senses and what role does each play?

2. Burton asserts that imagination or fantasy is "most powerful and strong" in two different groups of people. Who are they and how does imagination affect them? According to Burton, what faculty should have superior power over imagination in human beings and separate them from brutes or beasts?

3. How does Burton define sleep? What does he believe are the physical causes of dreams and what role does imagination play?

4. Compare Burton's explanation of the inner senses—especially imagination—with Duke Theseus's explanation of fantasy or imagination at the beginning of act 5, scene 1. Do the two men have similar perspectives? What is their attitude to the role of reason and its relationship to imagination? Do you think Shakespeare is sympathetic to this perspective? Why or why not?

5. How does Thomas Nashe initially define dreams in *The Terrors of the Night?* What does his language suggest about his attitude towards dreams? Find other words or phrases that indicate not only his explanation for dreams but his attitude towards them. Does he take dreams seriously or not? Does Shakespeare take dreams seriously in *A Midsummer Night's Dream?* Explain your position.

6. Make a list of the metaphors or analogies Nashe uses to describe dreams and night-mares.

7. How do Nashe's views about dreams compare with Robert Burton's? If the two men were having a discussion together, would they agree or disagree with one another? Explain.

8. Imagine that you are Thomas Nashe or Robert Burton and that you have just seen a performance of *A Midsummer Night's Dream.* Write a response to the play based on your beliefs and observations. Did you find the play enjoyable and entertaining or silly, foolish, and a waste of time? Provide reasons.

9. Choose one of the dream experiences described in Shakespeare's play—there are at least four—and consider how it might fit into the different traditions of Renaissance dream interpretation as defined in this chapter.

10. In his epilogue, Puck invites the audience to consider *A Midsummer Night's Dream* as a dream. Referring to the description of the literary dream frame narrative in this chapter, discuss what truth or wisdom the play might offer to its audience about love, imagination, or dream visions.

11. In Shakespeare's time, imagination received mixed reviews, and could be considered as a source of deception or creative invention. Discuss which view you think is most prominent in *A Midsummer Night's Dream* and provide examples to support your position.

12. John Aubrey tells stories about people's encounters with fairies. In *The Remains of Gentilism and Judaism,* what beliefs about fairies are represented in his tales? Make a list.

13. In "The Wiltshire Fairies," Aubrey recounts a story about Mr. Hart's experience with fairy rings and then provides a semiscientific explanation of how they came to be. The story and explanation appear contradictory. What does that suggest to you about beliefs in fairies and magic in Aubrey's time?

14. Compare Aubrey's references to changelings with the role of the changeling in *A Midsummer Night's Dream.* How do they differ? What do the differences suggest about Shakespeare's portrayal of fairies compared to popular folk beliefs represented by Aubrey?

15. In the ballad about Robin Goodfellow, Puck is a fairy and a practical joker. Which of his deeds are positive or benevolent and which are mischievous and harmful? Divide your page into two columns and make a list of each.

16. The ballad of Robin Goodfellow was probably written after *A Midsummer Night's Dream.* What parallels can you find between the two? Do you recognize any echoes of Shakespeare in the language of the ballad as well as in Puck's activities?

17. If you are musically inclined, compose a melody for the ballad of Robin Goodfellow and play it for your class.

18. Referring to this chapter, describe how Shakespeare's fairies differed from the common fairy beliefs of his time. Can you find any clues or hints in the play suggesting that Shakespeare's fairies had sinister rather than simply kind or good powers and purposes? Explain.

19. If you are artistically inclined, draw several pictures of fairies according to sixteenth-century folktale beliefs described in this chapter and according to the descriptions in *A Midsummer Night's Dream.* Provide a brief explanation for your artistic interpretation.

20. In Reginald Scot's version of the story about the English sailor and the witch, how does the witch lure the man into her trap and bewitch him? How is the spell broken? What happens to the witch?

21. Scot discounts the story of the sailor's bewitching. What arguments does he use to prove that the tale is untrue?

22. How does the sailor's bewitching in Scot's account compare to Bottom's transformation in *A Midsummer Night's Dream?* What are the similarities and differences?

23. What is Ambroise Paré's definition of a monster? Explain the role of imagination in his account of monstrous births. What examples does he offer?

24. How does Paré's view of the power of imagination compare with Robert Burton's, with Duke Theseus's, or with Shakespeare's as playwright of *A Midsummer Night's Dream?*

SUGGESTED READING

Briggs, K. M. *The Anatomy of Puck: An Examination of Fairy Beliefs among Shakespeare's Contemporaries and Successors.* London: Routledge and Kegan Paul, 1959.

———. *The Fairies in Tradition and Literature.* London: Routledge and Kegan Paul, 1967.

Garber, Marjorie B. *Dreams in Shakespeare: From Metaphor to Metamorphosis.* New Haven: Yale UP, 1974.

Kruger, Steven F. *Dreaming in the Middle Ages.* Cambridge: Cambridge UP, 1992.

Latham, Minor White. *The Elizabethan Fairies: The Fairies of Folklore and the Fairies of Shakespeare.* New York: Columbia UP, 1930.

Paster, Gail Kern, and Skiles Howard, eds. *A Midsummer Night's Dream: Texts and Contexts.* Bedford: St. Martin's, 1999.

Thomas, Keith. *Religion and the Decline of Magic.* New York: Charles Scribner's Sons, 1971.

Young, David P. *Something of Great Constancy: The Art of "A Midsummer Night's Dream."* New Haven: Yale UP, 1966.

6

Performance and Interpretation

In a play that focuses so much and so self-consciously on the act of performance, stage history merits discussion as an exploration into the many ways actors and directors over the centuries have engaged with Shakespeare's text, responding to it according to their own cultural climate and interpreting it according to their unique artistic vision. In some productions, there has been a deliberate attempt to recreate the so-called "Shakespearean" experience of *A Midsummer Night's Dream;* in other productions, Shakespeare's concept and language have been ignored or discarded almost altogether. Each choice reflects, in some measure, the perceived meaning of theater, the popular aspects of public entertainment in a particular time and place, and the challenges inherent within the play itself.

THE ELIZABETHAN STAGE

Virtually nothing is known about how *A Midsummer Night's Dream* was performed in Shakespeare's time except that the title page notes that it had been "sundry times publickly acted"; many scholars have also speculated about the possibility of an initial performance at an aristocratic wedding. Whether that speculation is true or not, many of Shakespeare's plays were performed both on the public stage and in the aristocratic context of court, and so it can be assumed that *A Midsummer Night's Dream* was exposed to a broad range of audiences. Chapter 4 addresses some of the culturally relevant aspects of play-acting in the Elizabethan period.

More can be said about Elizabethan performing, however, based on collected records contributing to English stage history. Acting companies such as the Chamberlain's Men, to which Shakespeare belonged during Elizabeth's reign, had to be flexible in their stage requirements. If they took their plays to court, a great hall of a palace became the acting space, or if they toured outside of London, a temporary platform became the stage. But the majority of public performances took place in London in open-air playhouses such as the Theatre (1576–1598) and the Globe (1599–1644), with an apron stage that extended out into the yard where the lowest paying spectators stood shoulder-to-shoulder to watch, while higher paying audience members sat in tiered galleries on benches, also shoulder-to-shoulder. As many as 2,000 to 3,000 people could watch a production crammed together in this fashion. The relatively close proximity of the audience to the stage and the lack of a curtain to draw between acts and scenes made for an intimate connection between spectators and players. Scene changes would have been marked simply by the characters' exits and entrances through doorways on either side of the back stage wall or through a third curtained opening between them.

Language also guided the actors and viewers alike about what they were expected to "see" as the setting of the play. Thus Theseus describes Titania's bower:

> I know a bank where the wild thyme blows,
> Where oxlips and the nodding violet grows,
> Quite overcanopied with luscious woodbine,
> Sweet musk roses, and with eglantine.
> There sleeps Titania sometimes of the night,
> Lulled in these flowers with dances and delight. (2.2.249–54)

Little more than these words would have been needed to set the scene, except the cooperative imaginations of players and audiences. Furthermore, because plays were performed in the afternoon during daylight hours, the central part of *A Midsummer Night's Dream* in the woods at night depended entirely on specific verbal references to darkness and the audience's willingness to accept and believe the illusion of time and place presented by the play. Elizabethan staging was simple but effective; by all accounts, theater was an enormously popular form of entertainment.

THE RESTORATION TO THE NINETEENTH CENTURY

Theatrical activity in England came to a close, however, in 1642 with the Civil War and the establishment of Oliver Cromwell's Puritan government, which forbade acting as idle and frivolous. Playhouses were destroyed, and when the monarchy was restored in 1660 with Charles II's return to the throne, play-going became an experience different from that before the war. Newer and fewer stages sported curtained arches like most modern stages, along with much more elaborate sets and smaller theater buildings. Higher admission fees meant that monied audiences came primarily from the upper and middle classes rather than from all walks of life as they had in Shakespeare's day.

A number of Shakespeare's plays were revived in this new era of theater, and *A Midsummer Night's Dream* was one of them. It was staged in 1662, and though we know nothing of how it was performed, Samuel Pepys records a response to it in his diary, saying that he vowed to never see it again "for it is the most insipid ridiculous play that ever I saw in my life." What we do know about that period of theatrical revival is that in most instances, the text of *A Midsummer Night's Dream* was either ignored or significantly revised, truncated, and adapted so as to barely resemble the original play. A production called *The Fairy Queen* was performed in 1692 as an operatic rendition set to the music of Henry Purcell (1658–1695). This version included only one third of the lines from Shakespeare's play, while adding characters representing Sleep, Night, Misery, and the four seasons, as well as a large Chinese chorus and six dancing monkeys. Clearly, there was little attempt or desire to remain true to Shakespeare's text. The lavish and lyrical Purcell production did establish a long-lasting fashion for operatic versions of *A Midsummer Night's Dream* in which spectacle proved more important than story line.

One of the particular challenges in the eighteenth century was the presence of the fairies in *A Midsummer Night's Dream* at a time of declining belief in magic and the supernatural with the rise of a scientific and skeptical way of thinking. This may, in part, explain why *A Midsummer Night's Dream* appeared not to be a popular entertainment in its original form for well over a century. Another challenge, which lasted longer than what has been coined the eighteenth-century "Age of Reason," was the lack of a central character to organize the many disparate groups within the comedy. Instead of the full text, therefore, what emerged were bits and pieces of Shakespeare's play, including a farce called "The Merry Conceited Humours of Bottom the Weaver"—which actually began before the 1642 closing of the theaters—a comic masque called "Pyramus and Thisby," and a short musical version called "The Fairies." The play itself—the original Shakespearean text—was considered by many to be a "closet drama" better read rather than acted because of its lyrical poetry.

In the nineteenth century, with the emergence of Romanticism—an artistic movement that stressed, among other ideas, the importance of dreams, renewed interest in the supernatural, and delight in wild landscapes expressed in painting and poetry—the cultural climate was more favorable to *A Midsummer*

Night's Dream and stage performances became more common again. At the same time, however, a Victorian sense of sexual decorum and propriety meant that the language and night escapades of the lovers were deemed inappropriate for public presentation and the lovers' part in the play was reduced. Even the word "bed" where it appeared in the text was changed or deleted. But in the 1840s, Madame Lucia Vestris directed a production of *A Midsummer Night's Dream* that reintroduced most of Shakespeare's text. Other songs were still added, however, and the music of Felix Mendelssohn's *Midsummer Night's Dream* replaced Purcell's earlier score. Grand spectacle, ballet, lavish realistic sets, and special effects such as flying fairies characterized the production. Oberon and Puck were cast as women, whereas, interestingly enough, in Shakespeare's time all the women's parts would have been played by men or boys because women were not allowed on stage. In general, the nineteenth century demonstrated a preference for gauze, gossamer child fairies, innocence, fantasy, and delicate music, all reflecting the Romantic sentiments of a period in which the chief aim of stage entertainments was to portray beauty and inspire delight.

THE TWENTIETH CENTURY AND BEYOND

The twentieth century saw the rise of new technology in the film and television industry that allowed for innovations in dramatic interpretation as well as expanded audiences. The camera made possible wide-angle and close-up shots that could present the illusion of "realistic" settings but also create visual symbolism that contributed to the overall production. Cultural, social, and political changes meant that the long-lasting Romantic perspective of the nineteenth century began to be subject to challenges and alternative perspectives. In fact, the first half of the twentieth century saw a clash in responses to the play, with some productions maintaining former traditions and others presenting new directions that were subject to both positive and negative reactions.

Harley Granville Barker (Stage, 1914); Max Reinhardt (Film, 1935)

Two productions that underline this tension in interpretation are the 1914 stage production directed by Harley Granville Barker and the 1935 film production by Max Reinhardt. Granville Barker chose radically to alter tradition primarily in his portrayal of the fairies and forest activity. He substituted Mendelssohn's embellished, romantic music with simpler English folk tunes and turned the fairies from charming innocent children in gossamer costumes to golden creatures who conjured up Oriental images and moved with mechanical gestures. They were not dainty but dignified. Puck, in contrast, was dressed in bright red, a rustic hobgoblin with a touch of the sinister that varied significantly from the child-cast Puck of the nineteenth century. Barker departed from the Victorian curtained arch stage and returned to the apron stage of the Elizabethan era, creating a stylized, dreamlike forest with trees made simply of hanging strips of green and purple silk against a cloth backdrop. With less cumbersome settings, the action of the play flowed more smoothly, not requiring long interruptions to change stage decorations between scenes. One of Granville Barker's chief contributions to twentieth-century productions of *A Midsummer Night's Dream,* therefore, was to include the whole text of the play without elaborate additions of unscripted characters, grand music, or lavish realistic sets. Because of his willingness to leave behind so many nineteenth-century traditions, he became one of the most notable innovators of his century as a director of this play. While some spectators were delighted with his achievement, others strongly opposed it.

Max Reinhardt's film version of *A Midsummer Night's Dream* in 1935 ignored many of Granville Barker's modernizing innovations and returned to some nineteenth-century impulses. The music again became delicate, the fairies shimmering, the imagery lush, and the overall impression one of fantasy and beauty. Reinhardt himself articulates the image he strove to present:

> In Shakespeare's lovely fantasy, I have always seen, above all, a cheering, hopeful reminder that since Life itself is a dream, we can escape it through our dreams within a dream. When stark reality weighs too heavily upon us, an all-wise Providence provides deliverance. Every one has a secret corner into which he can retire and find refuge in Fancy. "A Midsummer Night's Dream" is an invitation to escape reality, a plea for the glorious release to be found in sheer fantasy. (Jorgens 38)

Reinhardt's production is significant for its ballet and special effects, such as Titania's attendants dancing down a spiral moonbeam (Barnet 145). But the film also has some darker interpretive elements that varied from the Victorian style. Oberon, on his black horse, is sinister in many scenes. There is a nightmarish quality that erupts in strong moments of hatred and jealousy, the threat of rape, and the sexual humiliation of Titania (Jorgens 41). The combination of these darker moments along with the dominant comic tone confused some critics, but also offered a foretaste of darker interpretations of Shakespeare's comedy that were to follow World War II.

Peter Hall (Stage 1959, Film 1969) and Peter Brook (Stage 1970–1973)

The second half of the twentieth century was distinguished by darker comic versions of *A Midsummer Night's Dream* in keeping with a growing tendency to downplay sentimentality, emphasize anxiety and violence, and express greater openness about sexuality. Peter Hall's Royal Shakespeare Company rendition of the comedy first on stage and then on film sets the play in seventeenth-century England, endeavoring to recreate a Shakespearean atmosphere as well as suggest the connection rather than the distance between the court and the countryside. In the initial scene, Athens is portrayed not as a rational, civilized setting, but as a dull, sterile, gray place with no room for imagination or love. The forest, though magical, is a place where the lovers encounter muddy streams, fog, and discordant weather, not the ethereal beauty often portrayed in earlier productions. It is a place of wonder but also of disorientation, where the fairies are earthy, with an animal-like quality. The lovers seem silly and absurd, especially in the woods. The "mechanicals" are not the traditional bumbling fools who provide slapstick, sight-gag humor, but are earnest and serious. They do inspire humor, but also a sense of humanity in their naive attempts to cast and perform a play, and the aristocrats tend to sympathize with them rather than scorn their endeavor. By the last scene, Athens has changed because of the woodland magic. Sterility is gone, and the harmony of the various worlds comes through in the mechanicals' play and the fairy blessing. Hall's interpretation is not festive or sentimental, but it is true to the text of Shakespeare's play while offering innovations with close-up camera angles to suggest ambiguities about responses to the various characters.

Peter Brook's stage version in the 1970s takes even further an anti-Romantic view of *A Midsummer Night's Dream*. Brook sets his play in a white box with a circus theme. Oberon and Puck move across the stage space on trapezes transferring a spinning plate back and forth on wands instead of using a flower as the source of fairy magic. Puck relies on stilts to maneuver "invisibly" among the lovers, and a catwalk or observation deck across the back allows the actors to watch and respond to the play when they are not acting in it. Coiled wires serve as trees and a source of entrapment, while steel staircases on either side of the stage make it reminiscent of a prison. Gone is the greenery of fairyland; gone is any illusion of lavish "realistic" setting.

Moreover, there is a malevolent tone to the fairies' activity, and Bottom's dream becomes an erotic fantasy. In a casting choice that became common afterwards, Brook doubled up characters from the Athenian world and the forest. The actor of Theseus also played Oberon; Hippolyta and Titania shared the same actor; Athenian courtiers became woodland fairies; and Philostrate became Puck. This choice emphasized connections between the court world and the fairy world, suggesting that the midsummer night's events were perhaps the dream or nightmare of Theseus or Hippolyta or a reflection of their subconscious reality. Brook also broke down barriers between the stage and the audience. When Puck concludes, "Give me your hands," the players leave the stage and shake hands with the audience as a friendly gesture to close the play. Brook not only provided a radically darker version of *A Midsummer Night's Dream* than had appeared beforehand, but he emphasized theatricality—self-conscious acting—over the illusion of fantasy or a magical world. Next to Barker, he remains one of the greatest innovators of the twentieth century in his interpretation of *A Midsummer Night's Dream*. And like Granville Barker, he inspired both enthusiasm and fierce opposition to his production. Numerous performances since his stage debut of the comedy have either reacted against it or looked for ways to revision it.

Elijah Moshinsky (Film, 1981) and Michael Hoffman (Film, 1999)

Two other productions are worth noting because they are readily accessible and markedly different from each other. Elijah Moshinsky's BBC TV production, set in the seventeenth century, is a dark and serious rendition with a surprising lack of lightheartedness or humor. The library in the first scene creates a stifling, closed atmosphere that highlights Hermia and Lysander's need to escape for love. The forest is a potentially ominous place. Oberon seems dark and threatening, while Titania is regal in her flowing gown and long, golden hair. Placing the changeling child in the scene draws attention to the central cause of Titania and Oberon's disagreement in a similar way that Hall's film version drew attention to Titania's often-cut speech about bad weather to reinforce that source of the natural disturbances in the play. Giving the child a visible, vulnerable presence before Oberon's towering figure makes it difficult for audiences not to sympathize more with the fairy queen than the fairy king in the quarrel between them. To increase the sinister mood in the woods, Puck, as a half-naked faun, seems a mixture of animal and human. The pool provides an effective central focus to woodland activity, where the lovers and fairies return again and again, to the mud and slime that emphasizes the midsummer night's chaos and confusion. A most unusual perspective of this production portrays the craftsmen as sincere but ponderous and almost completely without humor. This is in keeping with the subdued tone of the performance, but means that there is virtually no cause for laughter throughout the play, or that if any laughter comes, it emerges more at the expense of the lovers, especially Helena, than the well-meaning craftsmen.

Michael Hoffman's 1999 Hollywood film, with its nineteenth-century Tuscany setting, returns to some of the earlier emphases on musical and visual appeal with an operatic score—including Mendelssohn—lush settings, lavish costumes, and special effects that only film can achieve. The star-studded cast brings romance to life with the lovers energized by their passions and the fairies appearing mysterious and exotic in their attire and deportment. In what seems to be a late-twentieth-century trend, the production gives an appealing sense of humanity to the craftsmen, extending scenes to focus on Bottom and emphasize his character, making him almost the central and most appealing role in the play. There is a richness and extravagance to this production that celebrates life's vitality and abundance—from the tables laden with food to the greenness of the woodland night to the small ring that Bottom keeps as a token of his indescribable dream.

What this survey of performances through the decades and centuries indicates is not only that Shakespeare's text lends itself to many interpretations from light fantasy to dark nightmare to melodrama, but that the temper of the times, the strength of tradition, the impact of stage precedents, and the unique vision of a director or actor all contribute to the particularity of any one rendition of the play. It cannot be said that productions of *A Midsummer Night's Dream* have evolved over time—suggesting that each new generation of entertainers improves on the last—but rather that any performance draws from and adds to the cultural climate in which it takes place. Dream or nightmare, romance or cruelty, violence or fantasy, humanity or absurdity—such choices reveal themselves because of what people take from Shakespeare's text and what they put of themselves into it.

The remainder of this chapter includes a series of excerpts from dramatic critics, observers, and directors describing the process of interpretation or commenting on the effect of a specific representation.

A MIDSUMMER NIGHT'S DREAM AS "CLOSET DRAMA"

A "closet drama" is read privately at home rather than watched on stage. William Hazlitt, a nineteenth-century literary and dramatic critic, believed that *A Midsummer Night's Dream* should be "closet drama" because its poetry and its magic were too beautiful to be presented effectively on stage. In short, he felt that while one's own imagination could meet the perfect or ideal dream that Shakespeare creates, any attempt to recreate that ideal could merely destroy it. This is an intriguing argument considering that Shakespeare wrote *A Midsummer Night's Dream* first and foremost as a play to be performed. It does raise interesting questions about how our imaginations work and play, the very topic that Shakespeare addresses especially in act 5 of the comedy. As you read Hazlitt, recall Theseus and Hippolyta's discussion about the role of imagination.

FROM WILLIAM HAZLITT, *CHARACTERS OF SHAKESPEARE'S PLAYS* (1916)

(Oxford: Oxford UP, 1816/1916) 103–4

The *Midsummer Night's Dream,* when acted, is converted from a delightful fiction into a dull pantomime. All that is finest in the play is lost in the representation. The spectacle was grand; but the spirit was evaporated, the genius was fled.—Poetry and the stage do not agree well together. The attempt to reconcile them in this instance fails not only of effect, but of decorum. The *ideal* can have no place upon the stage, which is a picture without perspective: everything there is in foreground. That which was merely an airy shape, a dream, a passing thought, immediately becomes an unmanageable reality. Where all is left to the imagination (as is the case in reading) every circumstance, near or remote, has an equal chance of being kept in mind, and tells according to the mixed impression of all that has been suggested. But the imagination cannot sufficiently qualify the actual impressions of the senses. Any offence given to the eye is not to be got rid of by explanation. Thus Bottom's head in the play is a fantastic illusion, produced by magic spells: on the stage, it is an ass's head, and nothing more; certainly a very strange costume for a gentleman to appear in. Fancy cannot be embodied any more than a simile can be painted; and it is as idle to attempt it as to personate *Wall* or *Moonshine.* Fairies are not incredible, but fairies six feet high are so. Monsters are not shocking, if they are seen at a proper distance. When ghosts appear at midday, when apparitions stalk along Cheapside, then may the *Midsummer Night's Dream* be represented without injury at Covent Garden or at Drury Lane. The boards of a theatre and the regions of fancy are not the same thing.

"A DREAMLIKE SPECTACLE"

William Winter was a stage critic with strong roots in the Victorian Romantic tradition. He saw Harley Granville Barker's 1914 stage production of *A Midsummer Night's Dream* and objected passionately to Granville Barker's interpretation, which departed from the realistic greenery and dainty fairies of the nineteenth century. Winter offers two contrasting views of the fairies and then provides a representative view of what the stage tradition of Shakespeare's play had become prior to Granville Barker's production. "Illusion" and "delight" are key words. The Romantic view of the stage was that it should create an illusion of reality into which one could escape and that the escape should be for the sole purpose of delight or pleasure.

FROM WILLIAM WINTER, *SHAKESPEARE ON THE STAGE* (1916)

(New York: Moffat, Yard, and Co., 1916)

The personal appearances and deportment of fairies and elves are matters of fancy and conjecture. It seems, however,—and certainly it is true for the purposes of Shakespeare's dream-play,—that as far as possible they should be represented in such a way as to suggest delicate, elusive, airy creatures, who, while obviously they feel human emotions and act from human motives, are purged of human grossness, are transcendent of mundane materiality, are finer, more ethereal, more dainty than men and women; creatures, in short, of which the form is gossamer and the spirit poetical. That, surely, is not an irrational ideal of beings who flit and "wander everywhere," . . . beings who "war with rere-mice for their leathern wings," combat with the newt, the blind-worm, the weaving spider, and the snail, dwell in "the quaint mazes in the wanton green," sport in "the spangled starlight sheen," "creep into acorn-cups and hide them there," and couch them on banks. . . .

In the visualization of Granville Barker's erratic fancy those evanescent creatures appeared in the persons, male and female, of children and adults, of various sizes, with "hair" made of ravelled rope and twisted tape, stiffened with glue; their bodies encased, variously, in cloth, leather, and gauze garments, and all,—clothing, shoes, sandals, "hair," faces and hands,—gilded! The effect was much as though a considerable number of steam-heat radiators, cast in human form, had become mechanically animate. . . . (289–90)

"A Midsummer Night's Dream" should be presented as a dreamlike spectacle: it should be made to move with ease and celerity through a sequence of handsome scenes, imbued with an atmosphere of poetry, charming with drollery,—never rough, obtrusive, or boisterous,—and every available means, spiritual and mechanical, should be used to create and sustain this effect. In the Barker presentment of it, since that was made by a skilful manager with the professional cooperation of experienced actors, there were a few—though only a few—features of merit; and it must not be forgotten that Shakespeare does much for *every* presentment of his plays. As a whole, however, this ostentatious and conceited exhibition of grotesque "novelty" was the very apotheosis of "parlor theatricals." Illusion was never created. The absurd scenery was destructive of all right effect. It is impossible for the mind to abandon itself to the enchantment of the acted drama and allow itself to drift with the representation, self-forgetful and delighted, when it is continually compelled to consider that trees are indicated by long festoons of gray cloth, wooded banks by wooden benches, and flitting sylphs by prancing gnomes that no more suggest fairies than so many coal-scuttles would! (295–96)

THE FAIRY PLAY

The following excerpt provides an interesting response to William Winter's antagonistic views above and to William Hazlitt's earlier comments on the opposition between the poetry of fairies and the stage. Below, Harley Granville Barker addresses the question about how to put the fairies on stage, but instead of saying, as Hazlitt does, that it cannot be done, he accepts it as a director's greatest challenge in producing *A Midsummer Night's Dream.* The key word here is "power." As Eric Salmon attends to Granville Barker's remarks, he indicates that what is most important is not what the fairies look like but that they convince viewers of their magical power, which is precisely what Salmon believes Granville Barker has achieved with his golden fairies and at which William Winter feels he has failed.

FROM ERIC SALMON, *GRANVILLE BARKER: A SECRET LIFE* (1983)

(London: Heinemann Educational Books, 1983) 215–16

Barker says:

Then come the fairies. Can even genius succeed in putting fairies on the stage? The pious commentators say not. This play...[is] freely quoted as impossible in the theatre. But, then, by some trick of reasoning they blame the theatre for it. I cannot follow that. If a play written for the stage cannot be put on the stage the playwright, it seems to me, has failed, be he who he may. Has Shakespeare failed or need the producer only pray for a little genius, too? The fairies are the producer's test. Let me confess that, though mainly love of the play, yet partly, too, a hope of passing that test has inspired the present production. Foolhardy one feels facing it. But if a method of staging can compass the difficulties of *A Midsummer Night's Dream,* surely its cause is won.

His way of meeting the challenge of the fairies was a highly original one and was the element in the production which provoked the most comment—not all of it favourable. But all of it proved Barker's point that the practical problem of presenting fairies on the stage was the *central* problem of the play: the play is a fairy play; the essence of its spirit lies in the magic and mystery of the woodland. Find a way of reaching the audience with that magic, convince the onlookers of the *power* of the fairies, the natural dwellers in the misty twilight, and the play comes magically to life. To do this, Barker jettisoned all the traditional cargo of sentimental prettiness that the play had acquired...: his fairies were adults, not children; they were strange, other-worldly, slightly sinister; they were unaccompanied by Mendelssohn; and they were gilded—all gold, from head to foot; faces, hands, everything.

PETER HALL'S *DREAM:* THE FAIRIES' QUARREL

Peter Hall's 1969 film version of *A Midsummer Night's Dream* allows for a darker interpretation of the play than some earlier productions, especially in the fairy scenes. Below he offers his explanation for departing from tradition and turning the woods into a damp, rainy, foggy setting of tangled vines and underbrush.

FROM ROGER MANVELL, *SHAKESPEARE AND THE FILM* (1979)

(New York: A. S. Barnes, 1979) 123

[Peter Hall]: I've tried in the *Dream* to get away completely from the expected Shakespearean setting, which is essentially nineteenth century and Pre-Raphaelite. The kind of approach associated with Mendelssohn's incidental music. That's how the *Dream* has always been presented, culminating in Reinhardt's stage productions, and his film of the 1930s. None of these people could have really looked at the text. Or if they did, they chose deliberately to disregard it. The *Dream* is quite clearly a play about an English summer in which the seasons have gone wrong. It is winter when it should be summer; everywhere is wet and muddy. This is described by Titania in a central speech. This is why I shot much of the film in the rain, during a bad-weather period lasting about six weeks. Titania's speech explaining this has often been cut in the past, yet it is the essence of the situation. The King and Queen of the Fairies, embodying animal nature, are quarrelling, and their quarrels have upset the balance of nature. This is what the play is all about. It is not a pretty, balletic affair, but erotic, physical, down to earth. All this, but with great charm and humour as well.

BOTTOM'S PART: PLAYING THE ACTOR

There is a doubleness about Bottom's part. An actor on stage plays well the role of Bottom rehearsing and performing badly as an actor on stage. The doubleness makes for interesting reflections about what it means to act and to do so effectively or ineffectively. The following excerpt from a book-length observation of the making of Peter Brook's *A Midsummer Night's Dream* captures some of the challenge and intensity involved in preparing the play for performance. In this segment, the actor has just played Bottom being turned into an ass, frightening others who in turn frighten him. Then the actor, David Waller, reacts angrily to the difficulty of playing the part well. David Selbourne, the writer who observes the scene, suggests that by successfully creating enchantment in the play, the actors, to a degree, lose themselves in the magic they have brought to life and then hardly know how to remove themselves from it or react to it. You may be able to appreciate this process if you have ever acted a role or imagined yourself to be someone else until the make-believe became so real you did not know for a moment whom you really were.

FROM DAVID SELBOURNE, *THE MAKING OF A MIDSUMMER NIGHT'S DREAM: AN EYE-WITNESS ACCOUNT OF PETER BROOK'S PRODUCTION FROM FIRST REHEARSAL TO FIRST NIGHT,* INTRODUCTION SIMON TRUSSLER (1982)

(London: Methuen, 1982) 145–46

[From the second day of the fourth week.]

The other mechanicals, and the haunting spirits too, were revived themselves by the new strength of character in their friend and victim. Rising above them, he was now terrorized and transformed at a pitch which in turn rose to reach him. "O Bottom, thou art changed!", says the quivering Snout the tinker, backing away (dwarfed) from this new colossus. And Bottom's "What do you see?" is now an anguished and angered bellow. Transfigured, he is both fearful and fearsome, terror-struck and striking terror. But to be in fear while unwittingly frightening others, in turns confounds and terrifies him; and in the confusion and disorder, of which our fears are also a part, the frisson of fear was redoubled, and became for a moment the purest horror.

Soon afterwards, exhausted by the acting pressures . . . the actor playing Bottom, David Waller, lost his temper. Pushing the spirits aside, he broke out of his role and began shouting that he did not know what he was doing. It was as if, in his shouts of anger, all the fears and hopes and confusions of the actors were confounded, while his voice seemed still to speak from deep within the disordered world of terrifying enchantment which, moments before, he had himself created. "This is to make an ass of me, to fright me if they could," he had said, frightened, looking to the spectators for reassurance. "But I will not stir from this place, do what they can. I will walk up and down here, and will sing, that they shall hear I am not afraid."

These words had already seemed to me to contain Shakespeare's own articles of faith, or an Hippocratic code for actors. And never more so than today, in the echo of Bottom's unanswered shouting.

A "SOMBER" *DREAM;* A "FROWSY" HELENA

Roger Warren comments on Elijah Moshinsky's interpretation of *A Mid-summer Night's Dream* in the BBC TV production. Without discrediting or panning the film, he notes that it has a somber tone, which is certainly an unusual perspective on Shakespeare's romantic comedy. Second, he notes that Helena is oddly "frowsy" or untidy in appearance, and, third, he focuses on the presence of the changeling child in the first scene between Titania and Oberon. As you read Warren's comments, imagine the effect onscreen of a "Helena" whose appearance contrasts rather than parallels Hermia's beauty, and of a changeling child whimpering in the arms of the fairy queen. Consider how these images compare with the ones in your mind or that you have seen in another film.

FROM ROGER WARREN, *A MIDSUMMER NIGHT'S DREAM: TEXT AND PERFORMANCE* (1983)

(London: Macmillan, 1983) 68, 69

[Moshinsky's] interpretation was rather low-key, serious, even sombre. When Lysander and Demetrius argued over Hermia, for instance, threat and counter-threat were spoken in hardly more than whispers, in obvious awe of a stern, inflexible Theseus; and when Hermia and Lysander planned to elope, they also spoke in secretive whispers, as if afraid of being overheard by court spies. Helena was oddly interpreted as a frowsy, bespectacled bluestocking. It wasn't surprising that Demetrius should have preferred Hermia; what was surprising was that he should have fallen for her in the first place. This unhappy figure, afraid of being left on the shelf, matched Helena's forsaken situation but not the lightweight language which she uses to express it. It was hard to believe that this gloomily studious Helena had ever listened to the song of the lark or noticed the hawthorn buds to which she refers to lyrically [I i 184–5]. This interpretation was an extreme indication of the prevailingly sombre tone, and the lack of gaiety and humour in this approach.

...Peter McEnery's Oberon, arriving on a sinister black horse "from the farthest steep of India," had long black hair which carried the faint suggestion of an Indian guru; in complete contrast, Helen Mirren was a ravishing golden-haired Titania. It was a good idea to have the changeling child present, as the cause of all the trouble, but a serious miscalculation to have Titania clutch him to her breast throughout the *whole* of the "forgeries of jealousy" speech, his shuffling and whining completely distracting attention from what Titania was saying.

HOLLYWOOD'S *DREAM*

The following is a full-length newspaper review of Michael Hoffman's 1999 Hollywood film version of Shakespeare's comedy. Part of it simply gives an overview of the plot, as any review does. But beyond that, Marc Horton offers high praise for the production. He finds the acting effective, especially Kevin Kline as Bottom, and considers the film to be very funny Shakespeare. Before you read the review, listen to a few comments of another reviewer, Steve Rhodes, who says that the humor in Hoffman's production is "too-cute-to-be-funny," that the rude mechanicals' play-within-the-play "is supposed to be laughably bad but is, instead, merely bad," and that the "mud wrestling" scene in the woods is "[l]ike so much of the movie...more weird than funny" (Rhodes, 2002). It is, of course, rare to find two movie reviewers who agree, but take note of the striking dissimilarities and weigh them against your reactions if you have already seen the movie.

FROM MARK HORTON "FAIRY MISTAKES PUT LOVERS IN A SPIN; SHAKESPEARE'S SUBLIME COMEDY SPRINKLES MAGICAL CONFUSION THROUGH A FOREST OF DREAMS"

Edmonton Journal, May 14, 1999

William Shakespeare's A Midsummer Night's Dream *****
Director: Michael Hoffman
Writer: Michael Hoffman, based on the play by William Shakespeare
Starring: Kevin Kline, Michelle Pfeiffer, Rupert Everett, Stanley Tucci, Calista Flockhart, Anna Friel, Christian Bale, Dominic West, David Strathairn, Sophie Marceau
Playing at: Cineplex Odeon
Classification: Parental guidance

*

As Bottom, Shakespeare's most comic creation, Kevin Kline is tops. The enchanting film *A Midsummer Night's Dream,* as bewitching a rendering of Shakespeare's magical play as you're likely to see, gives us a Bottom that's as unique as he is hilarious. And Kline's rich and layered performance is the first of the year that is certain of an Oscar nomination. His is a sensitive Bottom. Sure, the play takes suspension of disbelief—a major dose as fairies dance through the forest and the course of true love hits a bumpy patch or two—but if you're willing, this one will sweep you into Shakespeare's most sublime world.

Director Michael Hoffman, who has respectfully trimmed Shakespeare's play, moves the action to Tuscany at the turn of the century. It's a time of change, and the guests who have gathered for the wedding of an aristocrat are much taken with the latest invention in transportation: the bicycle. And when they go into the woods on midsummer night, they're in for a surprise bigger than the one at the teddy bear's picnic.

All the nonsense begins when Hermia (Anna Friel) and Lysander (Dominic West) flee into the forest to escape the wrath of Hermia's father. He's intent on her marrying Demetrius (Christian Bale) despite the fact she doesn't love the guy.

Demetrius goes in hot pursuit of Hermia while Helena (Calista Flockhart), who is passionately in love with Demetrius, also takes up the chase. The quartet of lovers find themselves in a part of the forest where fairies, elves and imps play. Part of the fantastical plot has the trickster fairy Puck (Stanley Tucci) administer a love potion that results in the wrong people falling in love with each other.

Complicating matters and putting this wonderfully rendered world on its head is the marital discord between Tatania [sic] (a radiant Michelle Pfeiffer) and Oberon (Rupert Everett), the king and queen of the fairies.

And through Puck's mis-sprinkling of the potion, Bottom becomes the donkey-eared lover of Titania. The world may never be the same again.

Now it's likely that if you've never had *A Midsummer Night's Dream* crammed into your noggin in some long-forgotten English class, all of this will seem supremely silly.

And it is. But it is such inventive silliness, such clever whimsy, that somehow it makes you believe in fairies... or very nearly.

Think Romeo and Juliet with jokes and happy-ever-after ending, where everyone ends up married to the right person, and you'll get the drift.

Central to this production is Kline as Bottom and his star turn as an actor and as a lover. His is a heartfelt performance, and while Bottom may be a shameless ham and a figure of ridicule in the village, there is an honesty in him that's special.

But the other performers also hit all their marks as well. Tucci's Puck is a meddling little scamp, fun-loving, occasionally exasperated; Everett makes you understand Oberon's marriage difficulties and Pfeiffer is splendid as Tatania [sic].

Flockhart as Helena is not unlike her Ally McBeal character—searching for love, and maybe looking in a few of the wrong places. The production is sumptuous to look at; the costumers [sic] are lavish and vivid. The soundtrack which uses Felix Mendelssohn's overture as its main theme is a winner, and opera fans will revel in the great swatches of Puccini and Verdi which are used to make clear just how powerful romantic longing can be. Mostly, though, this is the funniest Shakespeare you'll ever see. If you thought Shakespeare could never make you laugh, you'll gladly admit you were wrong.

TOPICS FOR WRITTEN AND ORAL DISCUSSION

1. Create a model of the Globe Theatre, the main stage for many performances of Shakespeare's plays during his lifetime. Research in books or on the Internet to learn more about its construction. Select material you wish to use, such as cardboard, paper, plaster, or wood. Include a presentation to the class about how the architecture of the theater affected the performance and reception of plays such as *A Midsummer Night's Dream.*

2. Create a comic book version of *A Midsummer Night's Dream,* deciding which scenes to depict and how many frames you need to cover the main details of the plot. Decide whether to use captions directly from the play or modern paraphrases.

3. *A Midsummer Night's Dream* has often been introduced to students younger than high school age as a tale of magic and fairies. Using either a comic book illustrated format or a shortened, simplified dramatic version of the play with a cast of fellow students, present the play to students from a younger class. Include what seems necessary to the plot as you "teach" it to other students, realizing that teaching is often an excellent way of learning. Discuss the outcome of the exercise. How did the audience respond? What did you learn? What might have worked better if done differently?

4. Pretend you have been hired in the publicity and promotions role for Shakespeare's Chamberlain's Men as they prepare to open *A Midsummer Night's Dream* in London in the mid-1590s. Design a poster to distribute to prominent public places or several posters that will appeal to different classes of playgoers. What might attract the lower classes, gentlemen, young apprentices, middle-class women? Which posters should go in the market, the local pub, the university, the queen's court?

5. Pretend to be a director of *A Midsummer Night's Dream* for its first production. Remember that stage props were minimal, sets were simple, and the stage jutted out into the theater yard with audiences on three sides and with three exit doors across the back stage wall. Choose an act or long scene and decide how it should be performed, writing notes or drawing stage diagrams to determine where characters will stand in relation to each other and the audience, what simple props might be necessary, and where and when the characters will enter and exit. Discuss what this exercise teachers you about the theater and about this play.

6. Listen to Henry Purcell's seventeenth-century music for *The Fairy Queen,* Felix Mendelssohn's nineteenth-century music for *A Midsummer Night's Dream,* or Benjamin Britten's 1960s operatic version of the play. Discuss how you feel the music captures or reflects aspects of the play, including actions and feelings. What interpretation of Shakespeare's comedy does the music encourage?

Alternatively, find different musical selections—classical, modern, or both—that you feel would be effective in a production of *A Midsummer Night's Dream.* Describe where the music should appear in the play and what effect your selections are designed to achieve.

7. Watch any film of *A Midsummer Night's Dream* and review it, considering how it has realized the theme and characters of Shakespeare's play and providing your own opinion as to its success or failure. What do you think the movie was attempting to achieve? How would you rate it in a movie guide?

8. Watch two film versions of *A Midsummer Night's Dream* and compare them. Consider their use of camera techniques, their presentation of the characters, their ability to engage you as audience, and their interpretation of comedy. Write your response in the form of an essay or hold a class discussion about the film version you preferred and why.

9. With a video camera, film a portion of *A Midsummer Night's Dream*—a scene or a portion of a long scene—paying attention to lighting and camera angles. Offer a written explanation of your choices and the effect you intended.

10. Design a collage of *A Midsummer Night's Dream,* incorporating symbolic images and various materials that depict your understanding and interpretation of the play.

11. Carefully study the language of a scene in *A Midsummer Night's Dream,* circling words that indicate setting, tone, and character positioning or relationship on stage. Discuss what this exercise teaches you about using the text to make decisions about producing the play.

12. Choose a partner. Imagine one of you is an Elizabethan male actor playing the role of Titania and the other is a nineteenth-century female actor playing the role of Oberon. Have an informal conversation or script a dialogue indicating some of the challenges or effects of playing the part of the opposite sex. Does it matter theatrically whether a male or a female plays these roles? Does it matter that young actors—children or teenagers—played adult parts? What are the cultural reasons behind the scripting choices that determine your role?

13. Summarize the reasons William Hazlitt provides for arguing that *A Midsummer Night's Dream* should be read rather than performed on stage. Discuss what his views indicate about his understanding of how imagination works and how it does not.

14. Construct a dialogue between one of the following pairs:

(a) William Hazlitt and Shakespeare regarding the staging of *A Midsummer Night's Dream* and the role of imagination
(b) William Hazlitt and Theseus, who does, after all, allow the "rude mechanicals" to perform "Pyramus and Thisby" on his wedding day
(c) William Hazlitt and Harley Granville Barker about casting fairies on stage

15. What is William Winter's view about how Shakespeare's fairies should be presented on stage? Why does he criticize Granville Barker's fairies in his 1914 production of *A Midsummer Night's Dream*? For Winter, what constitutes the ideal version of *A Midsummer Night's Dream*?

16. Film artist Max Reinhardt believed that " 'A Midsummer Night's Dream' is an invitation to escape reality, a plea for the glorious release to be found in pure fantasy."

Write a response to his comment, agreeing or disagreeing with his perspective and providing reasons, referring to the play itself to support your point of view.

17. Eric Salmon indicates that "the play is a fairy play; the essence of its spirit lies in the magic and mystery of the woodland." Discuss whether you accept his statement and why. Hold a classroom debate—especially if you have already viewed a production or two of the play—about how the fairies might best achieve the sense of magic and mystery they represent. Should the fairies be children or adults or a combination? Should they be exotic or regal? How should they be dressed? Should there be a somewhat dark, ominous, or sinister aspect to their presentation? Why or why not?

18. What interpretation does director Peter Hall take about the play's setting and atmosphere? Do you agree with him? Why or why not?

19. David Selbourne observes a rehearsal of Peter Brook's production of *A Midsummer Night's Dream* and describes actor David Waller playing one of Bottom's scenes. What does he suggest is the source of tension in assuming the role in a disordered "world of enchantment"? What has to happen for an actor successfully to become a character? Why is it so challenging and difficult?

20. Elijah Moshinksy's BBC film production of *A Midsummer Night's Dream* was, in Roger Warren's words, "low-key, serious, even sombre." Discuss whether you think this could be a fair and appropriate interpretation of the play or not. Provide reasons.

Especially if you have seen the BBC production, but even if you have not, discuss the effect of making Helena appear "frowsy," unattractive, and in a pair of glasses. Does Shakespeare's text support such an interpretation or not? Provide examples.

21. What is the effect of having Titania appear beautiful and delicate while Oberon appears dark, sinister, and powerful? Discuss in a small group the value or problem of such an interpretation. Would including a small changeling child in the first fairy scene affect your response to Titania and Oberon? How and why?

22. Watch Michael Hoffman's film *A Midsummer Night's Dream* and review it, referring to Marc Horton's review in this chapter but including your own observations about what you thought was effective or otherwise. How are the different worlds in the film version presented? What do you think of the extended scenes that focus on Bottom? Would you label this production as romantic, humorous, ridiculous, cute, weird, or something else?

23. Watch Hoffman's film as a group and then hold a debate in which one side agrees with Marc Horton that "this is the funniest Shakespeare you'll ever see" and the other side agreeing with reviewer Steve Rhodes who says that it is "too-cute-to-be-funny" and that "much of the movie...is more weird than funny." Provide argument and counter-argument, offering examples from the film and attempting to determine a framework for what constitutes "funny."

24. Peter Brook offered a radical "white box" set with a circus theme for his version of Shakespeare's play. Try to come up with your own creative rendition. What will the set be? What will costumes contribute? Is your interpretation dark comedy or light

fantasy? Will you emphasize dream or nightmare? Include drawings and/or written briefs to describe your vision of the play.

Once you have completed your scenario, meet with another student who has gone through the same exercise and discuss your different visions. Do they both seem to be supported by evidence in the play? Are there ways you can recognize that the world around you and your own values or ideals have influenced your approach?

SUGGESTED READING

Barnet, Sylvan. "*A Midsummer Night's Dream* on Stage and Screen," in *A Midsummer Night's Dream*. Ed. Wolfgang Clemen. A Signet Classic. New York: Penguin, 1986. 136–47.

Dawson, Anthony B. *Watching Shakespeare: A Playgoer's Guide.* New York: St. Martin's Press, 1988.

Griffiths, Trevor R. Introduction. *A Midsummer Night's Dream.* Cambridge: Cambridge UP, 1996. 1–80.

Jorgens, Jack J. *Shakespeare on Film.* Bloomington: Indiana UP, 1977.

Manvell, Roger. *Shakespeare and the Film.* New York: A. S. Barnes and Company, 1979.

Rhodes, Steve. "Review of *A Midsummer Night's Dream.*" http://www.All-Reviews. com/videos-3/Midsummer-Nights-Dream.htm. July 2002.

Selbourne, David. *The Making of A* Midsummer Night's Dream: *An Eye-Witness Account of Peter Brook's Production from First Rehearsal to First Night.* Intro. Simon Trussler. London: Methuen, 1982.

Warren, Roger. *A Midsummer Night's Dream: Text and Performance.* London: Macmillan Press, 1983.

Winter, William. *Shakespeare on the Stage.* Third series. New York: Moffat, Yard, and Co., 1916.

7

Contemporary
Applications

While the previous chapters have explored the historical context of *A Midsummer Night's Dream* from various angles and offered both dramatic analysis and a history of performance, this final chapter brings a modern context to the discussion of themes, concepts, and ideas. The topics included here suggest parallels between Shakespeare's play and concerns or issues in the present or in recent times. Connections presented are based on the assumption that we can further appreciate the play by expanding our vision of it to include popular or controversial elements that are evident around us or that touch us personally. By asking what engages us in the world today as *A Midsummer Night's Dream* has engaged people in the past and maybe still does, we open ourselves to new insights about subjects such as entertainment, relationships, and unusual or inexplicable phenomena that have a "magical" or mysterious quality to them.

Those three areas, in fact, constitute the three parts of this chapter. The first section looks at our contemporary entertainment industry, considering parallels to Shakespeare's sixteenth-century comic drama by exploring romance on screen and in popular novels, the television staple of half-hour situational comedies or "sitcoms," and the art and performance of stand-up comedians. Each of these popular forms has something in common with the various elements of *A Midsummer Night's Dream* and invites us to inquire into the range of universal or culturally specific qualities that shape the industry and activity of entertainment.

The second section examines relationships of love and friendship, especially among teens and their peers. Addressing issues about dating and body image, the discussion points towards the silly playfulness and utmost seriousness of attitudes and emotions surrounding professions of loyalty and first love. Jealousy in small doses may seem a silly or incidental response of human nature but, out of proportion, it can become a sign of serious behavior that leads to the dangers of abuse. Although such dangers are hardly the main focus of *A Midsummer Night's Dream,* the undercurrent of violence in the play and the outright accusations of jealousy between Oberon and Titania encourage us to regard extremes of both infatuation and abuse as realities that shape relationships at their most mature and immature stages.

The third section includes a broad range of topics from dream analysis to paranormal experiences to fantasy in literature. What holds these subjects together is a common thread of mystery or a quality of the unknown, the very thing that informs the plot of *A Midsummer Night's Dream.* Although Freud and Jung have helped define the meaning of dreams for modern times, we still live with perplexity about the composition of our own dreams and our ability or inability to remember them. Although science can give us information about electromagnetic fields in physical objects including our own bodies, we still marvel at paranormal phenomena such that, for example, one rare person can cause metal to bend through sheer mental energy while the rest of us cannot. And although common sense tells us that there is no such thing as magic, we readily embrace the magical worlds of fantasy created in *The Lord of the Rings* or the Harry Potter books because our imaginations have a great appetite for the mysterious wonders that lie beyond the possibilities of our day-to-day lives. This last chapter, then, allows connections with Shakespeare's play to meet us where we are and to draw us beyond our own boundaries, inviting us to explore what pleases us, what confounds us, and what allows us the freedom to grow.

THE ENTERTAINMENT INDUSTRY

Romance

Defining the passionate response between two lovers, the notion of romantic love that began as early as the eleventh century (see chapter 2 on "The Courtly Love Tradition") has weathered the cultural changes of centuries to sustain mass market appeal in the entertainment industry of the late twentieth and early twenty-first centuries. Romance continues to be an enduring topic both on screen and in popular fiction. The pattern of courtship, loss and confusion, and then finally fulfillment replays itself as a theme with multiple variations.

On screen, this theme takes the form of the "romantic comedy" genre. It relies on some of the same characteristics as the dramatic form that Shakespeare
helped create four centuries ago (see chapter 1 on "Romantic Comedy") in
which "love at first sight" ignites the plot and marriage establishes the happy
resolution or conclusion. Modern movies share with comedies such as *A Midsummer Night's Dream* love's irrationality—as an experience bordering on madness—that can be a source of both pain and liberation in a society whose
expectations appear stifling and repressive and whose demands make love-
inspired rebellion appear healthy. From Shakespeare's stage to today's cinema,
romantic comedy unfolds with often unexpected turns in the plot, and un-
foreseen changes and coincidences. What appears in *A Midsummer Night's
Dream* to be the intervention of fairy magic might today be considered to be
sheer dumb luck. But the result is not much different—a sense of futility in
any effort to analyze or agonize about what it all means. Love appears time-
lessly confusing and uncertain. The goal is not to figure it out but to celebrate
the sense of optimism about humanity portrayed in a view of harmony that
can be achieved through a meeting of hearts and minds in spite of recognized
human frailties and limitations.

While some patterns in romantic comedy have a long history, Hollywood
has also recognized and engaged in shifting priorities and possibilities by placing the genre of romance and intimacy within an ever-changing social and
economic culture. Some radical changes came with the "sexual revolution" that
began in the 1960s in which gender roles began to be redefined by a rise in
women's self-expression and social and economic power. Within this context,
the possibility of sexual pleasure detached from intimacy and commitment became much more acceptable. Some thought that the "romance" of romantic
comedy would get lost in the wake of these new sexual freedoms. Several decades later, new generations responded to fears of an AIDS epidemic by re-
treating somewhat from the urge to seek sexual pleasure without responsibility,
and romantic idealism sustained and regained its appeal. Along the way, divorce rates have risen and with them a growing suspicion or uncertainty about
the meaning of marriage. Observers have identified ways in which the movie
industry has reflected and responded to these changes. We now see romantic
comedies in which the "boy meets girl" pattern has been revised. We watch
stories that include as central characters career women who are not simply defined by the men in their lives. We see romantically attracted couples accompanied by children from previous marriages. We see lovers balancing and
sharing traditionally gender-ordained roles of female domesticity and male
economic power and responsibility. Moreover, what has been called "the new
romantic comedy" often includes in the search for love, a search also for self-
identity so that the conclusion is not only one of social harmony but one of

personal growth and self-awareness. The conclusion is less predictable—perhaps a commitment to friendship between man and woman rather than the expected ringing of wedding bells. Yet, ultimately, what we continue to see are stories with an element of fantasy or wish-fulfillment in which the banalities and complexities of real life simply vanish in the celebration of love.

Romance that finds its way into popular fiction retains the pattern of courtship, loss, and fulfillment that defines romantic comedy on stage or on screen but, interestingly enough, responds less fully than Hollywood to social issues and cultural changes. Perhaps the difference stems from the fact that reading is a private pastime while film is public entertainment. In the modern romance novel, the woman is the main character and her ideal is simply to be married to the right man. The narrative explores the interior psychological experience of the woman as the question of whether she will be united with her hero propels the plot forward. The readership is largely female and the genre is primarily considered escape fiction because it perpetuates a view of life that has little basis in reality. In the following excerpt from *Women's Gothic and Romantic Fiction,* Kay Mussell describes the general outline of the romantic novel. Notice what main conflicts may need to be addressed before the resolution through love is complete.

FROM KAY MUSSELL, *WOMEN'S GOTHIC AND ROMANTIC FICTION* (1981)

(Westport, CT: Greenwood Press, 1981) xi–xii.

The romantic novel features a woman who experiences love, courtship, and usually marriage. Typically, it takes one of two forms: the drama of courtship and marriage within a setting of domestic detail, or the story of an already-achieved marriage with difficulties between husband and wife being resolved at the end, and the wife rewarded with either a better marriage to her current husband or a new marriage with a new lover. There are some romantic novels, also, of the "antiromance" type...in which the heroine behaves in such a way that she cannot be rewarded with marriage in the end. These, too, are romances, although the inversion of the plot makes them serve as cautionary tales rather than as models to be emulated.

The story of a romantic novel begins with an assumption, unquestioned and unexamined except in a few books, that the necessary, preordained, and basic goal of any woman is to achieve a satisfying, mature, and all-fulfilling marriage. The primacy of romantic love in defining a woman's place in the world and her personal and moral worth is rarely in doubt in these books....

Love relationships may be impeded by the heroine's immaturity, by the hero's stiff-necked pride, by the machinations of family members who wish to keep lovers apart, by the scheming of women who rival the heroine for the attention of the hero, by existing impediments to a marriage (wives, husbands, embarrassing earlier lovers who refuse to relinquish their hold on the heroines), and, most of all, by misunderstandings between the potential lovers that must be resolved before they may admit their love for each other.

Sitcoms

The situation comedy or the "sitcom" is a genre particular to television. It is structured as a half-hour story in which a set group of characters faces a difficult "situation" or problem that turns comic in their efforts to address it but that is always happily resolved by the end of the program. There is a "feel good" atmosphere to the story line which, while it pokes fun at day-to-day human foibles, does so by playing to the range of emotions within the audience's comfort zone. Sitcoms are usually safe and predictable; that is a large part of their appeal. Often a "family" provides the center of the character interaction, although the family may be a typical one with parents and children or it may be another group that acts as a kind of surrogate, temporary "family"—for example, fellow employees at work, or a company of friends that spend their time together (Mitz 4). A variety of stock characters may appear, depending on the setting for the show: wacky neighbors, sensible mothers, lovable incompetents, harried or wise fathers, cranky old people, dumb blondes, and many more (Mitz 6). Often the sitcom is contemporary and up-to-date, but sometimes it is a throwback to a previous generation, such as the 1950s, the 1970s, or the 1990s. Then it can provide not only laughter but also nostalgia for a remembrance of the way things were. The comedy can be played strictly for fun or it can offer social commentary within the lighthearted plot. Shakespeare did not write sitcoms, but given the slapstick humor, confusion, and mistaken identities that inform his plots, it is easy to imagine that were he alive today he might be writing to stimulate half-hour laughs for television.

Three excerpts included below round out the definition of situation comedy. In *TV: The Most Popular Art,* Horace Newcomb explains the formula for the genre, with complication and confusion creating the humor of the story. He chooses to differentiate between situation comedy and domestic comedy while other critics see domestic comedy as simply a special type of sitcom. Notice how he distinguishes the two. Rick Mitz follows with a list of actions, behaviors, or circumstances that often appear as the "situational" component of the comedy that inspires laughter. Then Gerard Jones describes what sitcoms offer to modern audiences in an age when social values and relationships grow increasingly complex. Look for his explanation of why we watch sitcoms, how they make us feel, and why that is important.

FROM HORACE NEWCOMB, *TV: THE MOST POPULAR ART* (1974)

(Garden City, NY: Anchor Books, 1974)

In situation comedy the situation is simply the broad outline of events, the special funny "thing" that is happening this week to a special set of characters. The characters will appear at the same time the following week in another funny situation which will be entirely nondependent on what happens tonight....

In order for the situation to develop into something resembling a story, two other elements common to the formula must be added: complication and confusion. . . .

Complications in situation comedies may take many forms, but most generally they are involved with some sort of human error or mistake....

Events, the things that "happen" in sitcom, are composed solely of confusion, and the more thorough the confusion, the more the audience is let in on a joke that will backfire on the characters, the more comic the episode. Individual shows are frequently structured on various layers of confusion that can be generated out of a single complication. Like parentheses within parentheses, the characters slip into deeper and deeper confusion. Expression and reaction follow complication, gesture follows reaction, slapstick follows gesture. The broader the element, the louder the laughter. (31–34)

The complex family structures of domestic comedy generate innumerable problems in which to contrive plots. The problems build on the human failure syndrome we noted in the situation comedy, and the problem-solving paradigm carries directly into the other formulas. In the earlier form, however, the failures were centered in physical problems: mistaken identities, misplaced objects, physical mishaps, and so on. Though such problems also arise in domestic comedy, they establish far fewer of the plot structures than in sitcom. Here the problems are more likely to be mental and emotional. Failure takes place in the areas of complex human interaction, though the plots themselves could seldom be called complex. (52)

FROM RICK MITZ, *THE GREAT TV SITCOM BOOK* (1980)

(New York: Richard Marek Publishers, 1980)

Here's how Parke Levy ... described sitcoms: "A sitcom is a small hunk of life exaggerated for comic purposes. If you play it realistically, it comes out drama because very little in life itself is funny. People want a mirror held up to life, but at an angle so that it's humorous." (3)

Here's a list of a few of the things that make for laughs on sitcoms of today and yesterday:

PEOPLE EAVESDROPPING "Ah, the reason I have this glass held up to the wall is because ... my ear is ... thirsty."

PEOPLE SAYING THE TRUTH BY MISTAKE AND THEN COVERING UP "I hate him ... I mean, I *date* him."

ALL-IN-GOOD-FUN NARCISSISM "I told them I was the best darned anchorman in the country. I had to—I was under oath."

MISUNDERSTANDING "You mean Shirley isn't dead? But I thought ... "

MISTAKEN IDENTITY "You mean, you're not the Contessa? But I thought ... "

COINCIDENCES "Guess who I saw at the school dance last night who was supposed to be at the library studying for finals ... "

TOILET HUMOR Archie Bunker's toilet flushing.

AMNESIA "Cosmo—it's me, Henrietta."

IRONY "We've all been fired—except Ted."

RACIAL SLURS "I don't like no Hebes, spics or coons, y'hear?"

MALAPROPISMS "It's just a pigment of your imagination."

FUNNY COSTUMES "Look, that's Laverne dressed as a giant chicken."

SELZTER/PIE IN THE FACE "Wham!"

BAD SINGING "Sweet Ad-o-line!"

OUT-OF-THE-MOUTHS-OF-BABES "Mommy, I think Billy's having an identity crisis."

RECURRING LINES OR JOKES "God'll get you for that, Walter."

PLAYING DUMB "Gee, I didn't know it was loaded, Mr. Mooney."

GUEST STARS "Oh, gosh, Ethel—it's William Holden."

PRATFALLS "Well, you've certainly got the padding for it—only kidding, kid." (8)

FROM GERARD JONES, *HONEY, I'M HOME! SITCOMS:*
SELLING THE AMERICAN DREAM (1993)

(New York: St. Martin's Press, 1993) 4–5

The sitcom is more directly, of course, about families and workplaces than about society in the greater sense. But even the family has had to adapt to our times with many of the same tools that industry and government have used. Sex roles have blurred; economic rules have changed; generational conflicts have become steadily more complicated. Patriarchal authority is nearly dead, and tradition is weak. Negotiation, consensus, and compromise have become essential in managing the modern family. No problems, of course, are ever solved as easily as on television. Perhaps, with such methods, no fundamental problems are ever fully solved at all. But sitcoms at least give us clues to how to patch up our difficulties well enough to laugh together and get through the evening. The sitcom is a primer on managing our private lives by the systems of our new mass society.

The sitcom is also a mirror. A foggy mirror, to be sure, that misses a lot of our blemishes and care lines ... but one of its functions has always been to show the American family to itself, to open an alternate family room within our own, to let us stop and check ourselves over before we step back outside into the winds of change. Some shows hold up models of what our culture thinks we should be like. . . . Others enable us to dispel some anxiety by laughing affectionately at those who have even more trouble dealing with daily life than we do. . . . Both types reassure us that there are others out there like us, that we will always work out a way to get by.

The sitcom is a daydream. In an age when the family is threatened ... it's pleasant to have an imitation family to retreat into.

Stand-Up Comedians

Along with romantic comedy at the movies and sitcoms on television, stand-up comedy is yet another genre or form of humor and entertainment in our time. Sometimes we can catch a comedy sketch on a television variety show or late-night talk show. But most stand-up comics make their living on small stages in nightclubs or other comedy venues. If romantic comedy on film contemporizes Shakespeare's stage comedy, and sitcoms capture some of the laughter-engendering confusion so common in his comic plots, stand-up comedians work on the intimate relationship between performer and audience that Shakespeare knew so well but that today's screen—large or small—eliminates. Stand-up comics do not respect the difference between the real world and play world. Like Puck taking down the invisible barrier between the stage story and spectators at the end of *A Midsummer Night's Dream,* stand-up comics perform with bold directness to the people in front of them. Their chief goal is to be funny and make people laugh; they rise or fall according to their ability to spark that laughter by the material they prepare and by their sense of timing and delivery. The boldness of the comedian consists not only of his or her willingness to speak directly to the audience but also of a readiness to push beyond the comfort zone of people's emotions and feelings in precisely the way that sitcoms do not. Often comedians depend on the shock value of jokes or stories that violate social taboos. People laugh at their own discomfort. They laugh at hearing something said that they only dared to think. The comedian is today's version of Shakespeare's clown, trickster, or wise fool who relies solely on language and body gestures to surprise and entertain.

The two following excerpts provide perspectives on stand-up comedy. Jay Sankey asks the question, "What is funny?" and attempts to answer it with reflections on the relationship between tension and laughter. David Marc talks about the daring and vulnerability of comedians who have nothing to protect themselves from their own performance and its effect on the audience. He also mentions tension, but he uses words such as "wiseguy" and "bigmouth" to indicate how boldness defines this particular brand of humor.

FROM JAY SANKEY, *ZEN AND THE ART OF STAND-UP COMEDY* (1998)

(New York: Routledge/Theatre Arts Books, 1998) 1–3

In response to a question like "What is funny?" comics often say, "Funny is funny," and, though that doesn't say much, I would have to agree. Whatever makes someone laugh is comedy, at least to them. That's what makes laughter such a subjective and fascinating phenomenon. Certainly laughter is a mysterious, highly personal response to an amazing range of things, but in my view, laughter is first and foremost *a release of tension.* Something about what the person just saw or heard (or perhaps merely thought) made him tense on an emotional or psychological level, and then something in him "chose" to release or vent this tension in the form of laughter, rather than tears or anger or some other form.

On a more primary, perhaps even symbolic level I'd be tempted to say that laughter is often the result of a sudden and surprising witnessing of *things either coming together or coming apart.* The magician puts a coin in his hand, then opens his hand to show that the coin has somehow vanished, suddenly breaking with the crowd's presumptions, jarring their belief in what is "real." And in response, they laugh. The comic tells a joke challenging a convention or taboo, creating tension in the crowd, and people laugh. And when the clown steps on a banana peel and takes a truly frightening fall, again we feel tension and release it in laughter. The magician, the comic, and the clown all do things that create, on some level, tension inside the audience—tension that, with the appropriate trigger, can be artfully coaxed into laughter.

FROM DAVID MARC, *COMIC VISIONS: TELEVISION COMEDY AND AMERICAN CULTURE* (1989)

(Boston: Unwin Hyman, 1989) 13–14

Stand-up comedy continues to expose itself to human contact, and there is a heroic quality to this in the nuclear age. It is an art of the bravado personality in a world being organized to and for death. The cult of the wiseguy is brought to the formal dimension of art. If the threat of atomic doom has reduced us to powerless resentful children awaiting punishment, it is difficult to resist the bigmouth who can spit in the eye of civilization with a bit of grace (though the wince is unbearable when the attempt is feeble). Without the protection of the formal mask of a narrative drama, without a song, dance, or any other intermediary composition that creates distance between performer and performance, without even necessarily, some remarkable physical trait or ability to gratuitously display, the stand-up comedian addresses an audience as a naked self, eschewing the luxury of a clear-cut distinction between art and life. Good actors can be singled out of bad plays; good singers can put over bad songs. But in the case of the stand-up comedian, there is no dividing medium from message. When performing stand-up comedy, Steve Martin is Steve Martin is Steve Martin. . . .

Owing largely to the extra tensions created by the purposeful confusion of "play world" and "real world," few spectacles in modern show business are as compelling as the successful stand-up controlling the physical responses of a large group of people with the power of language. A monologue, like a sermon, asks the anonymous members of the assembly to spontaneously merge into a single emotional organism capable of reacting uniformly to the metaphor, wisdom, and worldview of one appointed personality. By the same token . . . few public spectacles are as pathetic as the stand-up laying an egg . . . suffering the brutality of mass rejection.

TOPICS FOR WRITTEN AND ORAL DISCUSSION

1. Consider the latest romantic comedy you have seen in the theater or on video. Discuss how it portrays love. How is the movie "romantic"? In what ways is it "comic"?

2. Consider two or three romantic comedies in a group discussion. Do the movies all follow the traditional "boy meets girl" pattern or are there ways that one movie or another plays with the conventions? Is there a wedding at the end? If not, how do the movies resolve into a "happily ever after" conclusion? Do they raise questions about romantic ideals as well as exploring relationships between men and women? Is there any self-awareness or personal growth or change in the main characters by the end of the movies?

3. Choose your favorite romantic comedy and explain why you like it. Then consider it according to the description of "Romance" in this chapter, as well as "Romantic Comedy" in chapter 1 and "The Courtly Love Tradition" in chapter 2. Do you see any connections that can help you appreciate how old this genre is and yet how contemporary it remains? Provide examples.

4. Compare *A Midsummer Night's Dream* to a modern-day romantic comedy. How are they alike? How are they dissimilar? Consider the portrayal of love, the depiction of male and female roles, "magic" transformation, and comic resolution. What stands in the way of love? How are the obstacles removed?

5. Imagine a meeting between one of Shakespeare's lovers—Hermia, Helena, Lysander, or Demetrius—and a lover from a modern romantic comedy. Choose a specific point in the play and the film—near the beginning, in the middle, or at the end. Act out a dialogue with a partner or compose a letter and a response. What are the reactions? Confusion? Wonderment? Dismay? Frustration? Outrage? Delirium?

6. What, according to Kay Mussell, distinguishes a romance from an anti-romance? What is the main objective in the plot of the romance and what obstacles might stand in the way before the lovers come together?

7. Hold a debate about the value of reading popular romance fiction. One side will argue against reading romance, including among its positions the way romance novels portray women. The other side will argue in support of romance fiction, suggesting, among other reasons, that escape fiction has its place or that reading romance is better than not reading at all.

8. Choose a romance novel and compare the relationships in it to the romantic relationships in *A Midsummer Night's Dream*. How are they alike and unalike? What obstacles stand in the way of love?

9. Write a romantic short story in which the heroine is a strong individual who meets someone to whom she is romantically attracted. How will your conclusion reflect her independence and her feelings for the man she has met?

10. Discuss why you think romance is almost entirely a genre for female readers. What appeals to male readers and why? Consider reasons for the differences. Then discuss

whether Shakespeare's *Midsummer Night's Dream* appeals more to the male or female students in your class or equally to both and suggest reasons.

11. According to Horace Newcomb, what is the basic formula for a sitcom? How does he distinguish domestic comedy from situation comedy? Think of examples of half-hour comedies presently on TV. Do you think they are sitcoms or domestic comedies or a hybrid of both? Provide specific examples to support your opinion.

12. Rick Mitz gives a list of "things that make for laughs on sitcoms." Sit with the list in front of the TV and watch a sitcom or two. Find as many examples of Mitz's suggestions as you can, and then take your report back to class at the end of the week. Share your findings in a small group and then summarize your group findings for the rest of the class.

13. Consider Mitz's list of comic behaviors and happenings in relationship to *A Midsummer Night's Dream*. Suggest ways in which Shakespeare's play is like a sitcom by finding examples of sitcom humor in the play. What do your findings indicate to you about sources of humor through the centuries? What seems universal? What seems culturally specific?

14. What are some of the changes Gerard Jones sees in modern society? What role does he see sitcoms playing in that context? Are they merely an escape or more than that?

15. Consider Jones's comments in relation to sitcoms you watch. Why do you watch them? Do your reasons match Jones's or offer a different perspective?

16. What is funny? Jay Sankey answers that question. What does he say? Discuss in small groups what you think "funny" is. Determine whether your responses are shared or individual. Is humor simply personal or can it be social? Can you think of examples of things coming together or apart that might spark laughter?

17. Do you have a favorite comedian? If so, what appeals to you about his or her humor? Write a paragraph that explains your position.

18. In *Comic Visions,* David Marc seems to admire comedians. Why?

19. Can you see similarities between how Puck behaves and what stand-up comedians do? Suggest examples.

SUGGESTED READING

Evans, Peter William, and Celestino Deleyto, eds. *Terms of Endearment: Hollywood Romantic Comedy of the 1980s and 1990s.* Edinburgh: Edinburgh University Press, 1998.

Jones, Gerard. *Honey, I'm Home! Sitcoms: Selling the American Dream.* New York: St. Martin's Press, 1992.

Karnick, Kristine Brunovska, and Henry Jenkins, eds. *Classical Hollywood Comedy.* New York: Routledge, 1995.

Marc, David. *Comic Visions: Television Comedy and American Culture.* Boston: Unwin Hyman, 1989.

Mitz, Rick. *The Great TV Sitcom Book.* New York: Richard Marek Publishers, 1980.

Mussell, Kay. *Women's Gothic and Romantic Fiction: A Reference Guide.* Westport, CT: Greenwood Press, 1981.

Newcomb, Horace. *TV: The Most Popular Art.* Garden City, NY: Anchor Books, 1974.

Sankey, Jay. *Zen and the Art of Stand-Up Comedy.* New York: Routledge/Theatre Arts Books, 1998.

RELATIONSHIPS OF LOVE AND FRIENDSHIP

Love and friendship are central issues in *A Midsummer Night's Dream,* especially among the four young people, Lysander, Hermia, Demetrius, and Helena. Lysander and Hermia consider Helena a close enough friend that they share with her their plans to escape into the woods and marry away from Athens. Later, when Lysander and Demetrius dote on Helena because of their magically induced infatuation for her, Helena speaks at length to Hermia, appealing to their long history of friendship, saying,

> O, is all forgot?
> All school days friendship, childhood innocence?
> We, Hermia, like two artificial gods,
> Have with our needles created both one flower,
> Both on one sampler, sitting on one cushion,
> Both warbling of one song, both in one key;
> As if our hands, our sides, voices, and minds,
> Had been incorporate. So we grew together,
> Like to a double cherry, seeming parted,
> But yet an union in partition....
> And will you rent our ancient love asunder,
> To join with men in scorning your poor friend? (3.2.201–16)

Friendship between Shakespeare's two young women seems in jeopardy because of confused, complicated expressions of love. But when day dawns, the four young people are friends again, and their animosities triggered by passions and fairies are resolved into harmonious partnerships.

What Shakespeare's young men and women suffer and celebrate are relationships of intimacy and uncertainty that teenagers and young adults experience with just as much passion and intensity today. Youthful relationships can change with the wind, or they can lead to life-long commitments that produce lasting friendships and healthy marriages. Teens suffer the vulnerability of peer pressure and fluctuate between mature and immature responses to each other and the world around them as they grow into greater understanding of who they are and how to respond to their changing hormones, emotions, and responsibilities.

Dating

Part of the process of growing up from adolescence to adulthood involves dating peers of the opposite sex and trying to discover how to respond to one another—and to one's friends and parents—within the new parameters of relationships between boyfriends and girlfriends. Insecurity and excitement are both part of the process. The two following selections capture some elements of attraction between teenagers as they struggle with ways of communicating their feelings for each other. The first selection, from Jeremy Daldry's *Teenage Guy's Survival Guide,* adopts the voice of a young man struggling for the courage to ask a girl out. The second excerpt, from Delia Ephron's *Teenage Romance or How to Die of Embarrassment,* takes the form of a girl's diary entries as she "falls in love" with a fellow classmate and then pours out her feelings of uncertainty and embarrassment. Then a third quotation from Jennifer Rozines Roy's *Romantic Breakup: It's Not the End of the World* draws distinctions between love and infatuation. Roy defines love in the context of "passion," "fantasy," and "reason," some of the very concepts that motivate and confuse Shakespeare's characters. To "dote in idolatry" as Helena does for Demetrius would appear to be a sign of the excesses of infatuation rather than true love. Roy's distinctions raise questions about the foundation and definition of modern romantic relationships, as well, such as those depicted in the following two excerpts. Reflect on whether the voices and observations from these excerpted sources sound familiar to you from your own classroom or personal experience and among the teens who are your friends.

FROM JEREMY DALDRY, *THE TEENAGE GUY'S SURVIVAL GUIDE* (1999)

(Boston: Little, Brown, and Co., 1999) 11–12

It's been scientifically proven that when any guy gets within two feet of a girl, she gives off a mysterious aura that turns a normal guy into a gibbering wreck who can't string two words together.

It's proven. It's science. Strange but true.

But you still want to talk to them.

You want to be close to them.

You want to hold their hands,

and go out on dates with them.

And kiss them, and cuddle them,

and kiss them, and kiss them some more.

And therein lies a very **BIG** problem: asking a girl out on a date.

Even when it's totally obvious that a girl has a huge crush on you, why do you find it so hard just to go up and ask her out?

I'll tell you why.

Because of the big **N.O.**

Because you're scared of being rejected or that the girl in question will tell her friends, who then will have a good laugh about you.

But it shouldn't be scary, because, let's face it: You probably know when a girl wants to be asked out.

No, you do, really. . . .

There are those funny little signs. Like?

Well, when you talk to the girl in question:

- She blushes, or she starts to play with her hair.
- She smiles when she sees you coming and "accidentally" touches you on the hand or the leg when you leave.
- She laughs at your lame jokes, asks lots of questions about you, and then listens really closely to whatever you've got to say.

There are tons and tons of little signs. You've just got to watch for them.

But wait a minute.

What is so wrong with a *girl* asking one of us *guys* out for a night on the town. . . ?

Nothing. Absolutely nothing.

FROM DELIA EPHRON, *TEENAGE ROMANCE OR HOW TO DIE OF EMBARRASSMENT* (1981)

(New York: Viking Press, 1981)

Dear Diary,

Remember I told you I wish I could find someone I really like. Well, diary, . . . I have!!!!!!!! He's in my French class so I guess I was wrong—French won't be my most boring, worst class after all. His name is Jeffrey Dobkin. Oh diary, you should see him. Brownish hair, taller than me (very important), blue eyes. I noticed him right away because who wouldn't. He's really popular. I mean really, really popular. Compared to him, I'm practically a zero in popularity. But when I first saw him up close, I didn't think I would like him. He just didn't seem like my type. But then I started thinking about him more and more and yesterday during algebra, which is my class after French, I was thinking about him and I just knew. Diary, I'm in love. Do you think that's weird? (19)

DD,

Jeffrey is running for class veep. I hope he wins. Guess what? I'm not positive but I think today in class Jeffrey might have noticed me. . . . (22)

DD,

Jeffrey won. I knew he would. . . . But oh, diary, I could die, I did the dumbest thing. Madame Flynn gave me the test papers to hand back and when I gave Jeffrey his, I said congratulations. I meant about the election but probably he thought it was about his test. Oh God, I feel like such a jerk. I wanted to disappear the moment I said it. . . .

If I could only explain!...Oh, this is dumb—one thing's for sure, when I talk I mess it up. I feel awful, diary. I really hate love. If this is it, I don't want it, I really don't. Goodnight, diary. This is your best friend with a broken heart signing off. (30–31)

FROM JENNIFER ROZINES ROY, *ROMANTIC BREAKUP: IT'S NOT THE END OF THE WORLD* (2000)

(Berkeley Heights, NJ: Enslow Publishers, Inc., 2000) 12

Love is a wonderful thing. It feels good, makes people happy, and is even good for your health! One long-term goal of dating is to find love. But true love takes time to develop. It comes in stages. The first phase is not really love. It is called infatuation. Infatuation is a state of attraction and passion that is not based on reason. It is a time of excitement and fantasy, in which each person imagines how perfect he or she is for the other....

It is not always possible to tell the difference between love and infatuation while a person is in a relationship. Both feel wonderful and offer emotional highs. But the first few months of a relationship are almost always infatuation.

Body Image

Body image seems to become especially important in teen years when, on the one hand, significant physiological and biological changes are occurring and, on the other hand, good looks and appearances are valued more than they have been in earlier childhood years. Though caring for one's body is important, the idealized Hollywood and Paris runway images are not a true reflection of the general population and attempting to imitate the physique or style of movie stars and models can lead to an unhealthy obsession and lack of self-acceptance. Peer pressure often feeds this unhealthy mentality as young people try to make friends, impress one another, or fit into the right crowd. Shakespeare's four lovers do not escape these concerns. At the peak of confusion and vulnerability in the fairy world, name-calling reveals Hermia's and Helena's self-image and their views of one another. Helena refers to Hermia as "puppet," "little," and "low," while Lysander joins in by calling his former lover "dwarf," "minimus," "bead," and "acorn" (3.2.288–329). Hermia responds to these jibes by being deeply hurt and offended. While Hermia is short and dark, Helena is apparently tall and fair, and the differences seem to matter. Nevertheless, Demetrius's shift from winning Helena's soul before the beginning of the play to declaring his love for Hermia in act 1 suggests that even while appearances seem to matter, they do not guarantee committed affection any more than they guarantee a healthy self-respect.

The following three quotations address this issue of body image in young people. In the first excerpt, Sandra Friedman explores roots of self-perception and body image in girls and women, describing what the female population accepts as their "model of perfection" and revealing how difficulties addressing feelings can lead to negative attitudes towards one's body. Kaz Cooke then offers a perspective on what it means to be "real gorgeous" and how that perspective is different than the "fake world" of TV, movies, and magazines. The third document is a newspaper article about young men and teenage boys obsessed with their looks. If girls obsess about being fat, boys obsess about bulking up. Notice what motivates boys in the article to try to change or improve their physique and what the results are, not only physically, but also mentally and emotionally.

FROM SANDRA FRIEDMAN, *WHEN GIRLS FEEL FAT: HELPING GIRLS THROUGH ADOLESCENCE* (1997)

(New York: HarperCollins, 1997)

Whenever I asked girls or women to share their image of the perfect person—regardless of their own race and ethnicity—they are almost always unanimous in their list. The perfect girl is Barbie. She is tall, thin, blond, white, beautiful, competent, confident, independent, young, athletic, sexy and powerful. She has big white teeth, big lips and big breasts. She makes a lot of money and doesn't need anybody else....

The model of perfection that is held out to girls is one-dimensional. It doesn't account for the sheer messiness, the ups and downs in the insecurities and stress of real life. Because this model is unattainable, girls always end up feeling as if there's something wrong with them, no matter how hard they try. Because none of the things that girls value, and none of the qualities that make up real female culture, are reflected back to them positively by society, girls soon learn to devalue themselves.... (35)

Girls approaching puberty are encouraged to repress their feelings, which stops them talking about the important issues in their lives. As they try to fit into the male culture, they lose their sense of identity and devalue the very qualities and characteristics that make them unique. These feelings don't just go away. Many girls associate the social restrictions that are imposed upon them with the inevitable weight gain and increase in body fat that occurs during puberty. They try to deal with the new restrictions in their lives by focusing on these changes in their bodies. They focus on a reflected external image instead of on their real internal selves. Girls deflect their feelings back onto their bodies and encode them in the language of fat. (37)

FROM KAZ COOKE, *REAL GORGEOUS: THE TRUTH ABOUT BODY AND BEAUTY* (1996)

(New York: Norton and Co., 1996)

You will see only one type of normal in the magazines and on television and in films. That's the estimated 5 percent of us, the model-shaped thin girls, with very long legs and wide shoulders. In years gone by we had actors ranging from Sophia Loren's shape to Mae West.... English and Australian actors tend to have more diverse shapes but we see mostly the American ideal on our screens, which is the thinnest with the most makeup and the most fussed-over hair. It is also the most fiddled-with image, the most removed from reality, from the fake world (the planet of *Melrose Place*).

We have to start looking at the real world again as well as watching the TV and reading the magazines. If we have our head stuck in that stuff all the time our idea of what is normal gets completely out of whack because we are seeing only the Five Percent. Go see women in the shopping mall.... Where did all the real people come from? See how differently shaped they are?...And if you really want to see life as it is, go and swim at a local pool or the beach or do an exercise class at a community gym, and have a look around you in the changing room. Here we are. The 95 percent. The 100 percent. All different. Real gorgeous. (12)

If you eat healthy food and have a few indulgences every now and again and if you also exercise three times a week for more than half an hour, you are at the size and shape you should be. This formula is agreed upon by doctors, nutritionists, and body-image consultants. If anybody tells you any different, they're either misled or trying to sell you something. (21)

FROM "GUYS JUST WANT TO BULK UP: TEENS GO TO EXTREMES TO MEET THE POSTER BOY IDEAL" (2001)

Edmonton Journal, August 14, 2001

Steven Bereznai
For Southam Newspapers

"Don't make me go South of the border. I feel like a criminal," a middle-aged man says as he pleads with Nuno Cunha who is tending the register at Toronto's Muscle Shoppe.

He's looking for something. Bodybuilding protein powders and energy drinks line the shelves but they are not enough for everyone trying to fulfill their muscle dream.

Cunha looks at the piece of paper the guy has slipped across the counter, presumably to solicit any illegal body building product, and he shakes his head. "We'll get shut down. Try Chinatown," the 20-year-old says.

Requests like these are reminiscent of Cunha's high school experience only a year ago. Thirteen and fourteen year-old boys would regularly ask him for body building tips and how to get their hands on "stuff."

"Teenagers, if they can get (steroids) they'll do it, no matter what they tell people. They're young, they're immortal," says Cunha, who spent up to $300 a month on supplements to build his body chemical free. His program was contrary to high school gossip that he and his buddy were using steroids.

For Cunha and thousands like him, the motivation for bulking up has nothing to do with sports medals. He wanted a rugged aesthetic to score in the social arena; to impress other guys and to attract girls.

At 16, Cunha weighed 130 lbs. at a height of 5′4″. A year later he tipped the scales at 175 lbs. and was one of the school yard's "big boys."

"I was a nobody the year before, I was just a little wimp," he remembers.

"Everybody knew me after (I started working out)...People wanted to be my friend. A lot of guys would ask me about working out...And when I went to parties girls would come up to me. It really boosted my self-confidence," he explains.

Chuna's [*sic*] experience is not unique. He is just one of many young men fighting the body image war that was once the bastion of young women.

The once freakish male bodies, which adorn the covers of bodybuilding magazines, have now become the ideal according to Dr. Brian Pronger, the resident philosopher in the University of Toronto's physical education department.

"Now it's an expectation. Even if people don't live up to (the muscle image), the desire to have those kinds of bodies is pervasive," he explains. Pronger is currently working on his second book, *Body Fascism, the Culture and Science of Physical Fitness*.

But this perfect aesthetic is not strictly about body builds. It is also about skin tones and the way the predominantly WASP magazine models affect youth from other races. Raymond Fong recently talked about growing up Chinese-Canadian at Beyond 2000, a male sexuality conference. He says he was pushed to unreasonable extremes in an attempt to become a clone of the white male poster boy ideal.

"My body didn't match what I saw at the time in papers, television shows, and ads that contained men of muscular build. It's a masculine, collegiate look, a nicely built look, a Caucasian look....By fitting into that I could escape the stereotype of being a thin, bony, and fragile Asian," he says.

At 12 he sold his soul to a 700 Club operator for $5 a month because she promised him that God would make him grow taller. Now 29, Fong shakes his head and smiles at his own naivete. "It was an act of desperation which of course caused an avalanche of junk mail from other evangelists. I got so jaded about religion I decided to forget whole shebang," he explains.

Perming and bleaching his hair at 17 was equally disastrous. The next year he saw the ad for Soloflex, with the toned guy in his little red shorts and thought "that's what I want to be." Unlike his height, hair, and skin tone, his build was one thing he could permanently change.

When he began attending The University of Toronto, Fong hit the weight room with a vengeance and gained 10 pounds of muscle. He has since done a photo spread for OG (*Oriental Guys,* a pictorial magazine of Asian male nudes) and is a poster boy for the Asian Community AIDS Service's safe sex campaign.

"I feel much better about myself (now). I don't think any of us are completely satisfied with ourselves, and anyone who says they are is lying, but I have now seen a side where Asians can be attractive," he says confidently.

It has been a long haul, but Fong is hopeful that by talking openly about what he has gone through, maybe younger guys will give themselves a break. The attitude of today's youth needs to be: 'If you don't find me attractive, its [*sic*] your loss. I have no time for people like you,' he says.

Steven Bereznai is a 25 year-old Toronto writer.

Jealousy and Abuse

In a world where friendships and romance meet as young people move towards adulthood, sometimes the angst and exhilaration of emotions and passions develop into the darker, more serious concern of jealousy and abuse. The midsummer madness that Shakespeare dramatizes in his comedy verges on violence as the young lovers lose all reason under the spell of fairy magic. Demetrius and Lysander challenge each other to a fight over their competing claims for Helena. Hermia threatens to scratch out Helena's eyes. And only fairy intervention dissolves the dangerous outcome that seems about to erupt. Even before the jealousy inspired by fairy juice, however, there is an undercurrent of potential harm. Demetrius threatens Helena with sexual abuse as she doggedly follows him, saying,

> You do impeach your modesty too much,
> To leave the city, and commit yourself
> Into the hands of one that loves you not,
> To trust the opportunity of night
> And the ill counsel of a desert place
> With the rich worth of your virginity. (2.1.214–19)

Even Hermia has to persuade Lysander to "Lie further off, in human modesty . . . [as]°/ Becomes a virtuous bachelor and a maid" (2.2.57–59) when they settle down to rest for awhile on their night's journey. An undercurrent of violence coexists with an attendant sense of vulnerability as words of love and hate are so readily exchanged.

It is important to recognize that love never expresses itself in harmful ways. Today the level of violence that occurs between people who are friends, or boyfriend and girlfriend, or husband and wife, is an alarming statistic, and a sign that love in the relationship has been lost or never existed. Violence is behavior that causes fear. Between couples who are romantically involved, it can take the form of emotional abuse in which insults, threats, name-calling, and humiliation begin to characterize the relationship. It can also involve physical abuse in which the verbal threats become real, or it can result in sexual abuse, which is any sexual activity that does not include mutual consent. The prevalence of abuse in our society means that virtually everyone knows someone who has suffered or is suffering from it. Teenagers are not immune and need to be aware of the dangers so that they can protect themselves and seek help for themselves or others. The one who abuses and the one who is abused both need help to address issues of self-esteem or underlying problems that lead to the need for power and control over others.

The following three passages discuss violence in romantic relationships, especially among teenagers. Jennifer Rozines Roy points out the nature of jealousy as a sign of an unhealthy relationship, and its danger as a trigger for violence. Nancy N. Rue identifies seven characteristics of an abusive relationship, indicating that the abuser can be male or female, although the victims of such violence are most often female. Karen Zeinert then provides a description of teen violence, including an account of an abusive relationship between two young people, Joyce and Eddie. Consider whether you are familiar with any abusive relationships, firsthand or secondhand, as you read these passages.

FROM JENNIFER ROZINES ROY, *ROMANTIC BREAKUP: IT'S NOT THE END OF THE WORLD* (2000)

(Berkeley Heights, NJ: Enslow Publishers, Inc., 2000) 20–21

Another behavior that occurs in an unhealthy relationship is jealousy. . . . [It] makes people suspicious and afraid of losing their partner to another person.

Jealous people act mistrustful and overly dependent on the other person. They often demand more devotion and reassurance than a healthy partner. They may manipulate their girlfriend or boyfriend into believing that their jealousy is a sign of the strength of their love. However, jealousy is not love. It is a complicated emotion that can lead to more serious dangers in a relationship.

When jealousy, possessiveness, and bullying are mistakenly believed to mean love, abuse often follows. Violence in dating is likely to be triggered by jealousy.

Although minor incidences of jealousy are an occasional part of many relationships (such as when a person's attention wanders to an attractive person), it is not a trait of a healthy, secure relationship and should not be tolerated. Both partners need to make a consistent effort to work through and resolve both the feelings and the actions that cause jealousy.

FROM NANCY N. RUE, *COPING WITH DATING VIOLENCE* (1989)

(New York: The Rosen Publishing Group, 1989) 18–19

Every relationship is different and if it's a violent one, its pattern of violence will probably be different from those of other violent relationships. But certain qualities are common to all abusive steadies. It's important to be able to recognize them.

1. A layer of gentleness often masks an abuser's potential to be brutal. The girl is usually surprised the first time he blows because he "seemed so nice at first," and so she tends to blame herself for bringing out the worst in him.

2. The incidents of violence are unpredictable. It's impossible to tell when they're coming.

3. The abuser is usually overwhelmingly jealous, not only of other guys but of the girl's family, friends, and anything that takes time away from him.

4. The abuser tends to conceal his handiwork, seldom hitting his girlfriend in the face unless the attack is particularly severe.

5. Alcohol is often involved, though not always.

6. Psychological abuse usually precedes the physical abuse. Name-calling, destruction of prized possessions, constant put-downs are not uncommon in violent relationships.

7. The abuser has to be in charge of the relationship, and his girlfriend believes that he is.

Our definitions and symptoms have so far implied that in a violent relationship the boy is the abuser and the girl is the victim. The first question most people ask when they hear that is, "Hey! What about girls being abusive to guys? I've known some pretty nasty girls! It happens, you know!"

Yes, it does happen, and everything this book says about the *abuser* applies to the girl who batters physically and emotionally just as it does to the boy. For the most part, however, . . . [a]buse of girls by boyfriends happens more often than the reverse.

FROM KAREN ZEINERT, *VICTIMS OF TEEN VIOLENCE* (1996)

(Springfield, NJ: Enslow Publishers, Inc., 1996) 49–50

The majority of victims of violent teens are other teenagers, and many of these victims have been abused and assaulted—even killed—by their friends. For example, experts on teen violence believe that one out of every four teenage girls may be in an abusive dating relationship, a relationship in which the girl's boyfriend uses psychological or physical means to control and intimidate her. These means may include insults and put-downs as well as slaps, punches, and even rape.

Joyce's case is typical:

> At first I was flattered my boyfriend Eddie seemed to care so much. Then Eddie began to find faults with little things I did, like the way I carried my books, the way I fixed my hair, why I talked to this person or that person. Then slowly, he started telling me what to do. At first, I did whatever he asked, hoping to please him. But he was never really pleased. He just criticized something else. Pretty soon, to keep from being scolded, I was asking his advice about everything. [from U.S. Department of Justice]

Because she had not been physically assaulted, Joyce refused to believe that she was in an abusive relationship. But when she finally found the courage to differ with Eddie and Eddie slapped her while ranting about all of her "faults," Joyce began to view the relationship very differently. Then she was afraid for her physical well-being, and she discussed the situation with a friend who encouraged her to break up with Eddie. Eddie was enraged when Joyce announced that she would no longer date him. Although he made some frightening threats, she refused to back down and was successful in ending their relationship.

TOPICS FOR WRITTEN AND ORAL DISCUSSION

1. According to Jeremy Daldry, what is the biggest problem a boy faces in asking a girl on a date? Do you agree? Can you speak from personal experience? What are some of the signs that a girl likes a boy? And what does Daldry suggest as a possible alternative to the fears boys face?

2. Discuss in small groups what standards or expectations teen boys and girls face when dating. Is it acceptable for a girl to ask a boy out? Why or why not? Should your parents have a voice in your dating life—whom you ask out, where you go, when you should be home? Why or why not?

3. Imagine both Helena and Demetrius leaving notes for their parents the night they go off into the woods after Lysander and Hermia. What might they say by way of explanation? Do you think the parental responses would be similar or would Helena's parents be more upset or concerned because she is a young woman? Suggest reasons.

4. The girl who writes the diary in Delia Ephron's *Teenage Romance or How to Die of Embarrassment* admits that after the first day she saw classmate Jeffrey Dobkin, she was "in love." Discuss what it means to you to be "in love." Consider Jennifer Rozines Roy's comments in *Romantic Breakup* about the difference between love and infatuation. In your opinion, does the diarist experience love or infatuation? Explain.

5. Consider any romantic relationships in which you have been involved. What did they feel like? Do you think you have known love or infatuation or can you tell the difference?

6. Why do you suppose communicating with someone to whom you feel attracted is so difficult? What embarrassing moments have you or one of your friends felt because of it?

7. Discuss the significance of love and infatuation in *A Midsummer Night's Dream.* Which of the two do you think the "lovers" experience and when? How do the words "maturity" and "immaturity" fit into your considerations of the play's romantic relationships? What do you think Shakespeare's view of romantic love is in the play?

8. Body image often becomes a "big deal" in teen years. What does Sandra Friedman suggest that girls and women see as "the model of perfection"? Why is this perception of idealism wrong, according to Friedman? And what does she indicate is one of the underlying problems that leads to this misconception about body image and feeling fat? Do you agree with her? Why or why not?

9. According to Kaz Cooke, what is the problem with using television and magazines as a guide for body image? What is her solution?

10. Do you think that you have an unhealthy body image? Do you know anyone among your peers who actually has a healthy body image? Consider why appearances seem to matter so much and offer your opinions. Share those opinions with others in your class and see whether your ideas are similar or different.

11. In our world, who decides what defines the beautiful or handsome? According to Sandra Friedman and the article "Boys Just Want to Bulk Up," what is the role of race

in models of body image? Is your view of what constitutes the handsome or beautiful race-related? Do you have any ideas why or why not?

12. In the article "Boys Just Want to Bulk Up," what is the male body image that teen boys strive to achieve? What are their motivations and how do they try to attain the ideal?

13. In *A Midsummer Night's Dream,* both Hermia and Helena are unhappy with their appearances and wish to be like the other. What is their motivation? Write a diary entry for one or the other in which they express their feelings about their own appearances and the attractive qualities of the other.

14. Discuss the power of peer pressure in your concerns about appearance and friendship. Are you strongly influenced by your peers or do you feel confident about your own desires and choices? Suggest reasons for your answer.

15. How does Jennifer Rozines Roy define jealousy? What dangers does it present?

16. Write an essay about the role of jealousy in *A Midsummer Night's Dream.*

17. Review the list of behaviors that Nancy N. Rue identifies in an abusive relationship and the example that Karen Zeinert provides of Joyce and Eddie. Consider whether you know anyone else or are yourself involved in an abusive relationship. Be sure to seek help from a school counselor or someone else you can trust if you have any concerns.

18. What role do you think self-esteem plays in abusive or potentially abusive relationships? How do you think you can build positive self-esteem or encourage it in others?

19. Discuss the significance of violence in *A Midsummer Night's Dream.* Does the fact that the play is a comedy make the potential violence seem insignificant or do you think Shakespeare wants you as readers and audience members to see the violence as an honest threat? What does the undercurrent of violence suggest about male and female relationships in the play?

20. Why do you think the words "love" and "hate" are so closely connected? Sometimes the relationship between the two can seem humorous as, for example, in the words of Ephron's young diarist who says, "I really hate love. If this is it, I don't want it, I really don't." Imagine one of Shakespeare's young lovers saying those lines. Where in the play would they feel that way? What would be their reasons?

SUGGESTED READING

Bell, Ruth. *Changing Bodies, Changing Lives: A Book for Teens on Sex and Relationships.* Third ed. New York: Times Books, 1998.

Cooke, Kaz. *Real Gorgeous: The Truth about Body and Beauty.* New York: Norton and Co., 1996.

Daldry, Jeremy. *The Teenage Guy's Survival Guide.* Boston: Little, Brown, and Co., 1999.

Ephron, Delia. *Teenage Romance or How to Die of Embarrassment.* New York: Viking Press, 1981.

Friedman, Sandra. *When Girls Feel Fat: Helping Girls through Adolescence.* San Francisco: HarperCollins, 2000.

Roy, Jennifer Rozines. *Romantic Breakup: It's Not the End of the World.* Berkeley Heights, NJ: Enslow Publishers, Inc., 2000.

Rue, Nancy N. *Coping with Dating Violence.* New York: The Rosen Publishing Group, 1989.

Zeinert, Karen. *Victims of Teen Violence.* Springfield, NJ: Enslow Publishers, Inc., 1996.

DREAMS, THE PARANORMAL, AND FANTASY

Dreams

Our modern understanding of dreams has been significantly influenced by two men who began their studies in the late nineteenth century, Sigmund Freud (1856–1939) and Carl Gustav Jung (1875–1961). Freud was an Austrian physician who is considered the father of psychoanalysis. Believing that there could be a science of the mind as well as a science of the body, he changed our perception of reality by suggesting that there existed an external objective reality and an internal psychological reality, both equally important. Although he did not invent the concept of the "unconscious," he brought it into common currency through his study of dreams, neuroses, and other psychical phenomena. He believed that all people had unexpressed, innate instincts or desires of which they were not necessarily aware because they occurred at an unconscious rather than a conscious level. In dreams, however, the censor that created the boundary between the conscious and unconscious realms became less alert, allowing unconscious material to pass through the boundary into expression. Dreams were to Freud, therefore, a special form of thinking in which meaningful details could be studied scientifically through a process of "dream work" or analysis that considered symbols within the dream and that looked for clues to repressed emotional problems.

Freud developed a single, comprehensive theory of dreams that had at its foundation a conviction that all dreams were a form of wish-fulfillment, granting at an unconscious level what could not be achieved in a conscious wakeful state. Freud believed that dreams appeared in disguise, concealing their real message, necessitating careful analysis by a dream specialist. He described dreams as having two levels, the "manifest" content or what the dreamer remembered and the "latent" content or the unconscious wishes and fantasies containing the important concealed meaning. Just as important in his theory as the idea of repressed or hidden meaning in dreams was the view that all neurotic behavior stemmed from childhood trauma or infantile sexual conflict which formed the crucial details disguised in dreams. While Freud is still recognized for his significant contribution to psychology, psychoanalysis, and the understanding of dreams, many scholars and practitioners today see limitations to his rigid theory. They are not so ready to believe, as Freud was, that early sexual conflict provides the significant meaning of all dreams. They also recognize the problems inherent in a theory that is so categorical that it leaves no room for alternative ideas and becomes self-fulfilling. In other words, because Freud expected to find hidden sexual meaning in every dream, that is what he found, and any other potential interpretation simply had no validity for him or his followers.

These limitations were the cause of a break in the professional relationship between Freud and the other influential scientist offering valuable insights into dream analysis, Carl Gustav Jung. Admiring Freud's work, Jung eventually found Freud's ideas too narrow and dogmatic and set out to develop his own theories about the unconscious level of reality that defines the dream world. Jung agreed with Freud that dreams contained repressed material but he disagreed that the repressed content was necessarily sexual. He felt that each dream should be considered individually, bearing in mind that the meaning of the dream could be subject to the dreamer's age, class, and other social factors, as well as personal experiences. Jung believed that all people were on a quest for wholeness or self-fulfillment and that dreams could offer wisdom or problem-solving in this process by allowing dreamers to recognize neglected aspects of their personalities or blind spots in their self-awareness. Whereas Freud believed that dreams concealed their messages in disguise, Jung felt dreams revealed important messages that sometimes contained layers of meaning.

Jung offered two valuable concepts to psychology and dream analysis: collective unconscious and archetypes. The collective unconscious refers to a deep level of unconsciousness far below the present consciousness of the individual and connecting him or her to an evolving history of unconsciousness with the rest of the human race. The related term, archetypes, refers to universal symbols or typical modes of perceiving that Jung recognized were shared by different cultures and generations because of their common collective unconscious. One important archetype is that of the shadow self, which, according to Jung, represented the dark side of an individual's personality. Often repressed at a conscious level, this "dark side" could appear in dreams. Because Jung believed that the desire and goal of an individual was to be integrated and whole, he felt that dreams could help sensitize people to the darker side of their personality and, therefore, integrate it into their conscious understanding of themselves rather than allowing it to overwhelm them.

While scientific research continues into the understanding of how dreams happen, what they do to sleep rhythms, and how they work to resolve conflicts and anxieties, Jung and Freud and their successors remain as key figures in any approach that focuses on the meaning of dreams. The following excerpts of writings by Freud and by and about Jung will help to clarify their theories and analyses of dreams. The first quotation from Freud's *Interpreta-*

tion of Dreams emphasizes that he felt, contrary to some of the views in his time, that dreams represented intelligible and intelligent activity. His simple example of thirst demonstrates how he viewed dreams as wish-fulfillments. The second more elaborate example in the quotation from *On Dreams* conveys Freud's view that the wish in the dream is often expressed in disguise and can only be understood through dream analysis. As you read, identify what wish is being satisfied for the woman dreamer, according to Freud's analysis. Of the two excerpted quotations about Jung, the first is Jung's own description of what he calls "taking up the context"—in other words, listening to the dreamer's specific associations with the dream in order to determine its significance and meaning. The second quotation summarizes Jung's view that dreams follow the structure of a drama, an idea that is particularly interesting in considering Shakespeare's reverse suggestion that the drama *A Midsummer Night's Dream* is like a dream.

FROM SIGMUND FREUD, *THE INTERPRETATION OF DREAMS,* TRANS. A. A. BRILL (1900/1994)

(New York: The Modern Library, 1900/1994) 33–35

The dream is not comparable to the irregular sounds of a musical instrument, which, instead of being played by the hand of a musician, is struck by some external force; the dream is not meaningless, not absurd, does not presuppose that one part of our store of ideas is dormant while another part begins to awake. It is a perfectly valid psychic phenomenon, actually a wish-fulfillment; it may be enrolled in the continuity of the intelligible psychic activities of the waking state; it is built up by a highly complicated intellectual activity....

If, in the evening, I eat anchovies, olives, or other strongly salted foods, I am thirsty at night, and therefore I wake. The waking, however, is preceded by a dream, which has always the same content, namely, that I am drinking. I am drinking long draughts of water; it tastes as delicious as only a cool drink can taste when one's throat is parched; and then I wake, and find that I have an actual desire to drink. The cause of the dream is thirst, which I perceive when I wake. From this sensation arises the wish to drink, and the dream shows me this wish as fulfilled. It thereby serves a function, the nature of which I soon surmise. I sleep well, and am not accustomed to being waked by a bodily need. If I succeed in appeasing my thirst by means of the dream that I am drinking, I need not wake up in order to satisfy that thirst. It is thus a *dream of convenience.* The dream takes the place of the action, as elsewhere in life. Unfortunately, the need of water to quench the thirst cannot be satisfied by a dream ... but the intention is the same.

FROM SIGMUND FREUD, *ON DREAMS,* TRANS. JAMES STRACHEY (1901/1952)

(New York: W. W. Norton and Co., Inc., 1901/1952) 91–92

An analysis of a dream [with distressing content] will show that we are dealing with well-disguised fulfillments of repressed wishes . . . ; it will also show how admirably the process of displacement is adapted for disguising wishes.

A girl had a dream of seeing her sister's only surviving child lying dead in the same surroundings in which a few years earlier she had, in fact, seen the dead body of her sister's *first* child. She felt no pain over this; but she naturally rejected the idea that this situation represented any wish of hers. Nor was there any need to suppose this. It had been beside the first child's coffin, however, that, years before, she had seen and spoken to the man she was in love with; if the second child died, she would no doubt meet the man again in her sister's house. She longed for such a meeting, but fought against the feeling. On the dream day she had bought a ticket for a lecture which was to be given by this same man, to whom she was still devoted. Her dream was a simple dream of impatience of the kind that often occurs before journeys, visits to the theater, and similar enjoyments that lie ahead. But in order to disguise this longing from her, the situation was displaced on to an event of a kind most unsuitable for producing a feeling of enjoyment, though it had in fact done so in the past. It is to be observed that the emotional behavior in the dream was appropriate to the real content which lay in the background and not to what was pushed into the foreground. The dream situation anticipated the meeting she had so long desired; it offered no basis for any painful feelings.

FROM CARL GUSTAV JUNG, *DREAMS,* TRANS. R. F. C. HULL (1974)

(Princeton, NJ: Princeton UP, 1974) 71–72

[F]or the purpose of ascertaining the meaning of the dream, I have developed a procedure which I call "taking up the context." This consists in making sure that every shade of meaning which each salient feature of the dream has for the dreamer is determined by the associations of the dreamer himself. I therefore proceed in the same way as I would in deciphering a difficult text. . . . To give an example: I was working once with a young man who mentioned in his anamnesis that he was happily engaged, and to a girl of "good" family. In his dreams she frequently appeared in very unflattering guise. The context showed that the dreamer's unconscious connected the figure of his bride with all kinds of scandalous stories from quite another source— which was incomprehensible to him and naturally also to me. But, from the constant repetition of such combinations, I had to conclude that, despite his conscious resistance, there existed in him an unconscious tendency to show his bride in this ambiguous light. . . . Although it was something he could not bear to think about, this suspicion of his bride seemed to me a point of such capital importance that I advised him to instigate some inquiries. These showed the suspicion to be well founded, and the shock of the unpleasant discovery did not kill the patient but, on the contrary, cured him of his neurosis and also of his bride. Thus, although the taking up of the context resulted in an "unthinkable" meaning and hence in an apparently nonsensical interpretation, it proved correct in the light of the facts which were subsequently disclosed. This is a case of exemplary simplicity, and it is superfluous to point out that only rarely do dreams have so simple a solution.

FROM ROBERT L. VAN DE CASTLE, *OUR DREAMING MIND* (1994)

(New York: Ballantine Books, 1994) 165–66

In one of his letters, Jung characterized the dream as a "drama taking place on one's interior stage." A drama is presented by means of a structure similar to that found in most dreams. A drama or dream usually has four components, according to Jung: (1) an opening scene which introduces the setting, characters, and initial situation of the main character; (2) the development of the plot; (3) the emergence of a major conflict; and (4) the response to the conflict by the main character. This outcome is called the *lysis*. . . .

Some dreams are too short or fragmentary to be explicated by this structural approach, but it can offer an excellent entry point into understanding a dream. The sequence in which the dream unfolds often corresponds to the stages of problem solving unconsciously selected by the dreamer in waking life. The dream opens with a statement, expressed metaphorically, to the effect of "here's the problem or issue I'm currently struggling with," then proceeds to indicate how the dreamer has been dealing with the problem. The lysis or ending of the dream portrays possible strategies that the dreamer might employ to cope with the issue presented in the opening scene.

The Paranormal

In Shakespeare's time, the supernatural represented that which could not be explained in the natural world, with some of the common supernatural beliefs being about fairies, witches, and monsters. People also displayed great fascination with spells, astrology, numerology, alchemy, prophecy, and divination. Although skeptics existed and a new scientific method of understanding the world was beginning to take shape, much of the Renaissance population accepted without question the reality of supernatural beings that bred superstitious ways of thinking. In our age, we have lived through several centuries of strong scientific influences that have caused us to discount many occurrences that cannot be proven by natural laws and through scientific experiment and explanation. Yet phenomena still exist that defy explanation according to natural laws, and there are people in our scientifically advanced western world who accept, study, or practice "arts" related to these mysterious phenomena, which fall under the broad category of the "paranormal," referring to what lies beyond normal experience as an unseen and unseeable reality.

The paranormal can take a number of forms. Perhaps one of the most interesting instances of the inexplicable, relative to Shakespeare's *Midsummer Night's Dream,* is a story about the existence of fairies supposedly photographed in Cottingley Glen in Yorkshire, England, in 1918. Two young cousins, Elsie and Frances, ages sixteen and ten, told others about fairies that entertained them at the foot of the garden, and, upon request, took a camera with them from which Elsie's father later developed five photographs of the girls individually in the presence of one or several miniature fairies that appeared to be real. The photographs have been preserved and can be viewed, for example, in James Randi's 1987 book, *Flim-Flam!,* where he recounts the elaborate investigation that took place after the photographs were produced to determine their authenticity. Experts were involved in the investigation, including Sir Arthur Conan Doyle, the writer of Sherlock Holmes mysteries. The experts tended to conclude that the fairies must be real for they could account for no trick of photography that could produce them otherwise, and British people at the time were captivated by the story. The cousins only eventually admitted that the photography was a hoax decades later, in the early 1980s, when they were in their seventies and eighties, but many British people in the Yorkshire area and undoubtedly other people around the world still believe in the existence of fairies in spite of the lack of evidence. The Cottingley fairies story has continued to engage imaginations late in the twentieth century with a novel and a film entitled *Photographing Fairies* released in the 1990s. James Randi, a professional illusionist and magician, discounts the incident of the two cousins along with any other paranormal experience. The following excerpt conveys his strong tone of skepticism in a book that was published about the same time the public learned that the cousins had constructed the fairies out of paper.

FROM JAMES RANDI, *FLIM-FLAM!: PSYCHICS, ESP, UNICORNS AND OTHER DELUSIONS* (1987)

(Buffalo, NY: Prometheus Books, 1987) 20

To sum up the case for the defense: Two unsophisticated girls unfamiliar with photographic trickery, with no motive at all, have photographed fairies and a gnome in the glen. The photographs have been examined by experts and declared unquestionably genuine and beyond any possibility of fakery. Whatever flaws the photos have are explainable, indeed, these apparent errors are further corroboration of the authenticity of the pictures. Doyle, creator of Sherlock Holmes, cannot be fooled by any fake; the man who thought like Holmes is a master detective and exceedingly logical. Frances and Elsie, still alive and well in England (aged 73 and 79 in 1980), have never admitted to any fakery, despite having no good reason, at this late date, to maintain their innocence if they played tricks on people long deceased. Finally, the girls lacked a reason to be dishonest. They made no money from the episode and to this day are anxious to play down the whole matter. They may even have suffered because of the controversy....

Does it all sound convincing? Yes, quite, if you choose to believe that the facts are as presented; that the experts were really competent, that Doyle was a logical thinker, that the photographs could not have been fabricated by the girls, and that there was no motive to do so. . . . In my opinion the facts as learned by the experts reveal that Elsie Wright and Frances Griffiths were clever little girls who lied rather convincingly and were believed by some naive and not-too-bright persons who were in a position to transform a simple hoax into a major deception that is recounted to this day.

Besides the question of the existence of fairies, other varieties of the paranormal address many behaviors or outcomes that defy common sense or scientific explanation, including ESP (extra sensory perception) which encompasses clairvoyance, the ability to see distant objects or concealed events without any known senses; telepathy, the ability to read minds; precognition, foretelling the future; and retrocognition, awareness of past events. Along with ESP, another element of paranormal experience is known as psychokinesis, in which the mind does not simply sense something directly but has the ability to cause objects to move. An example of psychokinesis is levitation or the ability of material bodies to fly or hover in the air. Larry Kettelcamp's account below about the Russian psychic Nelya Mikhailova describes an incidence of psychokinesis in which the psychic exercises "mind over matter." Gary Blackwood's quotation that follows offers a whole series of bizarre occurrences that seem, as Shakespeare's Theseus might say, "More strange than true" (5.1.2), though they have been documented in recent history.

FROM LARRY KETTELCAMP, *INVESTIGATING PSYCHICS: FIVE LIFE HISTORIES* (1977)

(New York: William Morrow and Co., 1977) 16–17

At the Utomskii Institute in Leningrad an unusual Russian psychic named Nelya Mikhailova was studied by Dr. Genady Sergeyf. Mikhailova had the remarkable ability to cause certain distant objects to move just by looking at them and concentrating. In one test a large aquarium was positioned six feet from Mikhailova. It was filled with salt water into which a raw egg was broken. She was asked to perform the impossible-sounding task of causing the egg white and egg yolk to separate and move apart. During the test, cameras photographed the activity, and she was wired with electronic devices to monitor her brain waves, heartbeat, and the electromagnetic field around her body. Although human beings are known to have weak magnetic fields, Mikhailova's in even her resting state was surprisingly powerful, being one tenth as strong as that of the earth itself.

As Mikhailova strained to affect the distant egg, her heartbeat first increased to four times its normal rate. Then, just as the egg began to separate, her electromagnetic field began to vary in intensity, or pulsate, at four cycles per second. Her heartbeat and brain waves also changed to the same four cycles per second. Though dizzy and exhausted, Mikhailova succeeded in causing the egg white and the egg yolk to move apart under the watchful eye of the camera.

FROM GARY L. BLACKWOOD, *SECRETS OF THE UNEXPLAINED: PARANORMAL POWERS* (1999)

(New York: Benchmark Books, 1999) 43–46

It might be useful to be a "human cork" like Angelo Faticoni, who could float in the water even with a twenty-pound cannonball lashed to his legs; of course, it would be unhandy if you wanted to go scuba diving....

But chances are you wouldn't be so happy to have some of the other strange powers that people have been blessed—or plagued—with. It would be inconvenient, to say the least, to be Jacqueline Priestman; she has so much static electricity in her body that she burns out electrical appliances, and her TV set changes channels whenever she gets near it.

Or imagine being Jennie Morgan, whose handshake delivered an electric shock that knocked people unconscious. Or Peter Strickland, whose presence makes computers and calculators go haywire. Or physicist Wolfgang Pauli who, when he walked into a laboratory, caused pieces of lab equipment to tumble off shelves and shatter.

Even worse, you could be like Bendetto Supino, the nine-year-old Italian boy whose bedclothes and furniture and comic books burst into flame when he stared at them.

And then there are the folks with "magnetic personalities." In the wake of the accident at the Soviet nuclear power plant at Chernobyl, a disturbing number of Russians have reported a newfound ability to make frying pans and irons and silverware stick to their bodies. Some even attract glass and plastic as well as metal. American Frank McKinstry was reportedly so magnetic that if he stood still, his feet stuck to the earth and had to be pried loose.

It's hard to imagine anyone wanting to duplicate the feats of Mirin Dajo. The Dutch mystic regularly allowed a sword to be driven through his body, with no lasting injury.... He repeated his daring demonstration some five hundred times before he died.

Although the above examples have appeared in recent history, the paranormal is not a modern phenomenon; psychic or mystical experiences have been reported for thousands of years. However, perhaps we find such strange encounters especially fascinating and simultaneously doubtful because we live in an era when so much within our awareness—from distant stars and galaxies to minute subparticles of energy—can be explained or known through physics, mathematics, and other scientific methods. Within our model of understanding, where do we put a report about someone who can bend spoons or other metal objects without touching them? How do we respond to the story of someone who can find an underground water or oil well, or even missing objects or bodies, simply by using a forked stick, a penny, or a bent coat hangar? What kind of response can we offer to the clairvoyance of someone who can describe or draw a map of a location simply by being given its latitude and longitude coordinates? Do we need to see with our own eyes even to begin believing that these accounts are real or can we accept the reports as possible and acknowledge that not every experience can be explained or understood? There may indeed be elements of reality that are unknown and entirely unknowable.

Science, of course, will continue to seek explanations, and society will continue to turn to psychic sources for occasional enlightenment. Detectives and police departments, for example, have relied on psychics to help solve crimes, and organizations such as the CIA have explored the possibility of using ESP as a spying tool. But as one expert, Brian Inglis, acknowledges,

> [I]t is safest to regard psi [paranormal phenomena] as the equivalent of the force which prompts people to fall in love: that is, something which happens to and through people, but cannot be laid on in the way that a piece of steel can be magnetized. Some people are more susceptible than others, and become the channel for psi; a few—mediums, or psychics—can sometimes switch on the current, as it were, at will. But nobody has ever been able to switch it on, and keep it on, sufficiently consistently to convert sceptics. (18–19)

Inglis's comment draws the important connection between the paranormal and love as two related and inexplicable experiences. In some ways, love or infatuation can be seen as the most common "paranormal state" because one person seems to be "under the spell" of another. When it comes to the subject of the paranormal and what it means, undoubtedly skeptics will always exist and believers will remain just as resolute. The debate between them perhaps can remind us of the discussion between Shakespeare's Theseus and Hippolyta in act 5 of *A Midsummer Night's Dream*. Theseus discounts the lovers' midsummer story, saying, "I never may believe°/ These antique fables, nor these fairy toys" (5.1.2–3), but Hippolyta disagrees with him, suggesting that the lovers' "story of the night told over" "grows to something of great constancy;°/ But, howsoever, strange and admirable" (5.1.23–27).

Fantasy

Fantasy is a genre of literature in which the story takes place in an imaginary world set apart from the one we know. Like our world, it contains good and evil and requires that characters make choices, but the setting or the geography of the place is make-believe and is filled with a sense of enchantment. Part of this enchantment comes from the beauty or strangeness of the natural world that is portrayed, and part of it comes from creatures portrayed that are unlike any in the human and animal kingdoms we know. In fantasy, animals can talk, trees can move, and fairies, dwarves, and elves dwell together. None of this seems surprising to us as we read a tale of fantasy because we suspend our disbelief in the same way that we do when we watch a play about midsummer madness, dreams, and fairies, or a play about love. Fantasy may not be factual but neither do we expect it to be. We expect, rather, that it is in some sense true, that the plot or the adventure and the outcome are experiences we can understand and identify with as parallel to our own world of conflict and decision, cause and effect, struggle and hope.

Fantasy usually features a character on a journey or quest for something that may not always be clear. The outcome of the quest matters urgently not only for the individual who seeks but for the imaginary world in which he or she dwells where some situation must be corrected or set right for the good of everyone. The character on the quest is like us in that he or she has shortcomings or limitations as well as a desire to do good. That character or hero's strength and endurance are tested in the course of the story and although other creatures or helpers happen along the way, the hero must ultimately rely on personal intelligence and imagination to pass the tests and fulfill the demands of the quest. Fantasy always includes within the quest pattern elements of magic and the supernatural. Sometimes the greatest delight for readers is being able to participate in this magic simply by following the adventures of the main characters and seeing through imagination the mystery or enchantment of the story unfold. The ultimate satisfaction comes in seeing "the world put right"—the world of love or survival, and life itself.

J. R. R. Tolkien is one of the most renowned crafters of fantasy in modern times. His story *The Hobbit* and his trilogy *The Lord of the Rings* established many of the patterns and archetypes for the imaginary world of the quest story that many subsequent authors would recreate in their own plots. Tolkien invents a place called Middle-earth where creatures called hobbits or halflings dwell in homes dug into the sides of hills in a region known as the Shire. They are simple creatures with simple desires for the small comforts of life: hearty food, a good pipe, and a warm hearth. They hardly seem like the type to seek adventures or willingly face dangers, and yet for Bilbo Baggins in *The Hobbit* and his nephew Frodo in *The Lord of the Rings,* adventure seems to choose them. They find themselves on a quest and encounter many obstacles and magical beings along the way. Bilbo has been chosen to help a band of dwarves regain for their leader Thorin the Kingdom under the Mountain and to destroy the dragon, Smaug, who dwells there guarding mountains of dwarf treasure. Frodo, in *The Lord of the Rings,* has an even greater task than Bilbo had. He must take a powerful ring that allows its wearer to become invisible and journey to the dark land of the evil ruler Sauron, where he must throw the ring into the fires of a mountain and destroy it before its evil powers destroy all the creatures of Middle-earth. Although the primary task belongs to Frodo, a supporting company of others travels with him and partakes of his adventures. This fellowship includes elves, dwarves, other hobbits, a wizard, and two men, one of whom is destined to become a king.

The two excerpts below, one from *The Hobbit* and the other from the first book in Tolkien's *Lord of the Rings* trilogy, *The Fellowship of the Ring,* capture some of the magic and enchantment of the world Tolkien has created and the sense of power and mystery that causes the hobbits to respond with uncertainty and sometimes with wonder. The first excerpt recounts Bilbo's journey alone down a dark tunnel in the great Mountain to the place where he discovers the den of Smaug the dragon. Pay particular attention to Bilbo's feelings as he responds to what he encounters. The second excerpt describes a conversation between Frodo and his faithful friend and servant, Sam, while they stay for awhile at Lorien, the forest home of the elves and their great queen, Galadriel. Notice how magic is depicted and how the hobbits react to it.

FROM J. R. R. TOLKIEN, *THE HOBBIT* (1937)

(London: HarperCollins, 1937/1999) 200–1

It was at this point that Bilbo stopped. Going on from there was the bravest thing he ever did. The tremendous things that happened afterwards were as nothing compared to it. He fought the real battle in the tunnel alone, before he ever saw the vast danger that lay in wait. At any rate after a short halt go on he did; and you can picture him coming to the end of the tunnel, an opening of much the same size and shape as the door above. Through it peeps the hobbit's little head. Before him lies the great bottommost cellar or dungeon-hall of the ancient dwarves right at the Mountain's root. It is almost dark so that its vastness can only be dimly guessed, but rising now from the near side of the rocky floor there is a great glow. The glow of Smaug!

* * *

There he lay, a vast red-golden dragon, fast asleep; a thrumming came from his jaws and nostrils, and wisps of smoke, but his fires were low in slumber. Beneath him, under all his limbs and his huge coiled tail, and about him on all sides stretching away across the unseen floors, lay countless piles of precious things, gold wrought and unwrought, gems and jewels, and silver red-stained in the ruddy light. . . .

To say that Bilbo's breath was taken away is no description at all. There are no words left to express his staggerment. . . . Bilbo had heard tell and sing of dragon-hoards before, but the splendour, the lust, the glory of such treasure had never yet come home to him. His heart was filled and pierced with enchantment and with the desire of dwarves; and he gazed motionless, almost forgetting the frightful guardian, at the gold beyond price and count.

FROM J. R. R. TOLKIEN, *THE LORD OF THE RINGS;* PART ONE: *THE FELLOWSHIP OF THE RING* (1954/55)

(London: Unwin Paperbacks, 1954/55/1966) 375–77

"What do you think of Elves now, Sam?" [Frodo] said. "I asked you the same question once before . . . but you have seen more of them since then."

"I have indeed!" said Sam. "And I reckon there's Elves and Elves. They're all elvish enough, but they're not all the same. . . . If there's magic about, it's right down deep, where I can't lay my hands on it. . . . I'd dearly love to see some Elf-magic, Mr. Frodo!"

. . . .

Even as [Frodo] spoke, they saw, as if she came in answer to their words, the Lady Galadriel approaching. Tall and white and fair she walked beneath the trees. She spoke no word, but beckoned to them.

Turning aside, she led them toward the southern slopes of the hill.... At the bottom, upon a low pedestal carved like a branching tree, stood a basin of silver, wide and shallow, and beside it stood a silver ewer.

With water from the stream Galadriel filled the basin to the brim, and breathed on it, and when the water was still again she spoke. "Here is the Mirror of Galadriel," she said. "I have brought you here so that you may look in it, if you will."...

"What shall we look for, and what shall we see?" asked Frodo, filled with awe.

"Many things I can command the Mirror to reveal," she answered, "and to some I can show what they desire to see. But the Mirror will also show things unbidden, and those are often stranger and more profitable than things which we wish to behold. What you will see, if you leave the Mirror free to work, I cannot tell. For it shows things that were, and things that are, and things that yet may be.... Do you wish to look?"

Since Tolkien, one of the most recent and highly popular writers of fantasy is J. K. Rowling in her series about Harry Potter, the boy who discovers on his eleventh birthday that he is a wizard, that the jagged scar on his forehead marks him as a gifted wizard because, as an infant, he escaped the curse of the dark lord, Voldemort, and that he is about to enter Hogwarts School of Witchcraft and Wizardry. Like Tolkien's Middle-earth, the imaginary world Rowling creates portrays a conflict between good and evil. Harry, like Tolkien's Bilbo and Frodo Baggins, is chosen to struggle against evil perpetuated by Voldemort and his followers. In each book in the series, Harry's courage is tested as he encounters the dark forces in new forms and must act against them. In the first book, *Harry Potter and the Sorcerer's Stone* (published in the United Kingdom as *Harry Potter and the Philosopher's Stone*), Harry and several other students at the school are caught breaking school rules, and for their punishment they must accompany Hagrid, the school's groundskeeper, into the Forbidden Forest to help solve the mystery about what is killing the unicorns inhabiting the forest. The excerpt below describes what happens when Harry meets the figure who has killed the unicorn and what source of magic saves him.

FROM J. K. ROWLING, *HARRY POTTER AND THE PHILOSOPHER'S STONE* (1997)

(London: Bloomsbury, 1997) 186–87

It was the unicorn all right, and it was dead. Harry had never seen anything so beautiful and sad.... its mane was spread pearly-white on the dark leaves.

Harry had taken one step towards it when a slithering sound made him freeze where he stood. A bush on the edge of the clearing quivered... Then, out of the shadows, a hooded figure came crawling across the ground like some stalking beast. Harry, Malfoy and Fang stood transfixed. The cloaked figure reached the unicorn, it lowered its head over the wound in the animal's side, and began to drink its blood.

"AAAAAAAAAAAGH!"

Malfoy let out a terrible scream and bolted—so did Fang. The hooded figure raised its head and looked right at Harry—unicorn blood was dribbling down its front. It got to its feet and came swiftly towards him—he couldn't move for fear.

Then a pain pierced his head like he'd never felt before, it was as though his scar was on fire—half-blinded, he staggered backwards. He heard hooves behind him, galloping, and something jumped clean over him, charging at the figure.

The pain in Harry's head was so bad he fell to his knees. It took a minute or two to pass. When he looked up, the figure had gone. A centaur was standing over him....

"Are you all right?" said the centaur, pulling Harry to his feet.

"Yes—thank you—what *was* that?"

The centaur didn't answer.... He looked carefully at Harry, his eyes lingering on the scar which stood out, livid, on Harry's forehead.

"You are the Potter boy," he said. "You had better get back to Hagrid. The forest is not safe at this time—especially for you. Can you ride? It will be quicker this way."

TOPICS FOR WRITTEN AND ORAL DISCUSSION

1. In *The Interpretation of Dreams,* to what does Sigmund Freud compare the dream phenomenon in order to argue that it is "a highly complicated intellectual activity"? What example does he use to express his idea that dreams are wish-fulfillments and what does he mean by a "dream of convenience"?

2. In the excerpt from *On Dreams,* Freud offers an analysis of a dream validating his view that the meaning of dreams is often disguised rather than transparent. What is the dream, how does he interpret its hidden meaning, and what is the "repressed wish" that he identifies? Does his interpretation seem credible to you or far-fetched? Give reasons.

3. Can you think of any dreams you have had recently in which there seems to be a wish fulfilled that was not or could not be fulfilled at your conscious level of reality?

4. Can you see the "dream" of the lovers or of Bottom in *A Midsummer Night's Dream* in Freud's terms as wish-fulfillments? If so, how? If not, why not?

5. What does Carl Jung mean by "taking up the context" of a dream? How does he do so in the example he offers in the selection from his *Dreams*? What does his interpretation lead the dreamer to do?

6. Have you had any dreams that have led you or inspired you to respond to them in a concrete way as Jung's male dreamer does? Describe the experience.

7. How does Jung characterize a dream as a drama? What patterns does he see as the same? How might you apply Jung's patterns to *A Midsummer Night's Dream,* using examples from the play for each stage of the dream? Discuss with your classmates whether this exercise gives you any new insight into Puck's epilogue, in which he invites audiences to think of the play as a "weak and idle theme,°/ No more yielding but a dream" (5.1.430–31).

8. Do your dreams ever have a dramatic structure, or are they, as Jung suggests, "too short or fragmentary to be explicated"? Do you believe that your dreams can be a way of problem-solving? Why or why not? Does there seem any value in the idea of approaching a problem or decision "by sleeping on it," as the expression goes?

9. Does your understanding of Freud's emphasis on an "unconscious" reality or Jung's concepts of the collective unconscious and archetypes allow you to analyze or interpret Hermia's dream (in 2.2.144–56) in a particular way? Do you lean more towards a Freudian or Jungian analysis?

Alternatively, imagine Hermia or Bottom in the office of Freud or Jung recounting their dreams. Script or act out the dialogue between the dreamer and the analyst.

10. Referring to the discussion on "The Psychology of Dreams" in chapter 5, compare the Renaissance understanding of dreams with our modern perspective shaped by Freud, Jung, and others. What are the similarities and differences? What kind of conversation might transpire between Robert Burton or Thomas Nashe (in chapter 5) and Sigmund Freud or Carl Jung?

11. Read the account of the Cottingley fairies in this chapter. Do you find it surprising that people in the twentieth century could believe in fairies by relying on photographs as proof? Why or why not?

Choose one of the following exercises:

(a) Watch a video of the film *Photographing Fairies* or read the novel of the same title and write a response, expressing your thoughts and feelings about the account.

(b) Imagine what it must have been like for the two cousins, Frances and Elsie, tricking many people from the time they were teenagers until they confessed their hoax in their late seventies and early eighties. Compose a series of letters between them over the years as they confide in each other about the secret they kept. Do you think they enjoyed the secrecy or found it a burden as they grew older? How did they feel about an innocent prank that eventually attracted the attention of a nation and the world? What made them finally decide to confess?

(c) Imagine that someone today appears with evidence of fairies. What form would the evidence take? Construct a series of newspaper reports, editorials, letters to the editor, and interviews reflecting the attitudes of believers and skeptics.

12. If Shakespeare were writing *A Midsummer Night's Dream* today, do you think he would still include fairies? What other possibilities might he choose from? Describe what this "modern" *Midsummer Night's Dream* might look like.

13. Reading Larry Kettelcamp's account of the Russian clairvoyant and Gary L. Blackwood's list of bizarre powers manifested by different people, explain your reaction to these anecdotes. Are you a skeptic? Are you amazed and intrigued? Do you know of anyone with unusual powers?

14. In the Renaissance, belief in the supernatural stimulated many superstitions. Do you have any superstitions? What are they, what are their origins, or with what do you associate them?

15. In this scientific age, how far do you let yourself believe in the unseeable or unknowable? Where do you draw your line between belief and disbelief?

16. Why do you think we encourage children to believe in the tooth fairy or Santa Claus or other "fairy tales" when we know they are not true? Do you think we lose our imaginations when we grow up or simply become more aware and realistic? How was Shakespeare, writing about fairies for an adult audience, encouraging his viewers to think about imagination?

17. In the excerpts included in this chapter, how do Bilbo's reaction to Smaug's treasure and Frodo and Sam's reaction to Galadriel and her mirror compare? What do their reactions suggest about the imaginary world of fantasy?

18. Compare Tolkien's description of Galadriel, queen of the elves, with Shakespeare's portrayal of Titania, queen of the fairies. What similarities and differences do you seen

in them and in their responses to those around them, including, in Shakespeare's play, the changeling child and his mother?

19. Harry Potter is taken into the Forbidden Forest at night. Shakespeare's characters also go at night into a dark wood that is in some ways forbidding. Why is it necessary that Rowling's and Shakespeare's characters go there, what happens to them while they are there, and how does that change them?

20. Consider the beasts in these tales of fantasy. Both unicorns and asses are horse-like creatures. Why do you suppose Shakespeare has Bottom turned into an ass instead of, for example, a unicorn? What are the different connotations associated with each animal? What does the unicorn seem to represent in *Harry Potter and the Philosopher's Stone*? What about the dragon, Smaug, in Tolkien's *Hobbit*?

21. Consider devices of magic in *A Midsummer Night's Dream* and in the fantasy tales excerpted in this chapter. What are they and what powers do they represent? If you have read or seen in movie version either of Tolkien's novels or one or more of the Harry Potter novels, discuss more extensively what magical devices appear throughout the stories, whether they seem good, evil, or neutral, and how they are identified with the various characters.

22. This chapter discusses fantasy as a genre about "quest" stories. If you are familiar with Tolkien's or J. K. Rowling's novels, compare and contrast the quest pattern in one of them with *A Midsummer Night's Dream* as a "quest" story. What do the questers seek, how do they find it, and how does it change them, if indeed it does?

23. Do you have dreams for yourself and your future? What are they? Are your dreams different from your parents'? From people in the past? How so?

SUGGESTED READING

Becker, Alida, ed. *A Tolkein Treasury*. Philadelphia, PA: Running Press, 1989.

Blackwood, Gary L. *Secrets of the Unexplained: Paranormal Powers*. New York: Benchmark Books, 1999.

Evans, Christopher, and Peter Evans. *Landscapes of the Night: How and Why We Dream*. London: Victor Gollancz, Ltd. 1983.

Freud, Sigmund. *The Interpretation of Dreams*. Trans. A. A. Brill. New York: The Modern Library, [1900] 1994.

Freud, Sigmund. *On Dreams*. Trans. James Strachey. New York: W. W. Norton and Co., Inc., [1901] 1952.

Inglis, Brian. *The Paranormal: An Encyclopedia of Psychic Phenomena*. New York: Granada, 1985.

Jung, C. G. *Dreams*. Trans. R. F. C. Hull. Princeton, NJ: Princeton UP, 1974.

Kettelkamp, Larry, *Investigating Psychics: Five Life Histories*. New York: William Morrow and Co., 1977.

Kronzek, Allan Zola, and Elizabeth Kronzek. *The Sorcerer's Companion: A Guide to the Magical World of Harry Potter.* New York: Broadway Books, 2001.

Randi, James. *Flim-Flam!: Psychics, ESP, Unicorns and Other Delusions.* Buffalo, NY: Prometheus Books, 1987.

Timmerman, John H. *Other Worlds: The Fantasy Genre.* Bowling Green, OH: Bowling Green UP, 1983.

Van de Castle, Robert L. *Our Dreaming Mind.* New York: Ballantine Books, 1994.

Index

About the Author

FAITH NOSTBAKKEN has taught at the University of Alberta, Canada. Her research focuses on Shakespeare and Renaissance drama, particularly the historical contexts. She is the author of two other books in Greenwood's Literature in Context series, *Understanding Macbeth* (1997) and *Understanding Othello* (2000).